SPARKS

IN THE

KITCHEN

SPARKS

IN THE

KITCHEN

Katy Sparks

WITH ANDREA STRONG

PHOTOGRAPHS BY QUENTIN BACON

ALFRED A. KNOPF · NEW YORK 2006

THIS IS A BORZOI BOOK
PUBLISHED BY ALFRED A. KNOPF

www.aaknopf.com

Library of Congress Cataloging-in-Publication Data

Sparks, Katy.
Sparks in the kitchen / by Katy Sparks with Andrea Strong.— 1st ed.
p.   cm.
Includes bibliographical references and index.
ISBN 1-4000-4355-7
1. Cookery.   I. Strong, Andrea.   II. Title.
TX714.S63325 2006
641.5—dc22   2005044080

Book design by M. Kristen Bearse

Manufactured in the United States of America
First Edition

Photographic credits: The photographs on the frontispiece and on pages
21, 32, 39, 67, 74, 75, 79, 87, 94, 95, 99, 109, 113, 125, 128, 148,
151, 163, 176, 197, 213, 217, 231, 238, 242, 295, 300, 313, 318, 321,
and the color insert are by Quentin Bacon. All other photographs
are courtesy Katy Sparks.

FOR MY PARENTS,
KIM AND SUE SPARKS

CONTENTS

Introduction 3

SMALL PLATES, SNACKS, AND COCKTAILS   25

SOUPS AND SALADS   69

FISH AND SHELLFISH   121

MEAT AND POULTRY   169

VEGETABLES AND SIDE DISHES   227

DRESSINGS, PICKLES, AND RELISHES   259

DESSERTS   287

Appendix: Stocks and Techniques 317

Sources 325

Bibliography 327

Katy's Acknowledgments 328

Andrea's Acknowledgments 331

Index 333

SPARKS

IN THE

KITCHEN

My family's farmland in Vermont in summer

INTRODUCTION

IT WILL BECOME CLEAR IN A VERY FEW PAGES that I wrote this book for my parents, Kim and Sue Sparks. The joy they take in family, friends, their Vermont farm, their memories of great meals and travels past, and their anticipation of trips and feasts to come have always inspired me. Whenever we can, my husband, Michael, our son, Luke, and I happily drive the many miles up the road to spend time with them. It's not just filial duty that brings me back home—my folks are a hell of a lot of fun!

I have chosen to spend a great deal of my life in the kitchen because this is where I feel most at home. It's the main room in my parents' house, and my mother spends most of her day there. It is Command Central: barometers, wind gauges, thermometers, and bird feeders to monitor; tall windows looking to the east to get the measure of what kind of day the sunrise will bring. When we were growing up, there was no mudroom or garage to ease the transition from outside—the kitchen door was the front door. Everything began there. Dinner guests would be met at the kitchen door by two little girls (my sister Liza and me), who would take their coats. Cocktails would be mixed. My brother would actively avoid all the hubbub until food was actually served. The kitchen island—which made a beautiful backdrop for Mom's hors d'oeuvres—is made out of teak that my uncle Pete retrieved from the deck of a decommissioned navy submarine. It has always been polished to a high sheen—and woe betide the young cook who forgot to put down a cutting board before slicing bread for a sandwich! There had been plans for an elegant walkway carved out of a natural rock ledge to lead into a mirrored hallway as the main entrance to the house, but the convenience of unloading groceries directly onto the kitchen table proved too compelling.

Building the house has been an ongoing labor. My father, a college professor, was able to have work done in stages as he wrote one best-selling textbook after another. To fill in the gaps, we as a family leveled out the dense Champlain Valley clay piles of the construction site and raked and seeded year after year until a semblance of lawn emerged. At the same time, we planted gardens, cared for horses, cattle, and chickens, and baled hay in the summer on our seventy-acre farm.

I was introduced early to the joys and very hard work of encouraging plants to grow, discouraging weeds, and preserving the soil. The seasons in Vermont are very distinct—and winter is the longest, which makes spring all the sweeter. My father is an amateur naturalist who knows every plant and animal species specific to our area. He once had a fantasy that we would take to the land and live off what we could hunt and gather. This fell on the deaf and unromantically disposed ears of his teenage brood and was soon abandoned. But we were taught to gather wild leeks, mushrooms, and daylily buds, and to seine for crawfish (my father paid handsomely for these: five cents each). And deep down, I did have a profoundly secure feeling that the land could sustain us if need be.

The gardens became specialized—an upper herb and lettuce garden where the drainage was good, and an asparagus bed on the north side, initially protected by a row of stately elms that, heartbreakingly, fell prey to disease and had to be cut down. And down by the barn were the "big vegetables": potatoes, corn, squashes, beans, peas, peppers, and the like. I was sent out in the summer evenings just before cocktail hour to pick the maturing green beans to ensure that we had a fine source of haricots verts for quite a few weeks.

With my father—
a banner year for morels

But my upbringing wasn't entirely spent on the farm. My parents moved us to Mainz, Germany, several times as my father was rotated into the directorship of Middlebury's School of German Studies abroad. There, my mother fell into the rhythm of shopping every day in the markets. One stop for bread, another for the sausages, a third for the freshest beer I never tasted (until many years later), and the farmers market on the Domplatz several days a week. It's a habit that she continues back home, where she drives the five miles into town every morning to shop for dinner and pick up a copy of the *New York Times.*

I have strong memories of our Mainz apartment, an arduous walk-up with miniature appliances and a small balcony overlooking the Domplatz, the central square of a beautiful Romanesque cathedral. We had a lot of fun picnicking on the living-room floor with a voluptuous spread of meats, cheeses, and crusty breads. It was a small place for five people, but it felt like the center of the universe to us kids.

We were not churchgoers as a family, but my sister and I did get some kind of religious training while in Mainz. We were whisked away Sunday mornings by Tante Hilde-gard and Tante Charlotte—two affectionate teachers at our Catholic kindergarten. They would pick us up in a VW bug and take us to some of central Germany's most gorgeous churches. Of course, being food obsessed as I am, my strongest memories of going to church are of the *Milchbrot* (rolls made with milk) that we were given to hold in our hands during the long Catholic mass and told we must not eat until after the service. I could smell their delicious yeasty aroma but couldn't taste them. As a five-year-old, I was forced to learn self-restraint—after all, I didn't want to be damned for all eternity because I ate my roll before mass was over. In retrospect, I'm amazed that I didn't overcompensate and become a baker rather than a chef.

My mother shopping in Mainz

At the other end of the spectrum from winters in central Europe, there were the summer vacations spent in a tent on Danny McPhee's cow pasture in Nova Scotia. This wasn't just *any* cow pasture—it was situated on a majestic bluff overlooking the Bay of Fundy, where we could almost see the lobsters we were going to have for dinner still crawling on the silty bottom of the ocean floor. We spent so many summers making the two-day drive from Vermont to Nova Scotia that the midway overnight stop at Carlos' Cabins became mythical for us kids. Mrs. Carlos made such amazing pies made from the local blueberries that just the thought of a slice was enough to keep the three of us from killing each other in the back of the Ford Bronco. I don't know how it happened, but one year I fell asleep in the car just as we were closing in on the cabins and my parents dumped me in bed instead of waking me up for pie. I had never felt such betrayal before in my young life—such grief and regret—and all for this piece of pie! I apparently made quite a stink about it and am teased to this day. But perhaps it helped to launch my food career—there was the drive in me to somehow catch up with that lost piece of pie.

After such a well-fed youth, college was a rude awakening. I found out that not everyone ate as well as I had at home, a fact that was reaffirmed every time I went to the dining hall. The prefab food there seemed to satisfy my roommates, but I took to crashing Le Château (a residence for serious French students, among whom I did not number) for *petit déjeuner* just to be around people who were as enamored of the rituals of the table as I was.

I didn't last long at Middlebury College. After my first year I dropped out and landed my first real job in a local café. It was easy to find work in the restaurant business, and it didn't take me long to realize that this was because the hours were long and hard and the pay was lousy. For the first couple of years, I was still nursing the self-inflicted wounds of my failure as a scholar, and I thought of the restaurant only as a place to make friends and collect a paycheck. But in lieu of a family life—my parents were again living in Mainz, and my brother and sister were at Princeton—the kitchen provided a very homelike environment. People chatting while performing tasks that didn't require too much concentration reminded me of shelling beans or pitting cherries with my mother at home. The days had a pleasant rhythm—a long ascent of preparation to the climax of service, then the denouement of the "family meal," which was always modest: a piece of chicken and a salad and, if we were very lucky, a glass of wine. The restaurant business adopted me as it has so many black sheep and wandering souls.

And so I began to heed the siren call of restaurants, hoping not to be dashed on the rocks. My first job out of culinary school at Johnson & Wales University in Providence, Rhode Island, was at Al Forno, a

The little girl who missed her slice of blueberry pie

rustic little Italian place on Steeple Street famous for its grilled pizzas and local ingredients like quahogs (local slang for clams), johnny-cakes and polenta made from cornmeal ground in a local gristmill, jalapeño sausages made on Federal Hill, and the freshest produce to be found in New England. It was at Al Forno that I learned that you use the space and equipment available to you and thereby develop an idiom. At Al Forno there were two unique (at least for an upscale restaurant in the mid-1980s) pieces of equipment: a wood-fired grill and a pizza oven. The chefs used each to its ultimate potential—they grilled the pizza and roasted just about everything else: quahogs, pastas, and desserts. As luck would have it, when I later assumed the kitchen at Quilty's I inherited a pizza oven. Thanks to my experience at Al Forno, I knew just what to do with it.

Aside from learning adaptability, I was schooled in the integrity of ingredients. The hallmark of good Italian cooking is maximizing the potential of really great raw materials. Much has been written on the subject—perhaps too much. It is easy to wax lyrical on the merits of this or that olive oil, but much harder to actually get out of the way enough to let the food's inherent quality speak for itself. The art of cooking is in understanding when and how to engage your skills.

While working in that tiny kitchen on Steeple Street, I learned how to apply just the right amount of flame to the food. It took me months to master wilting the spinach to the perfect degree—it still had the body and beauty of its full leaves, but it was transformed by heat and good olive oil into a gorgeous, glossy mound. I had never before imagined that a busy kitchen could make mashed potatoes to order or line up berries perfectly on a fruit tart for two just as the entrées were being cleared—but we did it. I'm still inspired by that intense devotion to the immediacy of cooking.

As a graduation present, my parents offered to fund a "belly tour" of France for a month. My friend and fellow culinary graduate Philip Kennedy and I flew into Mainz and picked up my parents' car. In a few blinks of the eye and more than a few heart palpitations on the autobahn (these people drive soooo fast), we were across the border into the Alsace region of France. I loved Strasbourg, with its border city charms—first German, then French, then German, then

French . . . It boasts beautiful architecture, and famous dishes like *choucroute garnie, Flammkuchen,* and frogs' legs or pike in Riesling. My parents had accompanied us this far and now boarded a train back to Mainz, leaving me with a fistful of Thomas Cook's traveler's checks and absolutely no need to be anywhere in particular. It was heaven. I wanted to spend a good amount of time in Burgundy since I am in love with the wines there, and we had a series of sublime two- and three-star meals. But in between these gastronomic feats of endurance, Philip and I would pull over at the side of the road and picnic on *saucissons à l'ail,* baguettes so crisp that they cut your palate, Camembert, and quaint little wines like Gevry Chambertin or Pommard. We had decided not to acquire any objets d'art while in France; instead we settled for a few inches around our waistlines.

The belly tour proceeded, and then we ended the trip in Paris, where we looked up my friend David Catton, a fellow Vermonter and a very close neighbor since childhood. We slept on the floor of David's adorable flat—no frills at all, but who needs frills when you're in PARIS! I was stunned at the city's beauty. I had been to lovely Vienna, but Paris is just a little more feminine somehow. Its beauty is seductive and remote at the same time—a lot like that of Catherine Deneuve. We ate poorly in Paris mainly because it was so expensive and we were out of money. But it really didn't matter; we loved every second of it.

After getting back from France, I set out on what I imagine is a pretty normal young cook's life: I apprenticed myself to the best chefs I could find all over the country. I was desperately poor most of the time, relying on birthday or Christmas checks mailed from home to afford even nonluxuries like boots or a winter coat. But there were little tastes of the good life. At Campagne, a Provençal restaurant at the Inn at the Market in Seattle, the owner Peter Lewis was a real gentleman. He would instruct his bartenders to pour for us cash-strapped souls in the kitchen whatever poison we wanted at the end of a particularly brutal Saturday night. I had a mad crush on the sous-chef, so began emulating his taste for single-barrel bourbons. I later moved on to Scotch and much later to gin. Peter also hosted what was probably the best restaurant staff party/outing of all time. Chef Susan Vanderbeek's mother had a house on Whidbey Island, which is in

My belly tour to Europe—
in Paris

Puget Sound—quite a distance from Seattle by boat or ferry. Peter hired two sailboats and stocked them with smoked salmon, bagels, caviar, and champagne. We all met at the dock at sunrise, and the people with families were loaded onto the bigger boat, the singles among us on the smaller. It was a gorgeous May morning, but with no wind to speak of, so it took us hours and hours to get to Whidbey. We all arrived sunburned and drunk, did a little damage to the amazing feast of king salmon and Dungeness crabs that Susan and her mother had prepared, and then had to get back aboard to head home to Seattle. We didn't sail into Elliott Bay until well after midnight, and that return trip—with my once rowdy coworkers getting more somber and more than a little pensive as the night sea wove a spell over us—is a memory I still cherish.

I loved everything about living in Seattle, but I loved my family more, and after two years on the opposite side of the country I wanted to move back east. My parents were back from Mainz, and I moved in with a boyfriend who had faithfully kept in touch with me while I pursued my culinary ambitions on the West Coast. He had just bought a small cabin on Lake Hortonia, twenty miles or so south of Middlebury, and since I was carless, he loaned me his 1978 Corvette Stingray. I didn't realize how attracted to speed and power I was until I had it at my disposal.

There was at that time a small gem of a restaurant in Middlebury called the Otter Creek Café. The chef-owners were a couple who had received their training in well-run kitchens in the Northeast. I was lucky to land there for the summer. Ben Wood, the chef, was serious

Picnicking with saucisson à l'ail

about cuisine and always in the kitchen, so I was definitely not afforded a slacker summer as I had hoped.

That summer I was in transition. I knew that I wanted to make cooking my career, and that I cared deeply about food and the restaurant business, but I didn't really know what to do next. Being back home at the age of twenty-five made me a little uneasy. Middlebury was where I had failed as a student, and it was a little weird to be cooking for those same professors. But I had graduated summa cum laude from culinary school, and that was something.

I worked the lunch shift at Ben's. As I was not particularly good at getting up early, this meant that I had to cover the twenty miles from the lake to the café in a ridiculously short amount of time. I was just so lucky that the state troopers didn't seem to like to be up that early either. But that's the great thing about a Vette—it corners beautifully even at high speeds and can be slowed down to a crawl pretty quickly when necessary. I think Ben knew I was always a little late for work—and the tip-off was the bain-marie (water bath). My first duty was to set it up with fresh cold water and bring it to a boil to keep the soups and sauces warm for lunch. By rights, it should have been ready to roll by the time Ben came in around ten a.m., but it was ever only lukewarm.

The experience at Ben's taught me speed and accuracy. Our lunch crowd wanted to get in and out. Customers were always popping into the kitchen to say hello. Many were friends of my parents, no doubt happy to see me working in a good place, but I think also wondering if cooking was just a youthful fling for me. It began to gnaw at me that no one was taking me that seriously as a professional. Or maybe, more honestly, I wasn't taking myself seriously. I felt that I needed a taste of the big leagues, and that meant New York.

I had no idea where to start, so I picked up Bryan Miller's compilation book of *New York Times* restaurant reviews and got to work making a list of places to stop by. I have always been a believer in the face-to-face introduction, so I printed résumés and started pounding the pavement. I decided that I would just present myself to various chefs between two and four in the afternoon. As a cook, I knew this would be the best time to find the chef at his or her least harried.

With Michael in Paris

I started with the two-star restaurants and quickly realized that I had been exposed to that level of cooking already in my travels. So I set my sights on the three- and four-star establishments. The first place I entered was Palio, then on 51st Street. It was a beautiful northern Italian restaurant; I was nicely greeted, and when I asked to see the chef, I was graciously escorted upstairs to the chef's office. But once I disclosed that I was a cook looking for work I was curtly told to fill out an application and please leave by way of the back loading docks. I had always been treated well as a cook, so I was a little shocked. But I pressed on, stopping at Le Cirque, where I stood awkwardly in the kitchen for quite a while before being told rather dismissively that no one could see me. As I walked outside and down the sidewalk a young cook ran after me and said, "You probably don't want to work here, but you should try the Quilted Giraffe," which was another four-star. I was getting a little weary for one day, but decided to drop by—it was still before four o'clock.

I found the chef-owner Barry Wine and his wife, Susan, discussing business at the bar, just inside the front door. I introduced myself and handed Barry a résumé, and he immediately offered to give me a tour of his kitchens. He introduced me to his staff and asked if I would like to come back later that week for a trail—a shift that a cook works without pay so the chef can assess her skills. I agreed immediately and scheduled one for the next day. During my trail I spent time with Barry's amazing crew. They were wonderfully bright and engaged cooks, and I count two of them among my best friends today—Ellen D'Aleo and Amir Ilan. And so Barry proved to be not only a mensch, but also an amazing force in my career. He was a master impresario and taught me that the restaurant business in New York is every bit as theatrical as Broadway. I also learned that you needn't ever be satisfied with good enough, that you can keep pushing and working until your food is sublime. It was an intense and wonderful year that I spent at the Quilted Giraffe, but my soul cried out for a different environment—one that felt a little more like home.

So I regrouped. I spent the mornings in a café on West Fourth Street, circling ads in the *New York Times* Help Wanted section. It was at this time that I met my husband, Michael. He was sitting at a table next to mine, I had my nose buried in the paper, wondering what I was going to do next, and I heard a voice say, "Do you always read the paper so assiduously?" I had to see who this person speaking to me was, so I lowered the paper and saw a somewhat rumpled, paint-stained, but absolutely adorable guy. Michael is a painter and his home and studio were just around the corner from the café. We started talking, and after seeing each other several more times in the café—I have to admit I started to get really good at guessing when he would be stopping by for a cappuccino—we had our first date. Well, the rest is history, and we now are the parents of Luke, born in 2000, who is absolutely adorable and wonderful too.

In the meantime, I also answered an ad for a line cook's job. The ad said to contact Bobby. And I thought, Bobby? Not even Chef Bobby? As soon as I met Bobby Flay, I knew that exciting things might be around the corner, although our first interview went only okay. We met at the future site of Mesa Grill—it was halfway through a renovation at the time. I scored a big point by knowing where to find that week's *New York Times* restaurant review (the *Times* had inexplicably moved it from its usual section), but I also lost points for arrogance. I had, after all, just finished a year in one of the best, most idiosyncratically creative restaurants in the world, and I guess I was just a little full of myself. So I didn't get the job, at least not right away. It was two weeks later when I checked my phone machine and heard Bobby's voice asking me to call him.

I was part of the opening team that launched Mesa Grill. Up to that point, I had virtually no experience with southwestern cooking— just one trip to New Mexico as a kid. But thankfully Bobby's food was Southwest by way of Fifth Avenue and Fifteenth Street—*very* New York. His buoyant, interpretive style reminded me of what Barry Wine was doing with French-Japanese fusion at the Quilted Giraffe. So I was delighted. As one of Bobby's line cooks it was my job to execute his vision as well as I could. For the opening, he divided us into teams to start fleshing out his recipes. I worked with Larry Manheim, who now runs the Mesa Grill kitchen in Las Vegas. Back then, we were very nervous about making the roasted garlic sauce just right as Bobby took the measure of his new crew. My habit is to take lots of notes and be very focused, and I guess I must have done fairly well at executing Bobby's recipes, because a few weeks later he asked me to be his sous-chef. At first, I actually declined (I can't believe it now), saying that I just wasn't ready for such a big job. But Bobby assured me he would guide me through my new responsibilities, and he did. After six months, I felt as if I had been born to the job. I was still cooking on the line three days a week and covering Bobby's expediting shifts the other two. Expediting in a high-volume restaurant, especially one where many of the line cooks were seasoned professionals who were older than me, was like learning to drive a high-performance car—and in the middle of a race. All the power and speed is there, but you have to know how to handle it. I made a lot of mistakes, but Bobby always made it clear that I had his full support, and I rode through the rough spots.

Bobby began to introduce me to the food industry's stars at various parties and culinary events. I met Gael Greene, Florence Fabricant, Alfred Portale, Andrew Nathan, Bruce and Erik Bromberg, Jonathan Waxman, Debra Ponzek, Matthew Kenney, Mildred Amico, Ariane Daguin, Robert Del Grande, Stephen Pyles, and Dean Fearing, to name just a few. It was a very exciting time, and I was beginning to feel part of the larger food community.

When Bobby and Lawrence Kretchmer planned to open a second restaurant, the Spanish-inspired Bolo, Bobby asked me to go along to Spain with him and his friend Paul Del Favero to do some research. I had no illusions about the trip—I knew that Bobby and Paul would tease me incessantly—and they didn't disappoint. Bobby was recovering from a bad cold, and he and Paul spent several afternoons sprawled out on their hotel room beds watching bullfights on TV while I went on pilgrimages to as many sights as I could walk to, and then we joined up every night for dinner. Once we got back to New York, it was fascinating to see how Bobby took the influences from Spain and wove them into his New York vernacular. By contrast, my own ideas felt still half-formed. I continued to enjoy every minute of working with Bobby and our fantastic crew, and yet I soon felt that I wanted and needed to express my own vision through the food I was making. I realized I had to take a stab at being a chef in my own right.

Despite my solid résumé, it was difficult to land the job I wanted. I had always worked in kitchens with bright, passionate, and witty people, and I wasn't willing to settle for anything less. It hadn't dawned on me yet that as the chef I would have to create this environment for myself by hiring great people. So I had a few false starts and learned a lot of lessons along the way—the most enduring one being that a business can only be as great as the people who create it. I needed good partners.

My first real chef position was at a restaurant called Solstice. The owners of Lox Around the Clock, a veritable New York institution for twenty-four-hour service of lox, bagels, and just about any other noshable you can think of, wanted to go upscale. They hired a fancy maître d' and me. The only ingredient missing was capital. They had none, and despite several very good reviews, they pulled the plug four months after we opened. But yet again, the people I met there made even this failure a wonderful experience. I met Steven Hall and Sam Firer, of the public relations firm the Hall Company. At that time, I was a fledgling chef and Steven and Sam had just launched their business; I think I was their second client. Once I met Steven, I realized I had found a kindred spirit—someone who loves our business, but can still see the ridiculous and humorous side of what we do. Once we started talking that day on the banquette at Solstice, we never really stopped. (My doctor still teases me that I'm the only mother who's had her publicist in the birth recovery room.)

I also met and befriended a talented and terribly witty Englishman named Bob Craft. He was hired as the dining room manager of Solstice, and I took to him immediately. I was down in the kitchen doing my tasting for the powers that be before I was hired and he ran downstairs and whispered, "Ask for a lot of money, they're loving it!" We became a real team, and have been sad that since Solstice closed we haven't had a chance to work together again; Bob now keeps tabs on the shenanigans of the restaurant business from the comfortable remove of Cambridge.

The silver lining in the quick demise of Solstice was that it led me to Quilty's. While at Solstice, I was reviewed by Gael Greene in *New York* magazine, and the review caught the eye of Sam Roberts, one of the owners of Quilty's in Princeton. Roberts and his partners, Jim English and Jason Unger, had by sheer grit, luck, and youthful energy made a big hit with their small bistro in Princeton and were looking to expand into New York. They arranged a meeting with me at the offices of the Hall Company. I wasn't sure what to expect, but it certainly wasn't two very young (late twenties), very nice-looking men. I was now in the business of sizing up prospective employers as much as they were me. I had to be really careful about my next project; I was tired of lost causes—they take even more energy than the successes. Steven and Sam were doing a fine job of singing my praises when Roberts abruptly asked if they could speak to me alone. The three of us had a good feeling about our first meeting with him. We made a deal swiftly—gut instinct being the better part of valor. In October, we were to take possession of a restaurant that was closing in SoHo, and planned to open Quilty's in early November. This was an unheard-of turnaround time for a serious restaurant. But we learned a lot about each other that month. I was relieved to find that they were men of their word, could get things done, and had both humor and intelligence. I needed to work with people who got what I was trying to do with my cuisine. I wanted it to be elegant and refined, yet jaunty and exciting. I wanted full creative freedom, and it was granted.

I was making a departure in style from any work that I had done before. I liked the food I was doing at Solstice, but felt a little constrained by the low price point. I spent the summer months working on my menu and liked what was emerging—*my* style. It wasn't Bobby's or Barry's or anyone else's—it was my own. Bobby had always told me that you couldn't have a successful restaurant in New York without having a strong identity to the food, like southwestern or French or Italian. He strongly believed that the dining public wanted to be informed about what the experience would be. I was conceited enough to believe that my cooking would be the draw—even though I didn't exactly know what to call it. From the beginning I have struggled to define it—it has too many influences and convergent styles—so I've settled on "Seasonal American." I would change the menu every season to keep my cuisine moving forward and to stimulate my cooks and the waitstaff about the food.

The next most important task before opening was to find a sous-chef. This is a chef's most important hire—the person who becomes the chef when she's not in the restaurant. He needs to be as good at technique, flavoring, and presentation as the chef, and as good a manager of an often motley crew. And he must also sublimate his ego somewhat. I found all of these qualities in Kevin Roth, a suitably quirky mix of intensity, bull strength, and tenderheartedness. Kevin helped me to launch Quilty's in a very solid way. We were under extreme time pressure, but we were able to train cooks and hammer out the details of my dishes before the door opened to the public on November 7, 1996.

I knew how important reviews were to the future of a restaurant. Ruth Reichl was the critic at the *New York Times,* and I found her work extremely well written and fun to read, but a little unpredictable. I had no idea if she would even come to Quilty's, much less review us favorably. We intentionally opened during the busy season. The first three months were chaotic and energizing. Sam and Jim were generous with their booze, and many a night ended up with the entire crew at the bar celebrating our good fortune to be working together. By the time Ms. Reichl came, we had gelled as a team and were working together pretty smoothly. She awarded us two stars, and business doubled. We believed that we had an instant hit on our hands, that we were the hottest ticket in town. Then came June.

That first summer was a very humbling experience. It was also when I really found out what Jim and Sam were made of. In my past experiences with owners, slow business meant recriminations. Usually the chef is asked to take a hatchet to the labor and food budgets. I knew this could be fatal for the young restaurant. The three of us agreed to scale back but not eviscerate. We didn't lay off a soul. Even more meaningful was the grace with which Jim and Sam accepted this downturn. They took on the responsibility of keeping staff morale up—it's not easy for waiters to exist on 20 percent of not very much. We only did one turn a night that summer. No one walked in the door until eight o'clock most nights. It was very gratifying that our staff believed that we would recover in the fall, that we were too good and too earnest to fail. And they were right.

We had five and a half years of terrific business with some of the greatest regulars ever. Peter Lucania's bar at Quilty's was populated with a wonderfully diverse group—uptowners, downtowners, artists and musicians, Wall Streeters, and the well-heeled from all over. I always loved coming to the bar after a long night and having Peter make me a martini. He made it with such care and skill that I felt I could finally shrug off all the day's pressures. It was also the time to catch up with Sam and Jim, who had been moving nonstop until that moment too. Alas, though, eventually fate intervened, and Quilty's closed its doors shortly after September 11, 2001.

Luke being introduced to the
Quilty's kitchen

But boy, what a run we had.

Early in 2002, I decided to take a stab at raising money for my own restaurant. The timing was not auspicious. The economy was in bad shape and everyone's psyche post-9/11 was in bad shape. I just didn't have the heart to work as someone else's chef. So I did various things to keep us afloat—catering and writing articles for cooking magazines. This work had its charms, but I missed having my own kitchen. I did get to spend loads of time with my then two-year-old son, and looking back at those years I am very grateful that I didn't get immersed in a new project right away. I didn't know how special those years with Luke would be. But ultimately I'm just not stay-at-home-mom material, and I kept looking for a way to reenter the business I love. I know that it is just a business for some people, but for me it is more—it's about setting a stage upon which people can create their own special moments, assisted by food that comforts, intrigues, or excites them, service that welcomes them, and an ambiance that envelops them. It's an organic process; we may have great nights and less-than-great nights, but we always plan a stellar performance when the curtain goes up.

My dream of opening a restaurant of my own has not yet become reality. More time and more disappointments would follow until early 2004, when Andrea Strong and I discussed writing a cookbook together.

Quite frankly, I was not interested in adding my two cents to the vast body of wonderful chef-written cookbooks unless I could share something unique and compelling about my own personal experience as a chef. But then, I thought, I am sort of in a rare position— I am a restaurant-trained chef, but have found myself cooking mainly out of my home for family and friends; perhaps the techniques and methods and recipes I developed for cooking at home, which drew on my experience as a professional chef, might be something people would benefit from (and enjoy) learning and reading about. So Andrea and I decided to give a book a try. Since then, we have spent a great deal of time together, and our friendship is one of the nicest things to happen to me in several years.

As a chef, I know firsthand that cookbooks made up of restaurant recipes that are meant to dazzle and excite often end up discouraging readers. Instead, they are more apt to make a reservation at the chef's restaurant. Such recipes can be expensive, time-consuming, and just plain daunting in their complexity. As a home cook, I have gone through the withdrawal of not having a brigade of sous-chefs, line cooks, and dishwashers to support my every culinary whim. And my husband adamantly refuses to wash every pot and pan in the house every time I make dinner, so I've had to think hard about how to cook and eat as I like without breaking the bank or straining my marriage!

My style of cooking, even when I'm working in a restaurant, has always been very straightforward. I focus primarily on finding great-tasting seasonal ingredients and transforming them with simple techniques. The hallmark of my style is combining flavors and textures in unexpected and surprising ways, such as in the dishes Oysters in Gewürztraminer Cream, crowned with a nest of crispy fried leeks, and Beet-Pickled Eggs, dipped in a spiced salt. And I'm very conscientious about how I store the food I've just purchased

to maintain its peak flavor. In this book I have included tips on how to keep ingredients like fresh herbs, mushrooms, and seafood in the best possible condition for as long as possible. You need to make an investment in your food, and I want to help you learn how to keep it in good shape. I also offer opinions about topics related to good food: fresh versus frozen meats and fish; fresh versus dried herbs;

sustainably raised meats and produce. And generally I just encourage you to go that extra distance to source out the best products you can find.

As much as I'm happy to share my knowledge about food and cooking with you, I want to share the pleasure I take in cooking even more. Even when I cook just for myself, I experience it as a celebration of life. I like how my favorite paring knife or French knife feels in my hand and smile when I see all the scars and nicks on the blades—these are hardworking tools. I enjoy shopping at the farmers market and chatting with the couple who grew the great tomatoes I'll be slicing for my salad tonight, or stopping by the Italian grocery to pick up a homemade salami, or taking a special trip to my favorite fishmonger to find out what fish came in today. Having contact with the people who procure and even grow our food is very satisfying. I still miss my connection to the Vermont land that I grew up on, and shopping for food in this way brings me a little closer to home.

While these recipes are inspired by my work in restaurants, where the customers expected to be dazzled with innovation and inspired combinations, this is essentially home cooking. There are a few dramatic dishes, like Foie Gras "Bonbons" with Fennel Kraut and Lingonberry Sauce and Sea Scallop Carpaccio with Lychee, Cucumber, and Caviar Vinaigrette, but the majority of the dishes are meditations on the ingredients themselves, such as Pan-Roasted Morels and Sweet Corn Soup with Crispy Shiitake Mushrooms, or dishes that are so satisfying and simple to make that they are part of my everyday repertoire, like Grilled Chicken in Marjoram Marinade and Pork Chops Smothered in Lentils.

Andrea created a wonderful device called "Weighing Your Options" to help you find new ways to use leftovers or to enjoy a riff or variation on the recipe, and I've included "Chef's Tricks" with many recipes—secret techniques of the trade that you can employ at home to make sure your fish has a nice brown sear, your chicken stock is rich and fragrant, your meat is tender and juicy, and more. I've also made sure to give you some advice on how long certain dishes can keep in the fridge or in some cases the freezer before they lose their quality. I want to make it as easy as possible for you to enjoy making and eating these dishes. So have fun and don't sweat the details. I still mess up from time to time and forget to put in an essential ingredient or amaze myself with my enduring capacity to find new ways to flub a recipe. But I always take pleasure in the process, reminding myself that I'll be cooking again tomorrow and can redeem myself then.

I hope you enjoy reading and cooking from this book as much as we have enjoyed writing it. And I hope that I've shared enough of my triumphs and struggles with you to shed some light on what really is a labor of love.

Katy Sparks
Brooklyn, New York

Smoked Trout Tartare with Cucumber, Feta, and Dill

Salt-Roasted Fingerling Potatoes with Crème Fraîche and Caviar

Sharp Cheddar and Sherry Crackers

Beet-Pickled Eggs with Spice-Seasoned Salt

Parsley-Stuffed Shrimp with Speck and Horseradish-Lemon Sauce

Chicken Liver Toasts with Cognac-Plumped Golden Raisins, Fried Capers, and Shallots

Smoked Salmon Flutes with Horseradish-Papaya Cream

Goat Cheese Spread with Caraway and Paprika

Beef Tartare with Anchovy Vinaigrette and Arugula

Palatschinken with Fresh Porcini and Pine Nuts

Chilled Oysters on the Half Shell with Apple Cider Mignonette and Grilled Spicy Sausage

Cold Fillet of Beef with Grated Apple and Blackberry-Horseradish Sauce

Roasted Black Mussels with Almond-Garlic-Thyme Butter

Zeke's Tyropitas

Grandma Sparks's Maryland Crab Cakes

Baked Smithfield Ham and Ham Spread

Goat Cheese Quesadillas with Smoked Salmon and Kumquat Relish

Grilled or Roasted Baby Artichokes with Lemon–Cracked Pepper Aioli

Pan-Roasted Morels

Broiled Shell-On Shrimp with Juniper, Black Pepper, and Citrus Dipping Salt

My Homemade Potato Chips

Homemade Gravlax with Fennel, Radish, and Marinated Chanterelles

Foie Gras "Bonbons" with Fennel Kraut and Lingonberry Sauce

COCKTAILS

My Martini • Highballs • Lemon and Lime Juice Drinks • Grandma Sparks's Eggnog

SMALL PLATES, SNACKS, AND COCKTAILS

I come from a family of snackers—grazers or noshers being the current terms. My mother's pantry overflows with nuts, cookies, crackers, and small, ancient tins of savory things. There are ribboned jars of fancy gourmet foods brought as gifts, the kind of thing my mother would never buy herself. She's an accomplished cook who loves to tinker with her own inventions. One of my favorite parts about a trip home to Vermont is seeing what small dishes my mother has just put together and is excited by: potted shrimp, roasted bell peppers with ginger and lemon zest, a fresh batch of Smithfield ham spread. There's a large pewter bowl of nuts in their shells down by the OED in case someone gets waylaid there and needs a few calories in them to turn the book's heavy pages. There are jars and small dishes filled with Hershey's Kisses, neighbors' home-made confections, and various kinds of mints scattered throughout the house—and not just for guests who might stop by. These candies are for when a little sugar rush can ease the transition from one chore to the next. Each vehicle, whether the farm truck, the sedan, or the fishing boat, has a box of Wheat Thins tucked into the passenger-door pocket. No trip could be safely launched without them. In Vermont, you don't know when you might get stranded in a snowdrift or forced to a full stop by a herd of cattle crossing the road to a fresh meadow. But, more likely, you'll just need a snack.

Life in the country is physically demanding, so the days are punctuated by cups of tea or coffee and a lunchtime shot of frozen vodka with a handful of pistachio nuts and the noon weather report. The body needs to be restored after raking leaves, feeding chickens, planting gardens, and repairing the weatherworn structures around the place. As a city dweller, I have to be careful to moderate my consumption of these daily rituals—I just don't need the constant refueling I

My parents' house in Vermont

did as a country girl. But when I'm up visiting the folks, I fall right back into that familiar pattern. It feels so natural to gather in the kitchen every few hours to reconnect, put on a kettle, and enjoy a small bite together.

As the day wears on, my folks will head to bed for a late-afternoon nap or the chance to get a chapter further into the newest spy thriller. My mother will have already planned what dinner will be, and the house gets very quiet and still for an hour or so. Then the kettle is on to rewarm and reawaken the snoozers, and the house starts to buzz again. Just around six is martini time. There have been other cocktails mixed in my parents' house, but rarely. The ritual is a martini and some kind of cocktail goody, a quick game of pool, and the anticipation of a good meal to come—often with good friends stopping by to share it.

I hope you will enjoy these small dishes, snacks, and cocktails to the fullest. If we were cooking together, we would all lift a glass and celebrate the moment.

Smoked Trout Tartare with Cucumber, Feta, and Dill

I love this dish because it's full of robust, smoky flavors. It is also a nice departure from smoked salmon. Trout takes on a wonderful richness when it is treated to some time in the smoker. When you combine the rich trout with crisp cucumber and briny feta, you have a real palate tickler that can be dressed down with a beer or gussied up with a glass of sparkling wine.

SERVES 6

Peel the cucumbers, slice them in half lengthwise, and run the tip of a spoon down the length of each half to remove the seeds. Cut half of 1 cucumber into ¼-inch dice and put in a big bowl. Add the rest of your ingredients—the trout, sherry vinegar, lemon juice, olive oil, feta, salt, pepper, dill, and orange zest. Toss everything together thoroughly in the bowl.

Remove a thin strip from the bottom of the remaining cucumber halves so they will sit up without tipping. Cut the cucumbers on a slight diagonal into 1-inch sections, and top each section with a teaspoon of the filling. Garnish with a strip of the red pepper.

NOTE: This recipe is ideal for parties because it can be made up to 2 hours ahead and refrigerated. Just take it out of the fridge 5 minutes before serving. The full flavors will be masked if it is kept too cold.

2 European-style hothouse cucumbers

¼ pound smoked trout, picked over for bones and diced small

1 tablespoon sherry vinegar

1 tablespoon lemon juice

2 tablespoons extra virgin olive oil

3 ounces Greek feta (not French feta, which is too mild)

Pinch of salt

Freshly ground black pepper to taste

3 tablespoons minced fresh dill

1 teaspoon freshly grated orange zest

for garnish
Half a red bell pepper, cut into a thin julienne

Salt-Roasted Fingerling Potatoes with Crème Fraîche and Caviar

This is not so much a recipe as an inspired combination. While certainly not unique to my repertoire, it is worth trumpeting to the world as loudly and often as possible. Good caviar is getting scarcer and more expensive, but I would urge you to wait to make this dish until you get your hands on all the best ingredients—fresh, small fingerling potatoes, good crème fraîche (not sour cream), and either Iranian or Russian caviar (sevruga, osetra, or beluga; see Sources and box on page 142). You will be rewarded for your efforts with the truly sublime: warm potatoes, cool crème fraîche, and the essential primordial flavor of the briny sweet-saltiness of the sturgeon eggs bursting in your mouth. And don't be stingy with that caviar, baby! Better to have two or three bites loaded up with caviar than spread the wealth too thin.

SERVES 6–8

2 cups coarse sea salt
   (see next page)
2 sprigs thyme
1 pound very small
   fingerling potatoes
   (Russian Banana and
   Ruby Crescent are both
   great)
¼ cup crème fraîche
   (see next page)
6 ounces caviar, your choice
¼ cup minced chives

Heat your oven to 375°F. Scatter the sea salt over a baking sheet, and lay the sprigs of thyme on top of the salt. Arrange the whole potatoes on top of the salt-thyme bed, and roast until they are tender—about 30 minutes. (Salt-roasting concentrates the flavors and helps infuse the herbs' aromas into whatever you are cooking.) Remove the potatoes from the oven and brush off any salt.

Make an X incision on top of each potato and squeeze gently to open it up slightly. Spoon a bit of crème fraîche in the X-marks-the-spot, add as much caviar as you dare, and garnish with chives. Serve while the potatoes are still warm. I can't think of a better accompanying beverage than ice-cold premium vodka—Prosit!

CRÈME FRAÎCHE

Crème fraîche is a luscious thickened cream with a subtle nutty flavor and a zippy tang, similar to sour cream. In France, where unpasteurized cream is used, the bacteria are present to naturally thicken it, but here in America, where all cream is pasteurized, buttermilk or sour cream is added to the cream to start the process of fermenting and thickening. Good-quality, commercially produced crème fraîche is readily available around the country, but it can be expensive, and it is easy to make on your own.

To prepare crème fraîche at home, combine 1 cup heavy cream with 1 tablespoon buttermilk in a glass container and let stand at room temperature for at least 8 hours (and up to 24) until it is very thick. Stir well. It can be stored, covered well, for up to 10 days in the fridge.

SALT

Kosher salt is my choice for a good all-purpose seasoning salt; I like the big flakes and the mild flavor. Both kosher salt and sea salt are better choices than traditional table salt, which has a harsh flavor and undesirable additives. When a special garnish or larger crystal is called for, I use any one of the various sea salts in my pantry. Each one has a slightly different taste, texture, and color, and all boast a high mineral content (a supposed healthful benefit), from magnesium and potassium to zinc and calcium. These are a few of my favorites:

- Maldon sea salt, from England: large, pyramidal crystals, easy to crumble
- Fleur de sel, from Brittany: the crème de la crème of salts—from the very top layer of the salt pond
- Alaea Hawaiian sea salt: red Hawaiian clay gives this salt a high mineral content and red color
- Maine sea salt: large crunchy crystals—great for garnishing pretzels and rolls
- Hallen Mon smoked sea salt, from Ireland: smoked over hardwood chips—it's just cool

Sharp Cheddar and Sherry Crackers

As a former Vermonter, I am a proud supporter of my home state's best native products. One of these is the world-class cheddar available from many committed artisans around the state. (Grafton Village Cheese and Shelburne Farms are two local producers that make great cheddars. See Sources.) I think the sharper the cheese, the better it is for this recipe. I keep a log or two of dough in the freezer so I can bake off a tray of these crackers to accompany a hearty soup for lunch.

SERVES 6

6 tablespoons unsalted butter, softened

10 ounces extra-sharp Vermont cheddar cheese, grated

1 tablespoon Dijon mustard

1 tablespoon kosher salt

1 tablespoon freshly ground black pepper

2 teaspoons paprika

3 tablespoons sherry*

2 tablespoons heavy cream

1⅓ cups flour

*For the sherry, I like amontillado best for this recipe, but a fino works well too. I wouldn't use a cream sherry, because it is too sweet.

Cream the butter with a wooden spoon. This step is worth the effort because it will make the dough dense, without air pockets, so the crackers turn out light and flaky. Once the butter is completely smooth (no lumps), fold in the cheese, mustard, salt, pepper, paprika, sherry, and cream. Mix together well with your spoon. Now, gently pour in the flour and mix again with your spoon, until all the ingredients are well combined.

Divide the dough into thirds and roll each into a log about 8 inches long; wrap each in foil. At this point, the dough can be frozen, but if you are going to proceed to bake the crackers, the rolls must be refrigerated for at least 3 hours.

When you are ready to bake the crackers, preheat your oven to 325°F. Remove a log from the refrigerator and slice it into ½-inch-thick rounds. Place the rounds on an ungreased cookie sheet and bake them for about 30 minutes, until they are a nice golden brown. You'll want to cool these slightly before serving—they taste better warm than piping hot, and you won't burn the roof of your mouth!

Beet-Pickled Eggs
with Spice-Seasoned Salt

While beet-pickled eggs may seem a bit odd at first glance, I encourage you to put your hesitation aside and try this recipe. I keep a jar of these beautiful pink-hued eggs in the fridge. They are a great tangy fix for a substantial salty craving, especially when dipped in the spice-seasoned salt. They look festive at parties and are a whimsical, updated bar classic.

SERVES 6

make the beet-pickled eggs

Cut off and discard the beet tops, but do not peel the beets. Put the beets in a large pot with enough cold water just to cover them, and then add your spices, vinegar, and salt and simmer until the beets are tender, about 30 minutes. Remove the beets and cool. Reserve the liquid.

In a separate pot, hard-cook the eggs. (My method is to start the eggs in a pot of cold water, and then simmer gently for 10 minutes once the water comes to a boil.) Cool your eggs immediately and shell them once they are not too hot to handle. Peel and slice the reserved beets, and put them back into the cooking liquid with the eggs. (It is fun to pack them in a glass jar so you can see the beautiful color begin to emerge.) When the eggs are a deep rosy shade (about 3 days), you'll know they are well pickled and ready to dig into. They will last in their pickling liquid, refrigerated, for up to 2 weeks.

make the spice-seasoned salt

Toss all the ingredients together and store at room temperature.

Serve the beet-pickled eggs in a ceramic bowl with an accompanying dish of the spice-seasoned salt, and you will have instant pink-egg-related cocktail conversation. You can also slice them and have them as a snack with some sliced red onion and hearty buttered bread, or toss them into a green salad for a burst of color and flavor.

for the eggs

6 medium-small beets
1 tablespoon whole black peppercorns
1 teaspoon coriander seed
1 teaspoon whole cloves
1 teaspoon mustard seeds
6 tablespoons cider vinegar
3 tablespoons kosher salt
8 large eggs

for the spice-seasoned salt

¼ cup kosher salt
1 tablespoon ground cumin
2 teaspoons ground coriander seed
1 teaspoon ground ginger
1 teaspoon freshly ground black pepper
1 teaspoon grated lemon peel

Parsley-Stuffed Shrimp
with Speck and Horseradish-Lemon Sauce

This is a boldly flavored appetizer or hors d'oeuvre that really wakes up the palate. When creating a small bite or a first course of a meal, I like to hit several flavor zones, and this starter is perfect because smoky, herbaceous, and tart are all at play here. What's also nice about this dish is that your kitchen will become filled with a wonderful aroma when you broil the shrimp. If possible, wait until guests have arrived to pop them in the oven; heads will turn and appetites will quickly become ignited. You could serve four of these shrimp with a small green salad and a baguette and have quite a fine lunch.

SERVES 6

*With Andrea in
my dining room*

prepare the shrimp

Peel and devein the shrimp, leaving their tails attached. Butterfly the shrimp by making a shallow cut lengthwise along their inside curve, being careful not to cut all the way through. Refrigerate.

Put the shallot, pine nuts, garlic, and bunch of parsley in your food processor and pulse to puree. Add the Parmesan and olive oil and pulse again, just to combine. Season with salt and pepper to taste.

make the horseradish-lemon sauce

Mix together all ingredients for the horseradish sauce in a small bowl, and set that aside while you prepare the shrimp.

Preheat your broiler. Place each shrimp on a work surface with the tail away from you. Fill the body of each butterflied shrimp with 1 teaspoon of the parsley mixture from the food processor. Wrap 1 thin piece of speck or bacon around each shrimp and secure with a toothpick. Repeat until all the shrimp have been stuffed.

Brush a broiler pan with a little olive oil and arrange your shrimp on the pan. Broil under high heat for 2 minutes or until the bacon begins to brown and the shrimp are opaque. Serve the shrimp hot on a platter with the horseradish sauce drizzled over the top, and if you are feeling decorative, some chopped parsley as well.

‹ leftover alert ›
Use any of the excess parsley mix to toss with pasta,
or spread it on good toasted bread
for a tasty little crostini.

for the shrimp

1 pound large shrimp
1 shallot
2 tablespoons toasted pine nuts
1 clove garlic
1 bunch fresh parsley, plus some chopped parsley for garnish if desired
1 tablespoon grated Parmesan cheese
2 tablespoons olive oil, plus more for greasing pan
Salt and freshly ground pepper to taste
½ pound speck or double-smoked bacon, thinly sliced*

for the horseradish-lemon sauce

Juice of 1 lemon
2 tablespoons prepared horseradish
1 teaspoon honey
2 tablespoons extra virgin olive oil
Salt and freshly ground pepper to taste

*Speck is smoked bacon, similar to prosciutto, made in Alto Adige, Italy. You can substitute regular bacon or prosciutto.

Chicken Liver Toasts with Cognac-Plumped Golden Raisins, Fried Capers, and Shallots

I like to make this pâté two or three days ahead to let the flavors really ripen. It will keep up to a week if stored refrigerated in small, well-wrapped crocks. If you can't find pancetta, don't substitute bacon, because I think the smokiness is too strong for the chicken livers. Use a bit of prosciutto instead. This dish is a gesture toward my assimilation into the Jewish deli culture of New York City; even a kid from Vermont can learn to love chicken liver.

SERVES 6–8 (MAKES ABOUT 2½ CUPS OF MOUSSE)

for the chicken liver mousse
1 pound cleaned chicken livers
2 cups cold milk
Salt and freshly ground pepper
¼ teaspoon ground coriander
¼ teaspoon ground anise
2 tablespoons vegetable oil
1 tablespoon butter
2 ounces pancetta or prosciutto
1 shallot, minced
1 teaspoon orange zest
1 tablespoon minced fresh sage
2 tablespoons unsalted butter, softened, for blending with cooked livers

make the chicken liver mousse
Soak livers in the cold milk for an hour. This removes some of the excess blood and tenderizes the livers.

Drain the soaked livers on paper towels. Season them well with salt, pepper, coriander, and anise. Heat vegetable oil and butter in a sauté pan. When the butter begins to sizzle, carefully place the livers in the pan and turn the heat down to medium-low. Cook the livers for 1 minute on each side. You want them to be medium-rare (still pink) on the inside and not too browned on the outside. Remove them from the pan.

Now, brown the pancetta or prosciutto in the same pan over medium-low heat while stirring, and cook it until it begins to crisp, but is not too firm. Scatter the shallots over the pancetta and sauté 1 minute longer. The orange zest and sage should be added at this point. Stir for 15–20 seconds. Remove the pancetta, shallots, orange zest, and sage from the pan and drain well on a plate covered with paper towels.

Put the liver and the pancetta mixture into a food processor and pulse to puree. Then pulse in the 2 tablespoons of softened butter. Pass this mixture through a sieve—you'll have to push it through with a bit of effort to remove any tough parts of the livers.

prepare the raisins

Bring the apple cider and cognac to a simmer, add the raisins and spices, and simmer gently until raisins have plumped up, about 10 minutes. Drain the raisins from the liquid, reserving the cooking juices. Fold the raisins into the chicken liver mousse, and taste for seasoning, adding more salt and pepper if necessary. Pack the mousse into an earthenware or glass crock, wrap well with plastic wrap, and store in fridge. I like to wait a few days before eating this, as time helps ripen the flavors.

for the cognac-plumped golden raisins

¼ cup cider or apple juice

3 tablespoons cognac

¼ cup golden raisins

1 stick cinnamon

2 whole cloves

fry the capers and shallots

Heat the vegetable oil in a deep casserole over medium heat until it shimmers, then slip in the capers and cook until they stop sizzling—this means their liquid has evaporated away and they are crisp. Scoop the capers up with a slotted spoon and drain them on paper towels. Dip the shallot rings in milk, then dredge them in some flour seasoned with salt and pepper. Fry them in the same oil until they turn golden brown. Drain on paper towels and season with salt.

When you are ready to serve the complete dish, take the chicken pâté out of the fridge a few minutes beforehand to let it warm up a bit, then spread it on crackers or crusty bread and top each with a pinch of the crispy shallots and capers. Both garnishes will keep a day or two at room temperature if stored in airtight containers.

for the fried capers and shallots

½ cup vegetable oil

3 tablespoons capers

3 shallots, thinly sliced into rings

¼ cup milk

1 cup flour

Salt and freshly ground pepper to taste

Smoked Salmon Flutes
with Horseradish-Papaya Cream

This is an easy-to-prepare, dramatic, high-impact dish. There aren't too many folks around who don't like the combination of smoked salmon and horseradish, and the papaya adds a sweet and exotic note. If papaya is not in season, any ripe stone fruit will work—nectarines, peaches, mangoes, or apricots.

SERVES 6

2 tablespoons warm water
1 tablespoon powdered gelatin
2 tablespoons prepared horseradish, drained of its liquid
½ cup heavy cream
1 ripe papaya, diced (about ½ cup), 1 tablespoon reserved for garnish
6 slices smoked salmon
1 tablespoon minced cilantro leaves

Put the 2 tablespoons warm water in a cup and sprinkle powdered gelatin evenly over the surface. Stir up once, and when the gelatin is no longer gritty but smooth in the water, combine it with the horseradish. Whip the cream until it comes to soft peaks, and then fold in the horseradish-gelatin mixture and the papaya.

Roll the salmon slices into flute or cone shapes and fill each with the horseradish cream using a spoon, a pastry bag, or even a ziplock bag with an edge snipped off. Let the flutes sit in the fridge for 30 minutes. Garnish with reserved diced papaya and the cilantro leaves.

Goat Cheese Spread with Caraway and Paprika

I'm not usually a fan of cheese spreads (I had a bad experience with Velveeta), but this one is easy to make and easy to like. This spread is based on a traditional Austrian dish, Liptauer, a farmer cheese spread commonly eaten as a snack in beer halls. My version is a bit more refined—using goat cheese instead—and it is a last-minute lifesaver if unexpected guests show up looking hungry.

SERVES 6

Place all of your ingredients in a food processor and puree for 1–2 minutes, until smooth. Spoon the cheese spread into a crock and let it sit overnight in the refrigerator. The spread will keep for a week (as long as you don't eat it all in one night). I like to serve it with a good dense rye bread, or even pretzels.

4 ounces fresh goat cheese
2 ounces small-curd cottage cheese
1 tablespoon minced white onion
1 clove garlic, germ removed, and minced (see Chef's Trick)
1 tablespoon minced dill, or other herb such as chervil, parsley, cilantro, or tarragon
2 teaspoons caraway seeds
1 tablespoon caraway-flavored aquavit or eau de vie (optional)
1 teaspoon Hungarian paprika
Salt and freshly ground black pepper

Chef's Trick When using raw garlic, it is important to remove the innermost green germ by splitting the clove in half and pulling out the tender inner shoot. The germ makes the garlic ferment slightly, leading to a bitter taste. When cooking garlic, the heat deactivates the germ, so it is not a problem.

Beef Tartare
with Anchovy Vinaigrette and Arugula

I eat less red meat than I used to, so when I do, I want it rare and of the best quality. Steak tartare is a treat because the garnishes enhance its essential, rich meatiness, and you don't need all that much to get your red meat fix. The pepperiness of the arugula is a nice foil for the rich beef.

SERVES 6

for the tartare

1 pound of the best-quality sirloin or fillet of beef from a reputable butcher or market*

2 tablespoons capers

¼ cup minced red onion

1 teaspoon Tabasco sauce

1 teaspoon Worcestershire sauce

1 teaspoon minced fresh tarragon

1 tablespoon olive oil

1 teaspoon Dijon mustard

Salt and freshly ground pepper to taste

*Sirloin will be a little more flavorful but not quite as tender as the fillet because it has a lot more marbling in it. The fillet is the opposite—it is more tender, but it lacks the intense beefy flavor of sirloin.

make the tartare

Have your butcher grind the meat fresh for you, or do it yourself by pulsing chunks of it in your food processor until it is just minced—not longer, or the texture will be lost. If you have a KitchenAid mixer with a grinder attachment, you can also process the meat that way.

Fold the meat in with the capers, onion, Tabasco, Worcestershire, tarragon, olive oil, and mustard in a medium-size bowl, and season with salt and pepper. Put the tartare in the fridge to let the flavors develop for a few minutes while you prepare the vinaigrette.

make the vinaigrette

Place the anchovies, garlic, lemon juice, and parsley in a blender and puree until smooth; slowly pulse in the olive oil. Add salt and pepper to taste.

Divide the tartare among 6 cold plates, pressing a little well into the center of each mound. Place the eggs in boiling water for just a minute; this will warm the yolks slightly. Separate the yolk from the white and rest a yolk in each well. Dress the arugula with the vinaigrette and surround the tartare with the leaves when you are ready to eat.

for the anchovy vinaigrette

4 anchovy fillets (see Sources)
1 clove garlic
2 tablespoons lemon juice
2 tablespoons minced parsley
1/4 cup olive oil
Salt and freshly ground pepper to taste

6 small eggs
1 bunch arugula, washed and dried

Pureeing in a handy home-size food processor

Palatschinken with Fresh Porcini and Pine Nuts

I've had a lifelong love affair with palatschinken—the Central European version of crepes. Simple to make, they can be prepared with an infinite variety of flavors and fillings, both sweet and savory. The classic sweet pancakes are filled with apricot jam, quark, or poppy seeds and dusted with powdered sugar. The savory ones are often rolled, sliced into strips, and used to garnish clear soups, or they are filled with a meat ragout or smoked fish and caviar. You need just three things to make good palatschinken: (1) a basic recipe, (2) a good crepe pan (see Note), and (3) a little practice.

NOTE: A good crepe pan is made of either carbon steel, blue steel, or copper, all of which conduct heat quickly and evenly. It will also have a good flat bottom and shallow sloping sides that make it easy to flip the crepe over. Lastly, it should have a tilted handle, to make it easy to swirl the batter evenly over the bottom. The blue steel and the carbon steel pans will season over time. You don't want to wash these in water—they will rust. Instead, just wipe the inside of the pan vigorously with a paper towel dipped in olive oil, with a little salt if you need some abrasive action.

This porcini mushroom recipe is one of my favorite savory versions. A firm, meaty mushroom, the porcini is amazingly good both fresh and dried. Here I use the fresh mushroom, which takes very well to roasting in generous thick slices. I make this special dish with friends and family milling about the kitchen with forks poised!

SERVES 6

for the palatschinken batter

3 eggs
1 cup milk
4 tablespoons melted butter
1 cup sifted flour
1 teaspoon curry powder
½ teaspoon salt
Freshly ground black pepper
Freshly ground nutmeg

make the palatschinken

Beat the eggs until frothy, then pour in the milk and 2 tablespoons of the melted butter. Stir in the flour, curry powder, salt, pepper, and nutmeg; keep stirring until the batter is smooth.

Warm the crepe pan over medium heat until it is hot. Dip a paper towel (folded into a small pad so you don't burn your fingers) in some of the remaining melted butter, and grease the pan. Carefully pour the batter into the pan and tilt or swirl until the batter coats the bottom. Cook your palatschinken over medium heat until the pancake browns on the bottom; the edges will begin to turn a caramel color (this whole process takes seconds). Flip it over using a flexible spatula, and brown the second side, which won't take quite as long as the first. Stack the crepes on a warm plate, one on top of another. You don't need to separate the crepes with parchment; there is enough butter that they will not stick together, and they will keep each other warm.

Continue this process with the remaining batter. Don't worry if the first one or two are part of a learning curve. Even the pros need a warm-up with crepes! And the torn ones make good snacks.

prepare the porcini filling

Trim off the bottom quarter inch of the mushroom stems. Brush the mushrooms with a damp towel to remove soil or debris. Cut them lengthwise into ½-inch-thick slices.

Heat your butter in a wide, shallow skillet. When it is bubbling, add the mushrooms. Don't add salt at this point, because it will draw out the moisture from the mushrooms and prevent browning, and this is where you'll get a lot of the glorious flavors of the porcini. Shake the mushrooms over medium heat for 2 minutes or until the bottoms brown, then turn them over. Toss in the shallots and cook the other side another 2 minutes. Season with salt and pepper. Remove the pan from the heat while pouring in the Madeira (that way you'll preserve your eyebrows). Return the pan to the heat, and the Madeira will quickly reduce to a syrup. Pour in the chicken stock, heavy cream, and thyme and reduce the sauce by boiling it until it is thick enough to coat a spoon—about 2 or 3 minutes. Once reduced, add the pine nuts, lemon zest, and parsley. Taste for seasoning and spoon some mushrooms and sauce over each crepe, fold into quarters, and serve hot with a spoonful of sauce drizzled on top.

for the porcini filling

1 pound fresh porcini*
2 tablespoons butter
2 shallots, minced
Salt and freshly ground
    pepper to taste
3 tablespoons Madeira
¼ cup chicken stock (see
    Appendix, or use
    organic, low-sodium
    boxed)
½ cup heavy cream
1 tablespoon minced fresh
    thyme
¼ cup toasted pine nuts
1 teaspoon lemon zest
1 tablespoon minced
    parsley

*Cremini mushrooms may be substituted, but they lend a more typical, less nuanced flavor. You could also use a combination of the two mushrooms.

Chilled Oysters on the Half Shell with Apple Cider Mignonette and Grilled Spicy Sausage

This dish is inspired by the Bordeaux region of France, where they pair chilled oysters with sizzling hot pork sausage, often studded with black truffle. I would never advise you to *not* add truffle, so if it is in your budget, please indulge; but if it isn't, don't fret. It is not necessary at all. Here is what *is* necessary: swallowing a chilled oyster with the mignonette and chasing it down with a mouthful of hot sausage and a bite of bread and butter. Repeat.

SERVES 6

for the sausage

1½ pounds trimmed, lean pork cut in small pieces

½ pound fatback, rind removed, cut in small pieces

1 tablespoon freshly ground black pepper

1 tablespoon lemon zest

1 tablespoon dried thyme

2 whole garlic cloves

2 dried hot red chiles, minced, or 1 teaspoon dried chile flakes

1 tablespoon kosher salt

3 tablespoons ice water

Olive oil, for frying

2 ounces fresh truffles, minced (optional)

make the sausage

This sausage is easy to make, and you can forgo the chore of stuffing casings by forming the sausage into meat patties.

Chill all your grinding equipment before beginning—this step is important, because it prevents the fat in the meat from melting, ensuring that your sausages won't be tough. Combine all the sausage ingredients except the salt and water. Chill well, for about 30 minutes. Grind the sausage ingredients through the medium plate of your grinder, adding salt and the 3 tablespoons of ice water as you go. Pinch off a small piece of the forcemeat and sauté until it is cooked through. Taste for seasoning. Now you'll want to add whatever salt and pepper to the raw meat you may want, because you won't be able to adjust your seasoning later.

Grind the mixture a second time through the same plate to further refine the texture of the sausage. After the meat is ground, fold in your minced truffles, if desired. Form the sausage into patties and chill them on a cookie sheet, preferably overnight or for at least 3 hours, before cooking. (The patties can be frozen for up to 2 months wrapped in wax paper and then placed in freezer bags. Defrost them completely before cooking.)

To cook the sausage, heat a cast-iron or thick-bottomed skillet with a thin coating of olive oil, and pan-fry the patties until well browned on the outside and just faintly pink on the inside—about 3 minutes per side.

make the mignonette
Toss the apple, shallots, vinegar, cider, and pepper together in a small bowl. Let mellow for about an hour at room temperature, before serving with the oysters and the sausage.

for the mignonette
1 green apple, peeled, cored, and diced fine
2 shallots, minced
¼ cup cider vinegar
¼ cup apple cider
1 tablespoon coarsely ground black pepper

18 East Coast oysters, shucked to order (see Appendix on techniques)

Cold Fillet of Beef with Grated Apple and Blackberry-Horseradish Sauce

for the blackberry-horseradish sauce

1 firm apple such as Gala or Fuji

3 tablespoons freshly grated horseradish root, or 2 tablespoons prepared horseradish, drained

1 tablespoon lemon juice

½ cup lightly crushed blackberries

1 teaspoon sugar

3 sage leaves, minced

1 teaspoon grated orange zest

Salt and pepper

3 tablespoons crème fraîche (see box on page 29)

for the roast beef

1 pound roasted, chilled fillet of beef, or leftover rib roast, cooked rare to medium-rare

1 medium loaf hearty rye bread, sliced

6–8 thinly sliced red radishes

2 tablespoons coarse sea salt, for passing

Freshly ground black pepper

This is one of those dishes that can either be made quite deliberately, or serendipitously when you have cold, leftover roasted beef tenderloin to take advantage of. Either way, it is a fun and flavorful little recipe. I serve this with buttered rye bread and radishes.

SERVES 6

Peel and grate the apple into a bowl, then mix in all the remaining sauce ingredients except the crème fraîche. Marinate for about half an hour at room temperature. Fold in the crème fraîche, and season to taste with salt and pepper.

Slice the beef very thin, and arrange it on a plate with the bread and radishes. Spoon the blackberry-horseradish sauce over the beef. Have a small bowl of coarse sea salt and some pepper at the table to pass around.

Roasted Black Mussels
with Almond-Garlic-Thyme Butter

For this mussel dish, I like to take the road less traveled—serving them on the half shell, topped with a flavorful butter and broiled until they are sizzling hot and aromatic—rather than following the more common wine-based *moule* recipes. I like to eat these fresh from the broiler and cool my palate with a crisp white wine. My favorites are Loire Valley Sancerre and Pouilly Fumé.

SERVES 6

Rinse the mussels in a colander under cold water. Most cultivated mussels don't have beards, but take a look anyway, and if you find any, be sure to pull them off.

Melt the butter in a wide skillet, then add the shallots and sauté them in the butter until tender. Add your mussels, wine, and bay leaf. Cover and steam until the mussels just open; start checking after 3 minutes. Remove the mussels from the broth, and reserve the liquid, which you can strain and freeze as a handy fish broth for soups, pastas, and the like. When the mussels are cool enough to handle, remove their top shells and discard. Arrange the mussels in their bottom shells in a gratin dish.

Put all ingredients for almond butter in a food processor—or, if you are a Luddite like me, mix with a wooden spoon. Dot each mussel with the almond butter, sprinkle each with the bread crumbs, and roast in a 450°F oven until the bread crumbs are a golden brown color, about 2 or 3 minutes. Serve immediately.

2 pounds Prince Edward
    Island mussels
2 teaspoons unsalted butter
2 shallots, thinly sliced
¼ cup dry white wine
1 bay leaf

for the almond butter
¼ cup toasted ground
    almonds
6 tablespoons unsalted
    butter, softened
1 tablespoon minced lemon
    zest
1 tablespoon minced fresh
    thyme leaves
1 tablespoon minced garlic
Salt and freshly ground
    black pepper

¼ cup fresh bread crumbs

Zeke's Tyropitas

My mother-in-law, Zeke Amendolara, showed me how to make these addictive little cheese turnovers. They are Greek in origin, but with the addition of a dry martini, very WASPy indeed! They freeze beautifully and will emerge golden and crispy from the oven in twenty minutes flat.

SERVES MANY (MAKES 36–48 SMALL TURNOVERS)

2 cups feta cheese

2 cups small-curd cottage cheese, drained

¼ cup grated Romano cheese

4 large eggs, beaten

2 tablespoons minced parsley

Salt and freshly ground pepper

1 box thawed phyllo pastry

2 sticks butter, melted

make the filling

Fold together the cheeses, eggs, parsley, and salt and pepper in a small bowl.

assemble the tyropitas

For every 6 turnovers, you should use 2 layers of phyllo, liberally brushing each layer with melted butter. To assemble, start at the shorter end of the phyllo rectangle and cut into 6 even strips. Beginning at the far left lower corner of each strip, place ½ teaspoon of filling, and like folding an American flag, begin making right-angle turns until you have reached the end of the strip and you have a triangle-shaped pastry. Brush the turnovers liberally with butter and place them on wax paper. When all the triangles have been made, place them between layers of wax paper in a box or snap-top container and freeze. They can also be baked and eaten right away.

Preheat your oven to 400°F, and bake the pastries for 12 minutes on an ungreased cookie sheet (they already have enough butter). If they have been frozen they can go directly from the freezer to the oven for 20 minutes. They will be a pale golden color and very hot inside, so be careful with the first bite!

Phyllo Dough Working with phyllo dough can be a frustrating experience if you ignore one important rule: Always defrost the dough slowly, overnight in your refrigerator. If you try to rush it you will lose half a box to sticky layers. Always keep the phyllo covered with a dry kitchen towel while working with it and brush layers liberally with melted butter.

Grandma Sparks's Maryland Crab Cakes

My grandmother, who lived her entire life just outside Baltimore, was a great cook, and these crab cakes were mainly responsible for burnishing her culinary reputation. You will be forgiven, dear reader, for thinking that the Sparks clan is obsessed with mayonnaise. And you may be right—so many of my family's culinary treasures use this humble but essential ingredient. We're a little particular about it too—unless you are willing to make your own, only Hellmann's (not Hellmann's Light—the real thing) will do. These crab cakes also depend on finding the freshest lump crabmeat (see Sources).

SERVES 6 (MAKES ABOUT 8–12 SMALL CAKES)

Carefully mix all of the crab cake ingredients together in a large bowl. Don't break up the crabmeat; big chunks are so much more satisfying to eat. When your crab cake batter is thoroughly mixed, let it rest for several hours in the refrigerator—this allows the bread cubes to soak up the moisture from the crab so they won't fall apart in the pan.

Shape your cakes into any size you wish—large ones for lunch, or tiny ones for hors d'oeuvres. When you're ready to serve them, heat a nonstick or heavy-bottomed skillet, add a generous amount of butter, and sauté the cakes over medium heat until golden brown, about 2 minutes per side.

‹ weighing your options ›

We serve our crab cakes with just a squeeze of lemon, but for a more assertive and modern accompaniment, you can pair them with Smoked Chile and Caper Remoulade (see page 271); it will give them a nice kick.

1 pound fresh lump crabmeat, picked over gently for any stray shells or cartilage

1 teaspoon salt

1 teaspoon Colman's dry mustard

½ teaspoon freshly ground black pepper

2 tablespoons Worcestershire sauce

1 egg, beaten

1 tablespoon mayonnaise (see headnote)

2 tablespoons chopped fresh parsley

2 slices fresh bread, crusts removed, diced into very small cubes

Butter, for sautéing

Baked Smithfield Ham and Ham Spread

We joke in my family that my mother really goes to the trouble of procuring a Smithfield ham, soaking it for twenty-four hours, and carefully baking it, just so we can grind it up and combine it with mayonnaise to spread on toast! In reality, having a desalinated (they are a salty beast) baked country ham in the fridge is very comforting—it keeps very well, and a thin slice with unsalted butter on good bread transports me to a simpler time. The grindings are precious and can be frozen for up to two months—just about when you'll need to pick up the phone and order another ham to be shipped out. We order from R. M. Felts Packing Company (see Sources) and request a "small" ham, which is usually about twelve pounds and takes about three days to be delivered.

prepare the ham

Soak the ham, completely immersed in cold water, at room temperature for twenty-four hours, changing the water every six hours. Does this mean you have to get up in the middle of the night? Yes! We want commitment here! (Just kidding. Change the water when you wake up.)

Bake the ham in a roasting pan at 325°F for about twenty minutes per pound. Test for temperature with a meat thermometer—you want it to reach 160°. You will wind up with a crackling, almost black-skinned beauty of a ham that should be chilled overnight in the fridge before you break into it. And it does feel like breaking in . . . you'll need a sharp knife and a strong wrist to crack the shell. My mother always calls my father up from the barn or his study to make the first cut. As part of the breaking-into-the-ham ritual, he sharpens his big carbon steel knife (which they purchased in France in the 1950s) and goes to work, cracking through the lacquered shell. When you break into your own ham, make the first slice at a slight angle right down to the bone. Slice as thin as possible and save all scraps and trimming for the grindings.

make the justly famous sparks ham spread

Grind the leftover ham scraps by pulsing small pieces in your food processor until it is fine. Combine equal parts ham grindings with mayonnaise. We dip into the spread with thin breadsticks at cocktail time or slather it on toast in the morning with eggs or anytime we want a salty, smoky snack.

NOTE: Some family friends have told me in the strictest confidence (don't tell my mother) that they actually adulterate this family treasure with some hot sauce with apparently good results.

Goat Cheese Quesadillas
with Smoked Salmon and Kumquat Relish

Eight 6-inch flour tortillas
12 ounces creamy goat
    cheese
½ small red onion, minced
Salt and freshly ground
    pepper

for the kumquat relish
1 dozen kumquats, sliced
    into rings with seeds
    removed
¼ fresh green chile, minced
1 small bunch cilantro
    leaves, minced

4 tablespoons vegetable oil
2 tablespoons butter
½ pound smoked salmon,
    cut into 24 small pieces
2 ounces salmon roe or
    caviar or per your
    preference and budget
    (see Sources, and box on
    page 142)

I have hijacked this essentially Mexican dish to allow for multicultural flavor combinations. It is so easy and satisfying to sandwich any number of good cheeses between two crispy sheets of tortilla. (Tortillas, by the way, keep very well in the freezer.) The quesadilla is a great vehicle for using up bits of cheese in your fridge as well as cooked leftovers like shrimp, chicken, beans, mushrooms—wherever your imagination takes you. Add a salsa and you have an impressive first course, or a light lunch.

This quesadilla is a fun and tasty one, and I have listed several others for you to try below as well. But I encourage you to create your own, enlisting the kids to help you.

SERVES 6

Trim the tortillas, going around the edge of an inverted bowl (it should just fit inside the outer edge of the tortillas) with a sharp knife; this makes a neater presentation. Spread 4 of the tortillas out on a work surface, and divide the goat cheese among them. Scatter the minced red onion over the cheese, season lightly with salt and pepper, and press the remaining 4 tortillas firmly over each bottom tortilla. Wrap the quesadillas with wax paper between them. They can be stored in the fridge at this point for a day or two.

make the relish
Combine the kumquats, chile, and cilantro in a small bowl, and stir gently.

cook the quesadillas
Heat an 8-inch nonstick pan or heavy-bottomed skillet over medium heat. Coat the pan with a film of vegetable oil, and when it gets hot, add a teaspoon of butter; when it sizzles, add a quesadilla (see Chef's Trick on next page). Using a spatula, peek at the under-

side periodically—you are looking for a golden brown color; this should take about 2 minutes. When the tortilla is brown, carefully turn the quesadilla over, tilting the skillet at 45 degrees, to prevent a "splashdown" of oil when the quesadilla hits the pan again; then brown the second side. Remove from the pan and drain on a paper towel. Cook the remaining quesadillas, adding more butter and oil as necessary. Keep the cooked ones warm in a 200°F oven, or simply assemble the garnishes and eat them as quickly as they come out of the skillet.

To serve, cut each quesadilla into sixths with a very sharp knife or pizza wheel, and place a slice of smoked salmon on each piece. Top the salmon with a spoonful of the kumquat relish and a dab of the caviar.

‹ weighing your options ›

The basic technique explained above is the same for all these recipes. One cautionary note: Keep the amount of filling to a reasonable level. Too much will make a soggy quesadilla, which is not a good quesadilla. The *italicized ingredients* are garnishes for topping the cooked quesadilla, and recipes for them are found in the Dressings, Pickles, and Relishes chapter.

- cooked shrimp or lobster with feta, hummus (store-bought is fine), and *Tomato and Citrus Salsa* (page 268)
- roasted wild mushrooms with ricotta cheese and a drizzle of *Red Chile Oil* (page 264)
- aged cheddar and Monterey Jack with pickled jalapeños and *Tomato, Basil, and Caper Salsa* (page 267)
- Taleggio cheese with *Dried Fig and Almond Chutney* (page 273)

Chef's Trick   Butter tends to burn and turn bitter when cooking at a high temperature. To prevent this, fry in a combination of vegetable oil and butter—what we in the business call "fortifying." The vegetable oil raises the smoking point of the butter and gives you that rich buttery flavor without the burn.

Grilled or Roasted Baby Artichokes with Lemon–Cracked Pepper Aioli

I love artichokes of all ages, but when they're really small—before the choke develops—they are particularly versatile. You'll want to cook them first in a simple white wine–based stock called court bouillon (see Appendix). After that, they can be marinated in the garlic and herb marinade below, and then either grilled or pan-roasted. Either way, you will be rewarded with a tender but crispy addition to a salad or antipasti plate. I also like to eat them simply, with a little salt and pepper, though my favorite pairing is a lemony aioli, so I have included a peppery version below as well. I always feel that I should be enjoying this on the veranda of my Provençal farmhouse . . . my imaginary Provençal farmhouse, that is.

SERVES 6

for the artichokes

2 dozen baby artichokes
6 cups court bouillon (see Appendix)

for the marinade

1 onion, sliced
5 cloves garlic, sliced
2 lemons, halved and juiced
1 bunch each fresh rosemary, thyme, and parsley, crushed with the back of a heavy knife (or 1 tablespoon each dried)
1 cup extra virgin olive oil

prepare the artichokes

Clean the baby artichokes by snapping off the tough outer leaves and cutting off their spiny tops. Place them in a bowl filled with acidulated water. (This is water that has a few drops of lemon juice mixed in, which will prevent the artichokes from discoloring.) When ready to cook, bring the court bouillon to a simmer. Remove the artichokes from the acidulated water and simmer them in the bouillon for about 25 minutes. Once they are tender, gently remove the artichokes from the pot and drain them upside down on paper towels. Cut the artichokes in half.

make the marinade

Combine all ingredients in a large glass jar, covered bowl, or Ziploc bag. Add the artichoke halves and marinate them for at least 2 hours, but overnight is best.

make the aioli

Pulse the garlic with the salt in a food processor. (The salt acts as an abrasive to help break down the garlic.) Add the bread and process until a somewhat coarse paste is made. Add the egg yolks and continue processing with the lemon zest and half of the fresh-squeezed juice. With the motor going, slowly pour in the oils, 1 tablespoon at a time, to form an emulsion. The aioli should begin to resemble a mayonnaise. Continue streaming in the oils until you have used them all up. Pour the aioli into a bowl and season with a generous amount of cracked pepper, and taste for seasoning: you may want to add a touch more salt or more of the reserved lemon juice at this point.

To serve, scrape the marinade off the artichokes and season lightly with salt and pepper. Prepare your grill or roasting pan, and when your surface is hot, grill or sear the chokes until they are nicely charred—about 2 minutes. Serve them on a colorful plate, with a dish of the lemon–cracked pepper aioli for dipping.

‹ leftover alert ›

The lemon–cracked pepper aioli makes a great sandwich spread and can also be used as a zippy accompaniment for crudités or even pretzels or chips. The grilled artichokes can be tossed in salads or pasta, or used as a side dish for grilled fish or meats.

for the lemon–cracked pepper aioli

2 garlic cloves, degermed (see Chef's Trick on page 37)

1 tablespoon kosher salt, or more to taste

½ slice sourdough bread, crust removed

2 egg yolks

Juice and zest of 1 lemon

½ cup vegetable oil, such as canola

1 cup extra virgin olive oil

Fresh cracked pepper to taste

Chef's Trick If you drizzle in your oil too quickly when making the aioli, you'll get something that resembles scrambled eggs. If, despite your best efforts, this happens, you can rescue the batch by starting over with a little more garlic and one more egg yolk, and using the broken aioli as the oil, adding it in drop by drop.

Pan-Roasted Morels

Several years ago, my father decided I had attained the appropriate maturity and discretion for him to share the location of his much-prized morel hunting grounds. Now every year, during the first week of May, my husband, son, and I get in the car and head north—fervently hoping that we've managed to divine the exact date when the morels will pop through the forest floor and into view. We had a banner haul this year, eighty-one of the little tan beauties under one decaying apple tree (they love dying fruit trees). They are best eaten a day or two after picking, since as they age they get drier and darker and less delicately flavored. Try to use the freshest morels you can find, whether under an old apple tree or in a gourmet market. Simple preparations are the best way to get the most out of this mushroom.

SERVES 6

4 tablespoons butter
½ pound morels
2 shallots, peeled and thinly sliced
1 teaspoon minced thyme
1 tablespoon cognac
¼ cup heavy cream
Salt and freshly ground black pepper
6 slices crusty bread, lightly toasted

Heat a 10-inch skillet over medium-high heat. Add the butter, and when it begins to sizzle, add the mushrooms. Leave them untouched for a minute or two.

After developing the fond (see Chef's Trick, next page) start shaking the pan periodically to keep the morels moving while they bubble and crackle and release their moisture. Gently stir in the shallots. Keep cooking the morels until they are tender and browned all over, about 4 minutes. At this point, add the thyme, cognac, and heavy cream, scraping the bottom of the pan with a spoon to get up all the browned bits—a technique known as deglazing. Reduce the cream lightly; it should be thickened within seconds. Season with salt and pepper, spoon over the toasted bread, and dig in. No garnishes required!

I like combining the morels with other spring flavors. For example, try a platter of simply steamed asparagus with a garnish of the roasted morels. Or, for a showstopper of an hors d'oeuvre, you can whip up these Morel Crostinis with Fava Bean Puree and Pecorino Romano: Remove the bean pods, then blanch the fresh beans and peel off the inner shell. Puree the beans in a blender with a mixture of herbs such as chervil, tarragon, and cilantro, then season with salt and pepper and a little extra virgin olive oil. Spread the fava puree on grilled or toasted crusty bread, top with the morels, and finish with a few thin shavings of Pecorino Romano. Voilà!

Chef's Trick When trying to achieve a nice browning with any food you cook, use a pan that has enough surface area so you are not crowding your ingredients and, subsequently, steaming them. Also, refrain from stirring too much. You want the food to have enough contact with the pan to develop what is called a *fond*—the delicious caramelized natural sugars that stick to the bottom of the pan. *Deglazing* is the technique of loosening the fond with water, stock, wine, booze, or other liquid and reintroducing it to your sauce or sauté.

Broiled Shell-On Shrimp with Juniper, Black Pepper, and Citrus Dipping Salt

I love the cross-cultural inspiration of this dish—it takes an Asian form, but with a somewhat Teutonic flavor. Broiling the shrimp in their shells amplifies their flavor, and marinating them first lends a wonderfully herbaceous complexity. This snack is great with lots of cold beer to quench your salt-induced thirst.

SERVES 6

1½–2 pounds shrimp
3 tablespoons olive oil
1 small white onion
2 cloves garlic, sliced
1 sprig each fresh parsley,
    thyme, and rosemary,
    crushed with the back
    of a knife

for the seasoned salt
¼ cup coarse sea salt
1 tablespoon finely ground
    juniper berries
1 tablespoon each finely
    grated lemon, orange,
    and lime zests
1 tablespoon freshly ground
    black pepper
1 teaspoon curry powder

Wash and dry the shrimp, but leave their shells on. Whisk the olive oil, onion, garlic, and herbs together in a big bowl, then toss in the shrimp, coating them in the marinade. Set the shrimp in the fridge for 1 hour.

Preheat broiler to medium heat. Mix together all of the seasoned salt ingredients in a small bowl. Spread the shrimp out on a broiler pan and cook 2 minutes per side. Cool slightly, then peel and devein the shrimp, leaving the tail attached as a "handle." (In my experience, people don't mind peeling their own shrimp. Just make sure you have some wet towels available.) Serve each person a share of the shrimp, and pass the bowl of seasoned salt.

‹ leftover alert ›
Leftover grilled shrimp are great on salads or tossed in with a big bowl of pasta.

My Homemade Potato Chips

There's no need to set up a deep fryer to make great potato chips—the oven is just fine. Part of the charm of homemade chips is that they're a little thicker and have more of a bite than chips from a bag. And best of all, you can serve them warm! Here's an opportunity for the yin-yang thing: warm potato chip with crème fraîche, a small slice of smoked salmon, smoked trout, or a bit of caviar, and a shot of very chilled vodka. Instant celebration.

SERVES 6–8

Preheat the oven to 400°F. Slice the potatoes into a bowl and immediately toss them with the oil. Season lightly with salt and arrange them in a single layer on a baking sheet. Bake in the oven until golden brown—about 12–15 minutes. Season again lightly with salt and pepper when they come out of the oven. Transfer to a rack to cool for maximum crispness.

2 medium Yukon Gold or Idaho potatoes, peeled and sliced into ⅛-inch slices on a mandoline or other handheld slicer
3 tablespoons olive, canola, or peanut oil
Salt and freshly ground pepper

‹ weighing your options ›

If you want to be a little more daring, don't limit yourself to salt and pepper—you can season with ancho chile powder, ground cumin, minced herbs, toasted sesame seeds, ground nori (toasted black seaweed sheets used to roll sushi)—really anything you like. Just be sure to season immediately after the chips come out of the oven, while there is still some residual oil for the spices to adhere to.

Homemade Gravlax
with Fennel, Radish, and Marinated Chanterelles

Making gravlax is my favorite way of preserving fish. While it may sound difficult, it is really so simple, and what's more, there are an infinite number of variations—combinations of herbs, spices, and liquors—that will impart all sorts of different styles and flavors to the fish at hand.

The goal is always the same when making gravlax: to saturate the fish with the flavor of the cure, while the salt and sugar draw out moisture to preserve it. This cure is achieved by time and pressure. (That's what they say about diamonds!) My version is flavored with juniper, orange peel, and hot pepper—notes that are bright and refreshing against the buttery richness of the salmon. Curing the fish in this way allows its natural flavors to shine through and is a nice change from smoked salmon. One last point: It is best to use farmed salmon for this recipe, because wild fish is too lean. See Sources for some of the best farmed salmon to buy.

SERVES 6
(OR MORE, DEPENDING ON HOW GOOD
YOU ARE ABOUT SHARING)

Two 3-pound farmed salmon
    fillets, skin on
⅓ cup salt
⅔ cup sugar
3 tablespoons crushed
    juniper berries
2 tablespoons crushed red
    chiles, or substitute
    dried chile flakes
1 cup chopped dill
Zest of 1 orange
¼ cup gin, or juniper
    schnapps

Lay 1 salmon fillet, skin side down, on the bottom of a nonreactive rectangular pan (glass is ideal). Mix together the salt, sugar, juniper berries, chiles, dill, and orange zest. Rub the fillet with half of this mixture, rubbing the remainder on the second fillet. Sprinkle each fillet with 2 tablespoons of gin. Place the second fillet, skin side down, on top of the first. Cover the fish well with plastic wrap and weigh it down with about 3 pounds of weight. Use cans of food or a stack of plates—just be sure to get the weight evenly distributed over the fillets.

Refrigerate the fish for 3 days, turning it over, so the top layer is now on the bottom, approximately every 12 hours. When ready to serve, scrape off the seasonings with the back of a knife, and slice the fish on the bias, as thin as possible.

make the fennel, radish, and marinated chanterelles

Heat 2 tablespoons of olive oil in a skillet. When hot, add the chanterelles; toss often until browned. Remove from heat. Add salt and pepper, dried currants, sherry vinegar, tarragon, and the remaining olive oil. Marinate for 1 hour at room temperature, and then fold in the fennel and radishes. Serve alongside the gravlax, with buttered rye bread.

for the fennel, radish, and marinated chanterelles

4 tablespoons olive oil
½ pound chanterelles, cleaned, trimmed, and cut in half
Salt and pepper to taste
1 tablespoon dried currants
1 tablespoon sherry vinegar
1 teaspoon minced tarragon
1 bulb fennel, thinly sliced
6 radishes, thinly sliced

‹ leftover alert ›

If you don't finish the gravlax, store it wrapped tightly in plastic in the fridge for up to ten days. There are plenty of ways to turn it into a new meal for another day. Here are a few of my favorite ways to use leftover gravlax:

- Serve it on buttered brown bread with thinly sliced red onion and radishes, a spritz of fresh lemon juice, and freshly ground black pepper.
- Cut into thin strips and toss with steamed new potatoes and chopped fresh herbs like dill, parsley, or basil.
- Drape slices over pieces of ripe avocado and grapefruit and drizzle with a good extra virgin olive oil for a great first course salad.
- Garnish the tops of the Goat Cheese Quesadillas on page 50 and serve with a little crème fraîche and caviar.

Foie Gras "Bonbons"
with Fennel Kraut and Lingonberry Sauce

Foie gras is not something I eat every day, but I do love it. This recipe for "bonbons" is something so fanciful and fun that it takes all the pretension out of the dish. Buy a whole foie gras, grade A, from a good producer (see Sources)—you'll have less waste and spend less time trying to dig out the veins.

SERVES 8

for the bonbons

One 1-pound grade A foie gras

Quatre épices, as needed (see Appendix)

Salt and freshly ground pepper to taste

1 box high-quality phyllo dough or strudel pastry, thawed (see box on page 46)

¼ pound unsalted butter

make the bonbons

Clean foie gras (see Appendix). Cut into 8 pieces of fairly equal weight—equal size will be nearly impossible, given foie's irregular shape. Season both sides of each piece with the quatre épices and marinate 30 minutes in fridge. Heat a thick-bottomed skillet over medium heat. Season the foie with salt and pepper. Press each piece onto the bottom of the skillet and keep your hand pressed against the pieces for a few seconds to generate a good sear. Sear the foie for 20 seconds on each side—you want good color but still rare liver. When you press on the liver with your fingertip, you should feel an initial softness on the surface, but still quite firm in the center. (As opposed to meat, which firms up as it cooks, foie gras softens as it cooks.) Drain the foie on paper towels.

Melt the butter. Place a sheet of phyllo on your work surface, covering the remaining dough with a towel while you work. Brush the sheet with melted butter, cover with a second sheet, and brush again with butter. Cut this 2-layered sheet into thirds and place one portion of foie gras on top of each rectangle. Roll the phyllo up into a cylinder and twist the ends like a fat bonbon. Brush the entire strudel generously with melted butter. Refrigerate each finished piece while you prepare the rest. When all are complete, transfer the bonbons to an ungreased baking sheet. When ready to bake, preheat oven to 400°F, and bake 10–12 minutes, until pastry is golden brown.

make the lingonberry sauce

Sauté the shallot and ginger in the butter until they are soft. Add the berries and sugar, then pour in your wine and port (taking the pan away from the flame to avoid a scorching incident) and boil rapidly to reduce by half. Add the stock and the sachet and simmer until you have reached a saucelike consistency. Remove the sachet and season sauce to taste with salt and pepper.

Serve the bonbons warm with the sauce and kraut on the side.

> **Chef's Trick** For this sachet you will need about 2 strips of orange zest, ¼ teaspoon coriander seeds, and 4–6 stems of cilantro. Use cheesecloth and butcher's twine to tie it all together. For more on sachets, see page 75.

for the lingonberry sauce

1 shallot, minced

1 teaspoon minced fresh ginger

2 tablespoons butter

½ cup fresh or frozen lingonberries, red currants, or other seasonal berries

1 tablespoon sugar

¼ cup red wine

¼ cup port

½ cup veal stock (see Appendix) or good commercial demi-glace (see Sources)

Sachet of orange zest, coriander seeds, and cilantro stems (see Chef's Trick)

Salt and pepper

for the fennel kraut, see page 231.

COCKTAILS

A well-made cocktail is as much a pleasure to me as a good glass of wine. But to be good, a cocktail must be mixed with care and some knowledge of the fundamentals. I can't think of anyone more talented in the fine art of cocktail making than my friend Peter Lucania. Peter was the head bartender at Quilty's for its five-and-a-half-year run, and I think he was as responsible for retaining our loyal and devoted customers through his charm and excellent drinks as I was through my cooking. For me, pulling up a stool at Peter's bar after a long shift in the kitchen was to be poised at the gateway between intense stress and the much-needed relief that would allow my shoulders to settle down to their proper position. Peter has generously agreed to share some tips of his trade with us here. This is by no means a comprehensive list of cocktails or even a proper survey—these are drinks that my friends and I enjoy that can be easily made at home.

Just as good cooking depends on certain fundamental techniques, making or "building" a good drink depends on the faithful execution of a series of simple but deliberate steps. The steps you take depend on the type of cocktail you're making. I'll outline three styles. The first is the stirred cocktail served straight up, which, for me, means one thing—a martini. Then there is the highball, a category that includes Bloody Marys, screwdrivers, madrases, and countless other variations. And finally there are the lemon and lime juice drinks, which for Andrea means one thing—a tart margarita. Cheers!

Martini hour at my parents'

MY MARTINI

My parents are gin martini drinkers, and in my case, the apple didn't fall far from the tree. My preferred brand is Beefeater, but any premium gin will make a good drink, with the proper technique. I have almost no interest in a vodka martini, since I think the flavor of even a few drops of dry vermouth tends to overpower the neutral flavor of the vodka, but I do enjoy a shot of frozen vodka from time to time—especially paired with caviar or smoked salmon. A good dry vermouth is the perfect foil for gin—and a fresh twist of lemon peel ties it all together.

So here we get to the basic procedure for a martini. You'll want to ice your glasses, since a straight-up drink loses a lot of its charm when it gets warm. My husband and I keep at least four martini glasses in the freezer (you never know when friends might pop by), but you can also chill your glasses with ice and cold water. Ice alone won't do the trick. By the way, this also applies to an ice bucket to chill champagne or wine—you need both ice and water to make enough contact to chill the bottle.

Next, you want to prepare a fresh twist, if using. I use a paring knife or vegetable peeler to carve off the zest—leaving the pith behind, which would lend a bitter flavor to your drink. Once your glass is chilled, dump out the ice and water and firmly squeeze the twist into the glass. Many people squeeze the zest over the finished drink, in which case the oils just float on top of the drink and don't blend in well. We've also seen far too many professional bartenders simply perch a dried-out spiral of lemon zest on the edge of the glass as some sort of decoration. A twist is definitely not just decoration; the flavor of the lemon oil is an essential ingredient in the drink.

Now that your glass is cold and the twist has performed its vital role, you need to mix the drink. Peter and I agree (sorry, Mr. Bond) that a drink of this type needs to be carefully stirred—not shaken. You need a bar glass filled with ice, a bar stirrer, and a wire strainer. (Truth be told, I've been known to mix a martini in a regular glass with a chopstick when absolutely pressed.) Once you pour the liquor into the glass, work quickly to stir the booze—you want to dilute it to just the right degree. If you stir it too little, the drink will be unpleasantly strong and very high in alcohol; stir it too much, and the cocktail loses flavor. I generally stir to the count of ten. Then pour the drink through either a wire strainer or whatever you have on hand, to keep the ice from dumping into your delicate stemware.

At this point there is only one more thing you have to do—get the glass to your lips without spilling any of the precious liquid. This is often best accomplished by going to your glass for that first sip rather than bringing the glass to you.

The recipe for a gin martini couldn't be easier. For each drink:

3 ounces Beefeater or other premium gin

A few drops of good-quality French vermouth (Noilly Prat)

Lemon twist or olives as desired

HIGHBALLS

Highballs tend to be more appropriate during a brunch or summer afternoon by the pool where you want to sip slowly on a chilled drink, whereas a straight-up or two would simply get you smashed. No recipes are required here; just follow this basic formula: Fill your highball glass with ice, pour in your liquor to measure $1/3$ of the way up the glass, and fill the remaining $2/3$ with your mixer. In the case of a Bloody Mary, use a good vodka and make your Bloody mix to taste using tomato juice, freshly ground black pepper, prepared horseradish, lemon juice, Tabasco and Worcestershire sauce, and a very small pinch of salt or celery salt. Few things are as idiosyncratic as a good Bloody, so go ahead and tinker with the proportions of the mix until it suits you.

A screwdriver is vodka and orange juice, a Harvey Wallbanger is a screwdriver topped with a splash of Galliano, and a sea breeze is vodka with grapefruit juice and a splash of cranberry juice—very refreshing.

LEMON AND LIME JUICE DRINKS

While I like my martini, Andrea loves a good margarita, a cocktail that falls into the category of lemon or lime juice drinks. Most bars these days will not go to the trouble of squeezing fresh citrus fruits and use a substitute called sour mix. I think this is an abomination—it tastes like chemicals to me. So when I have a margarita, I squeeze my own limes. But because fresh lime juice is quite tart, Peter and I both tend to balance the juice with simple syrup—which, true to its name, is simply sugar and water in equal proportions by volume. Just boil the water and let the sugar dissolve in it, cool, and store covered indefinitely. I've included Andrea's recipe as a contrast in style.

Peter's margarita also uses just a splash of orange juice, for a very well-rounded flavor. This is the drink where you get to use your metal shaker. Fill it with ice, pour in the ingredients, and shake vigorously for 15–20 seconds. You can then serve the drink straight up in a chilled glass (salted rim optional) or on the rocks.

Andrea's Margarita (Per Drink)

2 ounces El Tesoro Silver tequila (or another high-quality tequila, such as Patrón or Herradura)
1 ounce Cointreau or triple sec
1 ounce fresh-squeezed lime juice
Wedge of lime as a garnish

Peter's Margarita (Per Drink)

3 ounces high-quality tequila
1 ounce triple sec
Juice of 1 lime
Splash of orange juice
Splash of simple syrup

For either recipe, pour the ingredients into a shaker filled with ice and shake vigorously 15–20 times. Strain and pour over ice into a squat rocks glass, rimmed with salt or not. Garnish with a juicy wedge of lime.

GRANDMA SPARKS'S EGGNOG

This recipe is for a crowd of twenty or so people, because it's really no fun to drink eggnog alone. But the recipe does divide nicely in half or even into quarters. The most important thing is to let the eggnog mellow overnight and then fold in the whipped egg whites just before serving. There's quite a lot of booze in here, and it will taste raw if not left at least eight hours to age. Just a thought to leave you with: Despite the tremendously high calorie and cholesterol load in this beverage—or maybe because of it—my grandmother lived to the age of ninety-four!

18 eggs, separated
1½ pounds sugar
1 quart bourbon
1 pint brandy
1 pint rum
1 quart heavy cream
2 quarts milk
Whole nutmeg for grating

Whisk yolks and sugar together, and then gradually add the booze while stirring. Add the cream and milk. Whip ⅔ of the whites and fold in. Let age overnight in the fridge. Before serving, whip last ⅓ of whites, fold in, and grate some fresh nutmeg over top. I like to serve this in a large punch bowl with a ladle, so guests can help themselves to as much as they like.

SOUPS

Curried Cauliflower Soup with Garnishes

Sweet Corn Soup with Crispy Shiitake Mushrooms

Gazpacho with Avocado Sesame Relish

Summer Squash Soup with White Beans, Mango, and Basil

Celery Root Soup with Spiced Pear and Black Truffle

Lentil Soup with Red Chile Croutons and Crème Fraîche

Kabocha Squash Soup with Lemongrass and Ginger

Goulash Soup

Green Pea and Sorrel Soup

Cream of Fennel Soup with Mussels, Salmon, and Shrimp

Chilled Wild Leek Soup

SALADS

Arugula with Grilled Peaches, Goat Cheese, and Country Ham

Frisée Salad with Bacon-Wrapped Sea Scallops

Greek Salad with Roasted Olives and Rosemary-Skewered Shrimp

Salmon Carpaccio with Red Onion, Orange, and Avocado

Asparagus Vinaigrette with Lemon-Pistachio Dressing and Manchego Cheese

Composed Salad of Salsify, Seckel Pear,
and Serrano Ham in Brown Butter–Cardamom Dressing

Warm Lobster Salad with Golden Potatoes, Papaya, and Basil

Summer Tomato and Sweet Onion Salad with Creamy Herb Vinaigrette

Seasonal Country Salad with Spiced Walnuts

Roasted Baby Beets in Cayenne-Buttermilk Dressing

SOUPS AND SALADS

For me, soups and salads are the yin/yang of cooking. Soupmaking springs from "hearth and home" emotions. I enjoy the feeling of nurturing a soup along—standing over a steaming pot, gently skimming the surface, watching the individual ingredients slowly meld together into a rich and satisfying whole. Once it's done—a process that becomes easier and more creative as your experience grows—you are rewarded with a one-pot meal that will keep well in the refrigerator, feeding friends and family for days. Soups like Kabocha Squash Soup with Lemongrass and Ginger and Goulash Soup fulfill that old-fashioned notion of stocking the larder.

Salads bring out the opposite emotions in me—the sprightly, spontaneous, innovative side. I enjoy putting together ingredients that jump out at me at the farmers market: voluptuous peaches or tomatoes, shiny eggplant and squashes. The inspiration is the gorgeous food itself. Salads are not just for summer, though. The Warm Lobster Salad with Golden Potatoes, Papaya, and Basil and the Composed Salad of Salsify, Seckel Pear, and Serrano Ham are elegant fall/winter dishes that lighten up a substantial cold-weather meal.

I hope that this chapter brings out your nurturing side as well as your devil-may-care, spontaneous inner chef.

SOUPS

MAKING SOUP—A CHEF'S FOOLPROOF GUIDE

Most soups are easy to make once you learn a few basic techniques. You'll find that after you've put some soups together, a certain sequence of steps leads to success—a framework emerges that supports your creativity, and once you understand the method, you're free to experiment with whatever looks good to you at the market.

The Stock The first and most important step is to start with a good stock or broth. This can be a vegetable stock, chicken or beef broth, fish fumet, or, as in the case of the Cream of Fennel Soup with Mussels, Salmon, and Shrimp (page 90), the liquor from freshly opened mussels. Whatever your base is, it must be fresh and flavorful. In my lazier moments, I might buy a boxed organic low-sodium stock and "refresh" it with a sachet or bouquet garni of parsley stems, lemon zest, coriander seeds, and black peppercorns.

For all of the soup recipes below, I encourage you to make your own stock if you have the time and have stockpiled some of the basic ingredients (see Appendix)—you can make a lot of it and freeze it—or to substitute a good-quality, organic, low-sodium broth. Many are now sold in cartons or boxes in mainstream grocery stores; a few good brands are Imagine, Pacific, and Swanson.

Sweating Every soup begins with a flavor base, or foundation, that is created by *sweating aromatic vegetables*. These are good terms to know: *aromatic vegetables* are the supporting actors in the dish—not the stars of the show. They are most commonly leeks, onions, garlic, carrots, and celery. But they can be bolder flavors like ginger, lemongrass, fennel, and chiles, depending on the soup you're making. These aromatics give the soup a pleasing depth of flavor.

The process by which you slowly cook the aromatics in butter or oil is called *sweating*—a very slow sauté that allows the vegetables to release their liquid and their flavors. You may cover the pot briefly from time to time during sweating to capture the steam and to prevent drying out and browning the aromatics. Why not brown the vegetables? Well, sometimes, for aesthetic reasons, you might want a pale or blond soup. But most often, by not browning you avoid oversweetening the soup through caramelization and you accentuate the natural sweetness of the vegetables. Just after sweating, you will add any spices that you might be using, like curry, coriander, cumin. These spices want to "bloom" in the fat before a liquid is added.

Simmering and Skimming Now you're ready to add the stock or broth or even water. If you are using water, make sure it is from the cold tap; never start with hot water from the tap—it leaches more lead from the pipes and is also low in oxygen, which can leave a flat flavor. You'll bring your liquid to a boil, then reduce it to a simmer. The purpose of bringing the soup to a boil is to encourage impurities in the vegetables or proteins to rise to the surface, where they can be skimmed off. I never make a soup, stock, or sauce without having a ladle nearby. Skimming refines the flavor and the resulting texture by also removing any excess fat that if left in would leave a greasy feel on the palate. You'll be glad you tied up your spices and herbs in a sachet or bouquet garni as you skim—you won't need to count the peppercorns to make sure they're still in there!

To Puree or Not to Puree—That Is the Question Once your soup is fully cooked and the flavors have developed to your satisfaction, you will have a significant decision to make—to puree or not to puree. It's sort of like deciding whether to wear your hair up or down—you're sending a message. Chunky soups are homey, substantial, and comforting. Pureed soups are elegant and refined. The recipes in this chapter offer examples of both styles.

Garnish The last step is optional: garnishing the soup. Do you want a drizzle of fruity extra virgin olive oil, a fistful of garlicky croutons, a pool of piquant crème fraîche, or just a scattering of minced herbs? Imagine all the flavors dancing around in your mouth, and think of what might make the dish really sing. Does it need texture or brightness or herbaceousness? Let your senses guide you.

Curried Cauliflower Soup with Garnishes

2 tablespoons butter

1 clove garlic, mashed with a little salt

1 mild green chile, such as a poblano

1 tablespoon grated fresh ginger

1 leek, trimmed and white part thinly sliced

2 tablespoons Madras curry powder (see Sources)

1 tablespoon whole cumin seed (crushed with the back of a knife or saucepan)

1 large head cauliflower, cut into florets

1 small russet potato, peeled and diced

6 cups chicken stock (see Appendix, or use organic, low-sodium boxed)

for the garnishes

1 cup toasted unsalted cashews

½ cup toasted coconut

1 cup dried fruit, such as apricots, currants, figs, or raisins

½ cup cilantro leaves

½ cup sliced scallions

My mother delighted us back in the 1970s by introducing exotic cuisines to the dinner table. One night it was fondue, another night Cantonese pork stir-fry or chicken curry. I loved how she would present the curry surrounded by little bowls of garnish: toasted coconut, raisins, sliced bananas, and cashews. It was so exciting to participate in making the dish at the table.

SERVES 6

Heat the butter in a large saucepan or stockpot and stir in the garlic, chile, ginger, and leek. Sweat the vegetables until softened—about 5 minutes. Stir in the curry and the cumin seeds and cook 3 minutes longer, stirring occasionally. Add the cauliflower and potatoes, and pour in the stock. Simmer over medium-low heat for 40 minutes. Cool the soup and puree it in a blender, in batches if necessary, until smooth.

For extra richness, you can stir in half a cup of cream, whole-milk yogurt, or coconut milk, but it is really not necessary, because the addition of the potato lends a rich, smooth texture.

Serve the soup in bowls and arrange the garnishes in a condiment tray at the center of the table and let people dress up their own soup.

NOTE: This soup continues to improve in flavor up to 4 days, so double the recipe if you like. It also freezes quite well.

Sweet Corn Soup
with Crispy Shiitake Mushrooms

When it comes to corn, I know I'm spoiled. At home in Vermont, my mother would send me out to the garden to pick the Silver Queen or Butter and Sugar only after the water had come to a boil on the stove. Today, when I bring corn in from the farmers market here in Brooklyn, my son's eyes light up when he sees the fresh ears on our counter. The corn is so sweet that he eats it raw, straight off the cob. If I don't watch him carefully, it will all be gone, leaving me with nothing to cook.

To fully enjoy corn, freshness is critically important, because the natural sugars in corn convert to starch very soon after being picked. You can delay this inevitable progression by standing the ears upright in some water in your fridge, which fools the silly corn into thinking it's still on the stalk. But, alas, it catches on fairly quickly, so this trick will buy you only a day or two.

SERVES 6

make the soup

Cut the corn kernels off the cobs and reserve in a bowl. Put the cobs, milk, and chicken stock in a stockpot and bring to a simmer. Drop the sachet into the pot and let it all cook, simmering slowly, for 30 minutes. You want to extract as much flavor from the cobs as possible, but don't steep them too long or you will get a slightly woody aftertaste. Fish out the cobs and sachet and reserve the broth.

Melt the butter in a deep skillet. Sauté the onions, fennel, and jalapeño in the butter, being careful not to brown them. Stir in the reserved kernels and sweat the vegetables, stirring often. You may need to add a few tablespoons of the broth to keep the kernels moist as they sweat; this should take about 4 minutes. Taste a few kernels—they should still "pop" a little in your mouth but not crunch.

Pour the reserved broth into the skillet, turn off the heat, and let

for the soup

8 ears fresh local corn

3 cups whole milk

3 cups chicken stock (see Appendix, or use organic, low-sodium boxed)

Sachet of 3–4 cilantro stems, 8–12 coriander seeds, 1 strip orange zest

3 tablespoons butter

1 onion, minced

½ bulb fennel, diced fine

1 jalapeño, minced

Salt, freshly ground pepper, and freshly grated nutmeg to taste

the soup cool as the flavors develop. I puree ¾ of the soup, leaving the last ¼ unblended for texture. Season the soup with salt, pepper, and nutmeg.

for the shiitakes
½ pound shiitake
    mushrooms
1 cup pure canola or other
    vegetable oil
Salt
2–3 tablespoons cilantro
    leaves, chiffonade

make the crispy shiitakes

Remove the mushroom stems from the caps. Gently brush the caps with a damp towel to clean. Cut the caps into as thin strips as you can. Each 2-inch-diameter cap should yield approximately 15–18 of these thin strips—a julienne cut.

Heat the canola oil in an 8-inch-wide skillet until the oil shimmers on the surface. Test it for readiness by gently lowering a strip of shiitake into the oil—it should sizzle quickly and rise to the surface of the oil immediately. Fry the mushrooms in several batches; they're done when you see a golden brown color on them and hear almost no more sizzle from the pan. This will come to an end as the mushrooms lose their moisture. Frying in batches prevents the oil temperature from dropping too steeply. (When the oil is not hot enough for deep-frying or even shallow-frying, the food absorbs more of the oil than it should.)

Drain the mushrooms quickly on paper towels using a "spider"—a net screen with a handle. You can use a slotted spoon, but a spider will draw off less oil. Season the mushrooms immediately with salt while they are damp enough to hold on to it.

Serve the soup garnished with crispy shiitakes and cilantro.

‹ leftover alert ›
These crispy shiitakes can be kept
at room temperature in an airtight
container for two or three days.
They're great in an omelette or
sprinkled over a salad.

Spices and condiments at the ready

Chef's Trick   Do not underestimate the usefulness of sachets—little bundles of herbs and spices tied up in cheesecloth. They can really be a savior to the cook. I like to add sachets to stocks, soups, and sauces to invigorate them with flavor. They are convenient because when you have steeped in the desired amount of flavor, you can simply pull out the sachet rather than hunting around for the individual cloves, bay leaves, thyme stems, or peppercorns. I also like to drop a sachet filled with coriander seed, citrus zests, and herbs into a soup or sauce that's a day or two old; it really does wonders to perk up the flavors. This is a trick of the trade that you should readily employ at home—no one will ever know you're using leftovers.

Gazpacho
with Avocado Sesame Relish

When the humidity really descends on us here in Brooklyn, I make a giant batch of gazpacho to draw on for a few days. There is a lot of knife work involved, but, blessedly, the oven doesn't get turned on. The avocado relish lends a creamy balance to this cooling soup. I wait to make it until the tomatoes are really ripe—they are the essential ingredient here. It's also very important to remove the inner green germ from the garlic—it will cause the soup to ferment if left in. I learned this the hard way when I was the chef de cuisine at Bolo, a contemporary Spanish restaurant in New York City. I made a large batch of gazpacho without removing the germ from the garlic, and by the time we were ready for service that night, it was already bubbling over, starting to ferment. It was eighty-sixed from the menu, and I never left a germ in a clove of garlic again.

for the gazpacho

8 large red beefsteak
    tomatoes
3 cloves garlic, green germ
    removed
2 green tomatoes, seeded
    and diced
2 Spanish onions, diced
2 cucumbers, peeled, seeded,
    and diced
1 yellow bell pepper, seeded
    and diced
1 poblano pepper, diced*
1 papaya, diced (optional,
    but I like the musky
    sweetness)
2 jalapeños, diced*
Aged sherry vinegar and
    Tabasco to taste
Salt and freshly ground
    pepper

*When working with chile peppers like jalapeños and poblanos, leave the seeds in if you like a spicier soup; otherwise, remove.

SERVES 6

Pass the tomatoes through a food mill into a large bowl—this will remove the skins and seeds and make a nice puree. (A blender will yield an unappetizing-looking pink froth.)

Crush the garlic into a paste on your cutting board with a little salt (it acts as an abrasive, helping to break the garlic down) and stir it into the tomato puree. Add the remaining diced vegetables and the papaya (if using), seasoning and tasting the soup after adding each additional ingredient. Then stir in the sherry vinegar, Tabasco, and salt and pepper to taste.

Transfer the soup into either a glass or stainless steel vessel—you don't want a bowl of any material that will react with the acidity (such as aluminum or iron). You can wait an hour or so and taste the soup again to see how the flavors begin to meld. As the vegetables wilt into each other, the soup will change, so don't think your job as seasoner-in-chief is done—you'll want to taste it for salt and pepper every time you serve it.

make the croutons

Remove the crusts of the bread and cut into ½-inch cubes. Coat the bottom of a 10-inch skillet with olive oil and heat the oil until it shimmers. Toss in the cubes of bread and shake the skillet over medium heat until the croutons are a golden brown. Add the garlic and stir 20 seconds more. Season with salt and pepper.

make the avocado-sesame relish

Put all ingredients in a medium bowl and fold gently together. You want to leave the avocado in chunky, toothsome pieces rather than mashing it up as you would for a guacamole.

To serve, drizzle a little good fruity olive oil on top of the soup and pass around the garlicky croutons and the relish. Herbs like cilantro, tarragon, and chervil are always nice to add as a garnish, if you have any on hand.

for the croutons

1 small loaf peasant bread

Enough olive oil to coat a pan

1 clove garlic, mashed with salt

Salt and pepper

for the avocado-sesame relish

2 ripe avocados, peeled and pitted

½ medium red onion, minced

1 jalapeño, minced

Juice of ½ lime

2 teaspoons sesame oil

2 teaspoons toasted sesame seeds

1 tablespoon minced cilantro

Salt and freshly ground pepper

Fruity olive oil, for drizzling on top (see box on page 78)

‹ leftover alert ›
This relish is great on top of a quesadilla, with ceviche, or simply with an open bag of tortilla chips.

ON OLIVE OIL

You could spend a lifetime becoming an expert on the subject of olive oil, it is so vast. In an effort to simplify matters, let me tell you what I use and why.

Olive oil is one of the essential ingredients in my kitchen—I don't get very far without it. As much as I adore butter and am not shy about using it, I work with olive oil more often and even feel quite virtuous when I add a drizzle of extra virgin to finish a bruschetta, a soup, or a pasta. There are well-documented health benefits to this monounsaturated oil; it helps keep the heart and arteries well tuned. But I enjoy it first and foremost for its distinct flavors—each producer has a different style, much like producers of fine wine.

I keep three grades on hand, but in small quantities, because oils will become rancid if kept too long once opened. Try to replace your olive oils every three months (if you are cooking with them regularly, this time frame shouldn't be a problem). You can extend the shelf life of all your oils by refrigerating them. You'll just have to let them warm up a bit before using, since they will solidify somewhat when cold.

- I use **extra virgin olive oil** raw in salads, drizzled on pasta, and in soups as a last-minute invigoration. (In my recipes, when I call for a "fruity" olive oil, I mean extra virgin.) This oil should not be heated—heat would destroy the delicate flavor and aroma of the cold-pressed oil. The flavor notes should be fruity and peppery with no bitterness in the finish. Extra virgin oil is the first cold-pressed oil of the olive, with an acidity level of less than 1 percent. Fabulous oils are being produced in Italy, Spain, Greece, France, and California. Try a new one every once in a while—it's a lot like bringing the flavors of a particular part of the world to your table, as you become an "olive oil tourist."

- **Fino, or simply virgin olive oil,** is the oil you should use for cooking— but not high-heat frying, which is the job of the pure or light olive oils. Virgin oil is less expensive than extra virgin, and has higher acidity, but it is still an excellent oil. You'll need to do some taste comparisons to find the oil that you like—it should be neither too fruity nor too bitter. This is a lot like finding a good, reliable table wine that you like the price and quality of—it's nothing glamorous, but it does the job quite nicely.

- **Pure or light olive oil** is an excellent oil for both high-heat cooking and for making a mayonnaise, aioli, or other sauce where you don't want a pronounced olive flavor. At first I stuck up my nose at the idea of "light" anything. However, with this oil, you get the health benefits of olive oil, but in a refined product that has a very high smoking point, which is ideal for deep-frying.

Summer Squash Soup
with White Beans, Mango, and Basil

If you are a gardener, you know that there comes a time in the season where you just can't give away any more zucchini or yellow squash without endangering friendships. That is the time to make this soup. Although you can use canned white beans with success, I urge you to take the time to cook from the dried beans—with the addition of a smoked ham hock (or a piece of prosciutto or pancetta); they are divine. Mango and basil lend an exotic note to the humble squashes and beans. While most soups tend to improve with age, I think this is one soup that should be consumed within a day or two—the squashes are too fragile to improve in flavor past that.

SERVES 6

for the beans

½ pound white beans, like Great Northern or cannellini, covered in cold water and soaked overnight

1 small white onion, cut in half and stuck with 2 cloves

1 smoked ham hock

1 bay leaf

2 cloves garlic, smashed with the side of a knife

Salt

cook the beans

Put the soaked beans in a pot and cover with 2 inches of cold water. Add the onion, ham hock, bay leaf, and garlic and bring to a simmer. Skim off any foam that rises to the top, but be careful not to skim off the bay leaf. Simmer gently for 45 minutes to an hour, partially covering the pot with foil or a lid placed ajar. (Partially covering the beans while they cook makes them creamier.)

Remove from the heat and add the salt at this point, while the beans are still warm. Store any unused beans in this cooking liquid so they remain moist and absorb even more flavor.

make the soup

Heat the olive oil in a 6-quart pot. When the oil shimmers, stir in the onion and garlic and sauté until translucent. Add the zucchini, yellow squash, and mushrooms, and stir to coat with the onion and garlic mixture. Cook the squash 3–4 minutes. Adding a little salt at this point will help make the squash wilt.

Pour in the heated chicken stock and the cooked beans and simmer about 20 minutes. This is not a long-cooking soup. All the flavors develop their full potential fairly quickly.

Season with salt and freshly ground black pepper. Ladle the soup into bowls, add the diced mango, tear the basil leaves into the bowls, and drizzle with a nice fruity olive oil.

‹ weighing your options ›

A simple grating of Parmigiano-Reggiano gives a great salty accent to the soup, and the addition of fried croutons (see the recipe for gazpacho on page 76 for a quick and easy way to make your own) makes this soup hearty enough to be a meal in itself.

for the soup

3 tablespoons olive oil

1 large sweet onion (Vidalia or Walla Walla), diced

2 cloves garlic, minced

4 medium zucchini, diced

4 medium yellow squash, diced

8–10 shiitake mushroom caps, diced

6 cups chicken stock, heated* (see Appendix, or use organic, low-sodium boxed)

Salt and pepper

1/2 mango, diced

1/2 cup basil leaves

Extra virgin olive oil, for drizzling

*Green vegetables lose color very quickly when heated, so I like to preheat the stock when making this or any other green vegetable soup where maintaining color is important. It gives the squash a head start, helping it retain its bright color.

Celery Root Soup
with Spiced Pear and Black Truffle

This is an elegant soup for late fall and winter, when fresh black truffles are imported in some quantity; they're never cheap, though. You may choose to drizzle a bit of truffle oil over the surface of each serving if a big splurge is not in the cards. Fortunately, black truffles are so pungently aromatic that a little goes a long way, and you really only need a few paper-thin shavings per serving.

Celery root in its natural state is by no means pretty to look at; in fact, I have startled many a cashier at the grocery store with this unfamiliar, knobby, somewhat tufted root. But it's one of the most versatile vegetables—great in soups and purees, glazed with roasts, or julienned raw and dressed with mustard and crème fraîche for a wonderful piquant condiment called céleri rémoulade.

SERVES 6

for the soup

1 large celery root

3 tablespoons butter

2 leeks, white parts only, thinly sliced

6 cups chicken stock (see Appendix, or use organic, low-sodium boxed)

1 cup heavy cream

Salt, freshly ground pepper, and freshly grated nutmeg

make the soup

Using a vegetable peeler or paring knife, peel the celery root, then dice it. Hold the celery root in acidulated water—a bowlful of cold water with a few teaspoons of lemon juice—to keep it from discoloring.

Melt the butter in a heavy soup pot, stir in the leeks, and sweat them until very tender.

Drain and dry the celery root and add it to the leeks. Pour in the chicken stock and bring to a simmer. Cook the soup for 40 minutes or so, until the celery root is tender. Cool slightly and puree it in batches in a food processor or blender. Return the soup to the pot, and over medium heat stir in the cream. Bring the soup to a simmer and season with salt, pepper, and freshly grated nutmeg.

roast the pears

Preheat oven to 400°F. Peel and core the pears. Slice them lengthwise into ¼-inch-thick slices and reserve in a bowl. Melt the butter with the sugar and ginger, cinnamon, and coriander. Drizzle the spiced butter mixture over the pears, tossing very gently, being careful not to break the pears. Lay the pears out on an ungreased cookie sheet and roast until they are tender and a little golden. Season with freshly ground black pepper. Reserve for garnishing.

When you are ready to serve, gently warm up the soup—it shouldn't boil. Ladle it into bowls and garnish with a couple of slices of pear. Using a truffle shaver, shave the truffle onto the soup in front of each diner—this is a time-honored extravagance and deserves a little theatricality. If using truffle oil, drizzle it into each bowl.

for the spiced pears

2 firm-fleshed pears like Bosc or Anjou

3 tablespoons butter, melted

2 tablespoons light brown sugar

¼ teaspoon each ground ginger, ground cinnamon, and ground coriander

Freshly ground black pepper to taste

1 ounce fresh black truffle (about 1 small truffle), or 2 tablespoons black truffle oil (see Sources)

Lentil Soup
with Red Chile Croutons and Crème Fraîche

This is a rustic, uncomplicated soup at its base, but the addition of red chile croutons and a generous dollop of tart crème fraîche elevates it out of the ordinary. A piece of pork of some kind (pancetta, guanciale—cured pork jowl—or even lightly smoked bacon) is an essential ingredient; lentils are just not nearly as interesting without it. My favorite lentils are the French *lentilles du Puy,* which hold their shape when cooked and have a complex, mineral flavor. Nonetheless, brown lentils are a reasonable substitute. As with many such hearty soups, this one will continue to improve up to four days in the fridge. Just be sure to taste for seasoning every time you serve it—lentils and beans seem to have an inexhaustible ability to soak up salt and pepper.

SERVES 6

for the lentil soup

2 tablespoons olive oil

1 cup diced pancetta, guanciale, or lightly smoked bacon

2 cloves garlic, minced

1 small onion, diced

1 medium carrot, diced

1 small bulb fennel, diced

1 pound French or brown lentils

Heat the olive oil in a 6-quart stockpot. When it shimmers, add the pancetta (or other pork product) and render it halfway. (You don't want to get it crispy—just to render some of the fat.) Stir in the garlic, onion, carrot, and fennel and sauté 2–3 minutes, until the vegetables begin to soften. Stir in the lentils, pour in the chicken stock, add your bay leaves, and bring to a simmer. Skim off any foam that rises to the top. Simmer, skimming occasionally, for 45 minutes or until the lentils are thoroughly tender. At this point you can puree the soup if you care to, but I prefer leaving it as is. Season with salt, pepper, a small dash of sherry vinegar (this really helps to balance the starchiness of the lentils), and some minced thyme.

make the red chile croutons

Cut the bread into ½-inch cubes. Heat the butter and oil together in a 10-inch-wide skillet until the butter foams. Add the cubed bread and stir constantly until croutons are a golden brown. Evenly sprinkle in the chile powder, add the mashed garlic, then turn down the heat to low (to avoid burning the spice) and continue to cook for another minute. Season with salt and pepper and drain on paper towels. Sprinkle on a little more salt.

The croutons will keep 2–3 days if stored at room temperature in an airtight container.

To serve, ladle the soup into bowls and top with a dollop of crème fraîche. Pass around the red chile croutons.

10 cups chicken stock (see Appendix, or use organic, low-sodium boxed)

2 bay leaves

Salt and pepper to taste

Dash of aged sherry vinegar

Minced fresh thyme

for the red chile croutons

6 slices country bread, crusts removed

3 tablespoons butter

1 tablespoon olive oil

1 tablespoon ancho chile powder (see Sources)

1 clove garlic, mashed with salt

Salt and freshly ground pepper to taste

1 cup crème fraîche (see page 29)

Kabocha Squash Soup with Lemongrass and Ginger

I first encountered this Japanese variety of hard squash when I worked at the Quilted Giraffe, a four-star temple of French-Japanese fusion cuisine in 1980s New York. The kabocha, a large, round, squat-shaped dark green squash, has remarkable properties. It is as richly flavored as butternut, but with a silkier texture. It is grown primarily in California, so it's not quite as exotic as it sounds. I make this soup in the late fall and winter and have been pleased that my regular customers look forward to its debut every season.

2 large kabocha or butternut squash

3 tablespoons vegetable oil

Salt and pepper

2 leeks, trimmed, white part thinly sliced

2 tablespoons minced fresh ginger

¼ cup minced fresh lemongrass stalk

3 tablespoons butter

2 teaspoons curry powder

2 quarts chicken stock

One 12-ounce can unsweetened coconut milk

Sachet of 8–12 coriander seeds, 1 strip orange peel, 6–8 black peppercorns, and 3–4 cilantro stems

Honey and cinnamon to taste

SERVES 6

Preheat your oven to 400°F. (Yes, you are going to roast the squash. This extra step really deepens the flavor. It's worth it.)

Cut each squash in half. Be careful here—these squash are very hard, and if they slip out from under the knife you might get a nick (or worse). I place the squash on a dish towel on top of my cutting board. Remove the seeds and membranes. Rub the inside cavities with the vegetable oil and some salt and pepper. Place skin side down on a baking sheet, cover loosely with foil, and roast 45 minutes to an hour or until the flesh is very tender. Scoop out the roasted squash.

Sweat the leeks, ginger, and lemongrass in the butter in a 6-quart pot. When the aromatics are soft, stir in the curry and cook for 1–2 minutes. This amount of curry won't make the soup taste "curried," but it will lend some background notes to the final flavor.

Pour in the chicken stock and coconut milk and add the squash. Drop in the sachet and simmer for an hour, stirring occasionally. Cool the soup and puree it in batches in a blender until very smooth. Season to taste with honey (I just use a small amount), cinnamon, and salt and pepper.

What's for supper, Luke wants to know.

‹ weighing your options ›

When you have a nice, smooth, flavorful soup like this, you have a great canvas for garnishing options. I generally pair this fall/winter soup with other ingredients of that season—sautéed apple or pear slices, roasted chestnuts, roasted wild mushrooms, toasted pumpkin seeds with a drizzle of pumpkin seed oil, or a simple swirl of crème fraîche with orange zest.

Goulash Soup

When my mother would pull out her powder blue enameled Dutch oven, I knew we were in for her überdelicious goulash. If you want to warm up your entire household with the aromas of the old Austro-Hungarian Empire, this is the soup to make.

There are a few key ingredients you'll want to seek out to achieve the particular nuances of this soup. The first is very fresh Hungarian sweet paprika—Spanish won't do. The second is fresh whole caraway seed. The third is fresh marjoram—not often used in this country, but a remarkably interesting herb; it looks like oregano, but has a sweeter and more delicate flavor. Finally, an Austrian friend of mine said that he only uses the beef shin, because it yields so much gelatin into the broth and doesn't break down as much as chuck meat. I like to combine both. With its hearty flavors, this soup freezes well, so doubling the recipe can be a good idea.

1 pound beef, chuck or shin or a combination of both

1 tablespoon butter

1 tablespoon bacon fat, if you have it on hand, or use olive oil

1 large onion, diced

1 poblano chile or green bell pepper, diced

1 clove garlic, mashed with a little salt

2 tablespoons Hungarian sweet paprika

Salt and freshly ground pepper

1 tablespoon white vinegar

5 plum tomatoes, diced

2 tablespoons caraway seeds, crushed lightly with the side of a knife

2 quarts water

3 medium Yukon Gold potatoes, peeled and diced

2 tablespoons minced fresh marjoram

SERVES 6

Cut beef into small cubes—about an inch. Heat the butter and bacon fat in a 4-quart pot or enameled Dutch oven (of any color!) and sauté the onions and peppers until golden. Stir in the mashed garlic and sprinkle with the paprika. Cook 1 or 2 minutes longer to make the spice bloom. Add the beef, searing it with the vegetables, and let everything brown a bit.

Add the salt and pepper, and stir in the vinegar, tomatoes, caraway seeds, and water. Bring it all to a simmer, then cover and cook for an hour. Add the diced potato and cook 20 minutes or longer, until the potatoes are cooked and the meat is tender. Add the marjoram at the very end—its perfume will be lost if it goes in too early. Taste for seasoning, adding salt and pepper as needed.

‹ weighing your options ›

A slice of rye bread topped with the Goat Cheese Spread with Caraway and Paprika on page 37 is a wonderful accompaniment to this soup and makes for a more substantial meal.

A plate of cocktail snacks, clockwise from top: grilled baby artichokes with a bowl of lemon-cracked pepper aioli in the background; smoked salmon flutes with horseradish-papaya cream; roasted black mussels with almond-garlic-thyme butter

Greek salad with roasted olives and rosemary-skewered shrimp

Salmon four ways. Top left. sautéed on French lentils with mango and oil-cured olives; top right, grilled with wasabi-honey glaze; bottom left, paillard of salmon with sel gris and nectarine salsa; bottom right, oven-steamed filet with zucchini "noodles"

Simple roast chicken just out of the oven

Spiced lamb meatballs in eggplant "leaves" with yogurt sauce

Left, sugar snap peas with browned shallots, pancetta, and mint; right, squash roasted in foil packages

An assortment of flavored oils, vinegar, condiments, and chutney

Mohr im Hemd—"a Moor in a shirt"

Green Pea and Sorrel Soup

This soup is the result of my pondering the thorny problem of how to achieve a good-looking as well as good-tasting sorrel soup. I love the bright citrus flavor of sorrel, but am less fond of the murky green color it turns when cooked. I found that it pairs very nicely with sweet spring peas or even frozen petits pois, with the peas contributing their appealing vibrant greenness. I don't often advocate using frozen vegetables, but for some reason small green peas don't suffer too much from suspended animation and I prefer them to overgrown, overly starchy fresh peas if you can't find really young ones.

SERVES 6

prepare your ice bath
Set up a container larger than your soup pot and fill it with a combination of ice and water. This ice bath will be used to stop the pea soup from cooking and to fix its color—heat is the enemy of chlorophyll.

make the soup
Melt the butter in a nonreactive 4-quart saucepan. Sauté the shallots and ginger until lightly golden. Gently stir in the peas and sorrel. Then add the sachet and the heated chicken stock.

Simmer the soup for 10 minutes or until peas are just tender. Place the soup pot in the ice bath, stirring the soup until it cools down. Remove the sachet and puree the soup in a blender until smooth. Pass it through a sieve or strainer to remove any stringiness from the sorrel. Season with salt and pepper. Reheat gently if serving hot.

3 tablespoons butter
2 shallots, thinly sliced
2 teaspoons minced fresh ginger
1 pound shelled fresh young peas or good-quality frozen petits pois
3 cups fresh sorrel, chiffonade and firmly packed
Sachet of coriander seeds and orange zest
6 cups chicken stock, heated* (see Appendix, or use organic, low-sodium boxed)
Salt and pepper

*Green vegetables lose color very quickly when heated, so I preheat the stock when making this soup. It gives the peas a head start, helping them retain their bright color.

‹ weighing your options ›
You have a few nice options here. This soup is equally good hot or chilled. When serving cold, I top it with sliced hard-cooked egg and chilled shrimp, crawfish, or lobster meat. When serving it hot, a little whipped heavy cream floating on top is a nice rich foil for the tangy soup.

Cream of Fennel Soup
with Mussels, Salmon, and Shrimp

Fennel and seafood have such an affinity for one another—it seems like every Mediterranean fish stew or soup (Marseille's famous bouillabaisse, for instance) includes fennel as well as orange zest. The mussels in this soup produce enough briny broth that there is no need to resort to the overly salty canned or bottled clam stocks—I never use them. Use any substitute you like for the salmon and shrimp, but the mussels are the main building block of flavor here.

SERVES 6

for steaming the mussels

2 pounds cultivated black mussels*

2 shallots, sliced

1 cup dry white wine

1 bay leaf

1 sprig thyme

for the soup

2 tablespoons butter

1 tablespoon extra virgin olive oil

3 bulbs fennel, thinly sliced

1 large onion, thinly sliced

2 cloves garlic, mashed with salt

Pinch of salt

*The mussels should have little or no beard, scrubbed under cold water.

steam the mussels

Place the mussels, shallots, wine, bay leaf, and thyme in a 6-quart stockpot over medium-high heat, covered with a lid. Shake the pot periodically and lift the lid every couple of minutes to see how the mussels are doing. When they are all opened, they are done. Strain out the broth and reserve for the soup. Cool the mussels, then remove and discard the shells.

make the soup

Heat the butter and olive oil in a 4-quart stockpot. When the butter foams, add the fennel, onion, and garlic and a pinch of salt—this will help to wilt down the vegetables. When tender, add the saffron, orange zest, and Pernod (optional). Allow the Pernod to evaporate (about 1 minute).

Add the reserved mussel broth plus enough water to yield 6 cups total liquid and simmer for 40 minutes. Cool slightly and puree in a blender until smooth. Return the soup to a saucepan, and stir in the crème fraîche, first whisking a little warm soup into the crème fraîche to temper it (see Chef's Trick, next page), then adding it all to the soup. Bring to a simmer.

Season the salmon and shrimp with salt and pepper and gently lower them, on a spatula or spoon, into the simmering soup to poach. When they turn opaque, add the mussels and heat through. Ladle the soup into bowls, dividing the seafood evenly.

make the red pepper rouille
Place the roasted bell pepper and chile in a food processor with the garlic, bread, and vinegar. Process to a smooth paste. With the machine running, drizzle in the olive oil drop by drop until a mayonnaise-like consistency develops. Season to taste with salt and pepper. Spread on croutons, and you are ready to serve.

Small pinch saffron

1 tablespoon grated orange zest

2 tablespoons Pernod or any anise-flavored liqueur (optional)

1 cup crème fraîche (see box on page 29)

½ pound wild salmon fillet, cut into 1-inch slices

½ pound medium shrimp, peeled, deveined, and cut in half

Salt and pepper

for red pepper rouille

1 red bell pepper, roasted, peeled, and seeded

1 small red chile (Thai bird chile, chile de árbol, serrano), roasted and peeled

2 cloves garlic, mashed up with a little salt

1 slice country bread, crust removed

1 tablespoon aged red wine vinegar

6–8 tablespoons extra virgin olive oil

Salt and pepper

‹ weighing your options ›
If you are serving this soup to your family and just want a quick garnish, dice up a ripe tomato and combine it with sliced scallions, a dash of red wine vinegar, fruity olive oil, and torn basil leaves. If you are hosting more of a dinner party and want to make a more impressive garnish, you can serve this soup topped with croutons slathered in spicy rouille, like this red pepper recipe, for an intense flavor and gorgeous color.

Chef's Trick   Tempering is a way of equalizing temperatures between two ingredients to avoid curdling. Take a little hot broth and stir it into the cold ingredient—cream or eggs (or crème fraîche, in this case)—to equalize the temperature, and then you can safely add it to the whole batch.

Chilled Wild Leek Soup

This is my version of vichyssoise, the justly famous chilled leek and potato soup. Instead of leeks, I use ramps—the lovely wild leeks that are available in early spring, from late April through May. They are a remarkably pungent lily. When my father would take me out to hunt for them, the smell would perfume the forest air in our Vermont woods, giving them away.

SERVES 6

3 tablespoons butter

½ pound ramps, greens removed, stems sliced into ½-inch lengths*

3 medium Yukon Gold or russet potatoes, peeled and diced

4 cups chicken stock (see Appendix, or use organic, low-sodium boxed)

¼ cup each mint leaves, dill, cilantro, Italian parsley

2 cups whole-milk yogurt, preferably organic

Salt and pepper

*If you cannot find ramps, substitute regular leeks and add 2–3 thinly sliced shallots to your sauté, to approximate the sharper flavor of the ramps.

Melt the butter in a 4-quart stockpot. Toss in the ramps (or leeks and shallots) and sweat them until tender, about 8–10 minutes. Stir in the diced potato and pour in the chicken stock. Simmer 40 minutes.

Once the soup has cooled a bit, puree it with the herbs in batches in a blender until smooth. Pour out into a pot or serving bowl, and stir in the yogurt, thinning the soup with a little cold water if needed. Season with salt and pepper. Chill well before serving. Taste again for seasoning before serving.

A COOK'S TOOLS

I'm definitely not a minimalist in my approach to cooking tools—I can't open a drawer or cupboard at home without pots and pans spilling out as if to say, "Pick me! Pick me!" I think I still feel some sadness from when I left my family home to strike out on my own. Since then, I have tried to replace the loss of my mother's well-stocked and well-lived-in kitchen with meaningful objects drawn from my own lifetime of traveling and eating. It really helps to feel connected to the larger world by creating a personality in your kitchen—knowing that each spoon, knife, or pan has a story attached makes cooking a more companionable endeavor.

Many of my tools were purchased during trips to Paris at a shop called Dehillerin. I still remember my first visit there, when my eyes just about popped out of my head. This mecca for passionate cooks houses miles of copper cookware, from the minute saucier no bigger than your fist to the gargantuan stockpot—the biggest of which could fit three portly chefs inside. Every major city has some version of this kind of place—New York has Bridge Kitchenware and JB Prince, Seattle has Sur La Table, and everywhere has Williams-Sonoma.

The famous cookware shop in Paris

Another source for distinctive cookware is flea markets. They are particularly interesting in big cities, where just by buying a cooking vessel you feel like you are connecting to someone else's history. You are just picking up where the last cook left off, benefiting from all the flavors of the past, while seasoning with your own spices. I mean this metaphorically, of course—a good scrubbing is always in order!

As a younger cook, I bought into the gadget craze: a special tool to peel garlic, another to pit cherries, a third to channel out citrus zests. I've weeded out all those in favor of a couple of good knives—they can do anything the fancy tools do, and don't involve digging around in the abyss known as the "stuff drawer."

When choosing your knives, you'll want an assortment of carbon (a softer steel, which can be harder to find) and stainless (harder steel) knives. Carbon knives are best for slicing and deboning. These knives tend to lose their edge quickly, but a few strokes on a honing steel and they are back in shape.

For chef's knives, I like Wüsthof-Trident or Henckel, and I find the eight- and ten-inch blades the most useful. These will hold a sharp edge, but are notoriously hard to sharpen unless you know what you are doing. The regular use of a honing steel is a good idea—I keep mine right next to my cutting board and give a few swipes after slicing each vegetable or so. You want to hold the knife at a fifteen- to twenty-degree angle to the steel and go from the heel of the knife to the tip in one movement. A good honing steel has a handguard to protect you from an errant swipe, but even in my earliest and most awkward days as a cook, I never hurt myself on a honing steel. (Can openers, yes.)

As I have already confessed, my kitchen is stocked with lots of gadgets, but I find that I really reach for the same handful of tools most of the time. These are my essential Cook's Tools:

Knives

- paring knife: I like a sturdy, not too flexible blade about two and a half inches long
- ten-inch chef's knife: this is the all-purpose chopping and dicing workhorse
- boning knife: this should be quite flexible and about five inches long
- serrated knife for slicing bread and soft textures like ripe tomatoes and fruit

Pots and Pans (I like the All-Clad and Sitram brands)

- ten-inch high-gauge stainless-steel sauté pan
- twelve-inch high-gauge stainless-steel sauté pan
- ten-inch nonstick skillet, for eggs and anything you want to get good browning on without using too much oil or butter
- It's worth spending a little extra to buy a well-made and thick-bottomed nonstick pan; again, All-Clad makes a good one.

Saucepans with Lids

- two-quart for sauces
- four-quart for soups
- ten-quart for stocks
- enameled Dutch oven for casseroles and braises
- twelve-inch cast-iron pan for anything you want a good crust on

- Finally, I have a Japanese mandoline for paper-thin slices of garlic, ribbon cuts of zucchini, or julienne of just about anything.

SALADS

AN INSIDER'S GUIDE TO THE VINAIGRETTE

My father has taught me many things, but the lesson that is most valuable to me is this: If you flatter your child by telling her what wonderful salad dressing she makes, you'll never have to do it again yourself. I'm working on this with my son, Luke. As it stands, he's my chief salad spinner and pepper grinder and I'm promoting him to dressing whisker next. I encourage you to do the same with your kids—it gets them involved in the cooking process and also leaves less work for you to do.

On to the world of the vinaigrette. It seems many people—including my coauthor, Andrea—are a little nervous about vinaigrettes, as if it were a math test. "Is it two parts oil to one part vinegar, or three parts vinegar to half part oil—oh, I'll never get it!" she wails. Unfortunately, there's no definite formula, since there is such variety in vinegars and oils. But, as a very general rule, I tend to use three parts oil to one part vinegar—I like a reasonably tart dressing. You will just have to taste your way along; adding mustard, for example, sharpens the dressing, so you may use less vinegar. Also, what you are dressing will dictate the sort of vinaigrette you make. Very tender greens benefit from a dressing using heavy cream in place of the oil, and lemon juice in place of the vinegar with a few snipped fresh herbs tossed in for good measure. Spicy greens like arugula and sturdier lettuces garnished with cheese and ham can take on a dressing of some substance, like Aged Sherry-Walnut Vinaigrette (page 261), and for salads composed of fruit or summer vegetables, I like to use an aged balsamic vinegar and extra virgin olive oil, simply whisked together with good salt and pepper.

I often begin my vinaigrettes with shallots—they are a good foundation flavor. After mincing them, I add a hefty pinch of salt to encourage the shallots to wilt and dissolve their flavor quickly into the dressing. In lieu of salt, I may substitute minced anchovies or anchovy paste for a wonderful brininess; a little is not detectable as a fish taste, it just adds a certain full-bodied flavor. Because nut oils like walnut or hazelnut are so strong in flavor, I always cut them by at least 50 percent with olive oil or another, blander oil like canola or safflower.

If you are serving a salad with your roast chicken, add a few spoonfuls of the roasting juices to your vinaigrette—it's a wonderful way to get depth of flavor. Likewise with any pan drippings from your sauté pan if you happen to have just seared a piece of duck breast, quail, or foie gras.

Arugula with Grilled Peaches, Goat Cheese, and Country Ham

I love the peppery bite of arugula, and I loved it even more when my father taught me its nickname, "rocket"—presumably called that because it will bolt or "take off like a rocket" if your garden is not regularly harvested. To pair up with such a spicy green, I like to use a fresh, creamy, and tangy goat cheese. There are lots of wonderful artisanal cheese makers popping up all over the country, so try to find goat cheese that is made in your state. Vermont Butter & Cheese Company makes great chèvre (and even quark, which is sort of a German cream cheese). New York has Coach Farm, which makes wonderful aged and fresh goat cheeses, and California has many as well, including Laura Chenel and Cypress Grove. Whichever you choose, chèvre is a fresh goat cheese that should be eaten as soon as it is made. As for the peaches, we all know how hard it can be to find a really great peach these days. Is it just childhood memories that haunt us, or did peaches use to be a lot better? At any rate, grilling even less than sublime peaches will help sweeten them up by concentrating their flavor and lending them a delicious smokiness.

SERVES 6

1 pound young arugula
(look for medium-size,
bright green leaves)
3 ripe peaches
2 tablespoons olive oil, for
grilling
¼ teaspoon ground
cardamom (optional;
cardamom is a great
spice for fruit)
Salt and pepper

Preheat your grill.

Fill a sink with cold water, and wash the arugula several times—it is often quite sandy. Arugula bruises easily, so I avoid using a salad spinner, drying it on paper towels instead.

Cut the peaches (they can remain unpeeled) in half lengthwise and remove the pits. Dress them with 2 tablespoons olive oil, ground cardamom (if using), and salt and pepper. Place them skin side down on a hot charcoal grill or on a hot cast-iron grill pan on your stove. Turn peaches over after 2 minutes and grill the flesh side for another 2.

make the dressing

Whisk the salt into the balsamic vinegar to dissolve, then whisk in the oil and pepper.

make the salad

Arrange the arugula on a platter or on individual plates. Drizzle liberally with the dressing, reserving some for the top. Slice each peach half into thirds, tucking them in between the arugula rather than laying them on top—you don't want to squash the greens. Do the same with the ham and the cheese. Drizzle the remaining dressing over the salad and serve immediately. Arugula wilts easily when dressed, so prepare this salad just before serving.

for the dressing

3 tablespoons aged balsamic vinegar

Salt and pepper

6 tablespoons extra virgin olive oil

6–12 slices of country ham (Smithfield is ideal; see recipe on page 48)

6 ounces fresh goat cheese, crumbled with a fork

The Handy Grill Pan A grill pan is a great foul-weather substitute for an outdoor grill. I have several of different shapes and sizes. You can even scatter sprigs of rosemary onto the pan and let them smoke a bit before adding your food. It will add another dimension of flavor, and get you that much closer to the taste of charcoal grilling.

Frisée Salad with Bacon-Wrapped Sea Scallops

Bacon with sea scallops is one of those divine combinations that no mere mortal could have conceived. The quality of each ingredient is important: seek out "dry" sea scallops, meaning that they have not been soaked in a bleaching solution that makes them soggy and waterlogged. Ask your fish supplier for the "10–20" size (between ten and twenty scallops per pound). The bigger the better for this salad. I use applewood-smoked bacon, but any good single-smoked product will do; you don't need the super-sweet big commercial brands—the scallops are sweet enough. The aged sherry vinaigrette is tart and deeply flavored and balances the richness of the scallops. Sherry vinegar has the highest acid of almost all vinegars, so a little goes a long way. There is something bold and even romantic about this dish—it's the swashbuckler of the salad world!

SERVES 6

1 head frisée (also known as curly endive)

1 small head Boston or Bibb lettuce

1 Belgian endive, preferably with red edges

1½ pounds dry sea scallops, 10–20 size

¼ pound bacon

Olive oil, for broiling or grilling

Salt and pepper

½ cup Aged Sherry–Walnut Vinaigrette (see page 261)

Wash the frisée, Boston or Bibb lettuce, and Belgian endive and tear or cut into bite-size pieces. Spin dry.

Remove the adductor muscle from the scallops if still attached—this is the small, hard, cream-colored tab on the side of the scallop that held it to its shell.

Cut the bacon strips into lengths that will wrap once around each scallop with a little left over to secure with a toothpick—wrap the bacon strip around the scallop's circumference rather than the diameter (do we remember our geometry?).

Preheat broiler or grill. (The scallops are equally good grilled or even pan-fried, but broiling is a good way to keep bacon splatter to a minimum.) Line a broiling tray with foil, brush a thin coat of olive oil on each scallop, season lightly with salt and pepper, and broil, grill, or fry for 2 minutes per side. Scallops should still be translucent in the center when you take them off the heat—they will become tough and rubbery if cooked too long.

Dress the lettuces in the vinaigrette and arrange them on a platter or on individual plates. Top with the warm wrapped scallops.

‹ weighing your options ›

This salad is made for a variety of garnishes. Depending on the season, you can toss in some fresh fruit—thinly sliced pear or apple in the fall, mango in the winter, and stone fruits like nectarines or peaches in the spring and summer. Toasted nuts are a great addition if you have some on hand. Sautéed or roasted sweet corn shaved off the cob makes this salad a light entrée.

Greek Salad with Roasted Olives and Rosemary-Skewered Shrimp

I can never resist ordering a Greek salad whenever I go to a diner here in New York. There's something wonderful about the crisp lettuce and briny feta. And I'm an olive freak from way back. My favorite sandwich from my Vermont childhood was cream cheese with olives—you know, the ones stuffed with pimentos. My son, Luke, has inherited my love of brine—he hovers around my martini, eyeing the olives until I give them up. Shopping for olives in New York City yields an embarrassment of riches. There are so many great ones to choose from: oil cured, salt cured, brine cured, or even raw, so you can cure your own. I won't ask you to go that far, but by creating a flavorful marinade and roasting them, any meaty olive is transformed into something special. This version of Greek salad is fairly sophisticated and so pretty when arranged on a large platter at a summer cookout.

SERVES 6

for the rosemary-skewered shrimp

1½ pounds large shrimp, peeled

6 long, sturdy branches of rosemary, to act as skewers

3 tablespoons olive oil, for brushing on skewers

1 tablespoon ancho chile powder (see Sources)

Salt and pepper

for the vinaigrette

Pinch of salt

1 shallot, minced

Juice of 1 lemon

1 tablespoon aged red wine vinegar

⅔ cup olive oil

1 tablespoon minced fresh oregano, or 2 teaspoons dried

Salt and pepper

grill the shrimp

Heat your grill. Thread 4–5 shrimp on each rosemary skewer, folding the shrimp head to tail to form a U shape. Whisk together the olive oil and ancho powder and brush it on the shrimp skewers. Season with salt and pepper just before grilling. Grill 2 minutes each side, until shrimp is opaque throughout.

make the vinaigrette

Sprinkle a good pinch of salt directly over the shallots before adding the other ingredients. That way, they give up their flavor more quickly to the dressing. After salting the shallots, combine them with the rest of the ingredients in a medium-size bowl and whisk together, vigorously. Before dressing your salad, whisk again to combine.

make the olives

Stir together all the ingredients for the marinade and toss with olives in a casserole dish. Roast the olives in the oven at 400°F for 20 minutes.

arrange the salad

To serve, arrange the lettuce, tomatoes, red onion, cucumber, fennel (if using), and crumbled feta on a large platter. Stir or shake the vinaigrette and drizzle it evenly over the salad, reserving some to dress the grilled shrimp. Gently prop the skewers on pieces of tomato or cucumber so as not to deflate the greens. Garnish with the warm, oven-roasted olives.

‹ weighing your options ›

This salad is a great vehicle for other skewered grilled items: chicken, vegetables such as sweet peppers and portobello mushrooms, or even nice pieces of leg of lamb. Grilled quail is also particularly delicious treated this way.

for the olives

6 cloves garlic, thinly sliced

1 medium hot dried chile pod, such as New Mexico or guajillo (see Sources)

Zest and juice of 1 orange

3 tablespoons minced fresh thyme

½ cup olive oil

1 teaspoon crushed fennel seed (optional)

1 pound meaty black olives, such as Gaeta, Kalamata, or Nyons

for the salad

1 head romaine, washed, dried, and torn into bite-size pieces

2 beefsteak tomatoes—1 red and 1 yellow, if available—cut into wedges

1 red onion, thinly sliced

1 cucumber, peeled, seeded, and diced

1 small bulb fennel, thinly sliced (optional)

8 ounces feta, preferably Greek, crumbled

Salmon Carpaccio
with Red Onion, Orange, and Avocado

I had my first salmon carpaccio while on my honeymoon in Venice in 1993. The timeless atmosphere of that amazing city, as well as being a newlywed, left quite an impression on me—I still make this dish for my husband, Michael, whenever I need to send him a romantic vibe! Up to that point, I had assumed that carpaccio was always fillet of beef, thinly pounded and dressed with a creamy anchovy dressing. While the original classic is terrific, I make this version more often. Salmon is very well suited to carpaccio, since it is full flavored and its firm texture allows it to be pounded thin without turning to mush. (You'll still need to be gentle, though.) Good salmon is available year-round, and although I prefer wild king salmon, farm-raised will do nicely. I encourage you to play with different dressings and combinations of garnishes. I generally choose something reasonably strong flavored like citrus to balance the wonderful rich oiliness of the salmon.

SERVES 6

for the carpaccio
1½ pounds salmon fillet, skinned, pinbones removed

make the carpaccio
Trim any brown-colored flesh from the salmon—this will most likely be on the skin side. Place the fillet on a cutting board, and, using a slicing knife, make ¼-inch-thick slices across the fillet. The slices should go straight up and down, not at an angle. You should end up with 18–24 slices, but don't be alarmed if you have more or less—the pounding evens things out.

Pull off 6 squares of plastic wrap and place ⅙ of the salmon on each square, leaving about ¼ inch of space between the slices. (They will fuse together when pounded out.) Place a second piece of plastic on each portion of salmon and, using a mallet, gently pound the salmon until it is ⅛ inch thick all over.

Using a 6-inch-diameter plate or bowl, trim the salmon carpaccio into a neat circle with the tip of a sharp knife by cutting through both layers of plastic. Keep the salmon, wrapped in plastic, in the refrigerator until ready to dress.

make the vinaigrette
In a small bowl, whisk together the vinegar, reserved citrus juices, minced jalapeño, olive oil, herbs, and salt and pepper.

assemble the salad
Dress the watercress or arugula and the avocado with 2 tablespoons of the vinaigrette, and season with salt and pepper. Take the carpaccio out of the fridge. Peel off one side of the plastic wrap, then invert the salmon onto a plate, and peel off the second piece of plastic. Season with salt and pepper and drizzle a bit of the vinaigrette evenly over the surface. Repeat with the remaining carpaccio. Place the watercress, citrus sections, red onion, and avocado in a neat mound just off center on each carpaccio so the beautiful pink color is visible. Serve immediately.

for the vinaigrette
3 tablespoons rice vinegar
2 navel or blood oranges, sectioned; juices reserved
1 small jalapeño, minced
6 tablespoons extra virgin olive oil
2 tablespoons minced fresh cilantro or basil
Salt and pepper

for the salad
1 bunch watercress or arugula, washed and dried
2 ripe California Haas avocados, peeled and diced
1 small red onion, thinly sliced

‹ weighing your options ›
Grapefruit is a nice alternative to the oranges. Also, some thinly shaved fennel or thinly sliced radishes can substitute for the greens—anything fresh and crisp that you have on hand will work well.

Asparagus Vinaigrette
with Lemon-Pistachio Dressing and Manchego Cheese

My father keeps a well-tended asparagus bed on the north side of the house. The process of creating an asparagus bed made such an impression on me as a kid—digging the trenches, burying the crowns of asparagus, and creating a mound to keep them well covered by earth for three years, when the first harvest is ready. I felt such awe and admiration that my father could plant something and have the patience and character to wait several years to enjoy the fruits of his labor. I'm an instant-gratification girl, and I struggle with it still. I think that is why I'm attracted to the restaurant business, with all its Sturm und Drang—it's very Now, Now, Now!

SERVES 6

1 shallot, minced

2 teaspoons minced fresh ginger

Pinch of salt

Juice of 1 lemon

1/3 cup extra virgin olive oil

Salt and pepper

1½ pounds local asparagus, cooked (see box on next page)

¼ pound Manchego cheese, or aged goat cheese or Pecorino Romano, sliced thin

½ cup toasted pistachios, from Turkey or California

2–3 tablespoons Red Chile Oil (see recipe on page 264; optional)

Put the shallot and the ginger in a medium bowl and sprinkle them with the salt. Drizzle in the lemon juice and olive oil and whisk well. Taste for seasoning, adding salt and pepper as you see fit.

To serve, divide the chilled asparagus among 6 plates, or set them up on a decorative platter, with all the spears aligned. Season with salt and pepper, drizzle on the vinaigrette, and top with thin slices of Manchego cheese. (A great trick is to use a vegetable peeler for the cheese—you get thin shavings in a flash.) Scatter some toasted pistachios on top and garnish with a little red chile oil, if desired.

‹ chef's trick on toasting nuts ›

While many cooks like to toast nuts in a skillet, I find that this method tends to be uneven. I prefer to use an oven at 350°F. If the oven is too cool, the nuts will overdry, leaving them brittle and flavorless, but if it is too hot, you'll get browning on the surface and an untoasted center. The best temperature is 350°—you want it to be just right.

Cooking Asparagus There are many schools of thought on how to cook asparagus. Some cooks steam the spears standing up, some quench them in lots of boiling, salted water. I find that cooking asparagus lying down in a shallow amount of well-salted water works the best. (I also like to choose asparagus that are on the fatter side—more middle and less peel.) This method conserves as much asparagus flavor as possible and allows you to test for doneness easily by poking a stalk with the tip of a sharp knife—when the knife slides out effortlessly, the asparagus is done. I don't believe in "al dente" asparagus—I find that the flavor doesn't fully develop until they are cooked until just tender. I avoid "shocking" the asparagus in ice water, which can damage the texture. Instead, I lay them out single file on a plate or two, and pop them in the fridge or freezer for a few minutes. (Just don't forget they're in the freezer!)

Composed Salad of Salsify, Seckel Pear, and Serrano Ham in Brown Butter–Cardamom Dressing

I came up with this elegant salad for a dinner I made at the James Beard House here in New York. Cooking for the first time at "The House," as we call it, is like a chef's coming-out party. You are introduced to the culinary establishment, and a big fuss is made. In return, the chef shows off her best dishes while cramming as many talented cooks as possible into Mr. Beard's tiny townhouse kitchen, preparing dinner for up to eighty guests in the intimate upstairs dining room. It's quite a feat by all—the staff of The House and the visiting chefs. I've cooked there many times now, and I still get butterflies.

1 pound black salsify root
(see box on next page)
6 Seckel pears*
2 tablespoons butter
1 tablespoon light brown
sugar
¼ teaspoon ground star
anise
¼ teaspoon ground
cinnamon
Salt and pepper
6–12 slices Serrano ham (see
Sources)
¼ pound mixed organic
lettuces
3 tablespoons Aged
Sherry–Walnut
Vinaigrette (see recipe
on page 261)

*You can substitute any pear, but
Seckels are the perfect size.

SERVES 6

cook the salsify

Pour about 2 inches of salted water in a pot and set on the stove to boil. Scrub and peel the salsify, and cut it into 3-inch lengths on the bias to make quill shapes (like penne pasta). Drop the pieces in acidulated water—cold water mixed with lemon juice—as they are cut. Drain and place in a steaming basket over the boiling water. Cover and steam until tender, about 15–20 minutes. Remove as they are ready; the smaller roots will cook faster. Don't overcook or you will have mushy salsify—practically no fun at all.

sauté the pears

Peel and core the pears, then cut each in half lengthwise. Each salad will have 2 halves. Heat the butter in a 10-inch skillet, stir the sugar and spices into the butter, and when the sugar melts, add the pears. Cook just a minute on each side—this will prevent the pears from browning while keeping them fresh-tasting. Season lightly with salt and pepper.

‹ weighing your options ›
To make this salad into a light lunch or a dinner entrée,
include a sheep's milk or goat cheese and a few of the
Spiced Walnuts on page 116.

make the vinaigrette

Heat the butter in a small saucepan over medium heat and cook until the butter solids begin to brown, then add the cardamom. Continue to cook until the butter is the color of toasted hazelnuts. Take the saucepan off the heat and stir in the lemon juice, truffle oil (if using) or hazelnut oil, and salt and pepper.

To serve, arrange the salsify, pears, and ham on individual plates or one platter. Drizzle the vinaigrette over the top. Toss the greens in the vinaigrette and garnish each plate with a small amount of the greens. Serve at room temperature.

for the vinaigrette

4 tablespoons butter

¼ teaspoon ground cardamom

2 tablespoons lemon juice

1 tablespoon white truffle oil (see box on page 156; optional), or substitute hazelnut oil

Salt and pepper

Salsify in front, celery root in back

Salsify If you are not familiar with salsify, I imagine you might want to know more about it. Salsify used to be more readily used in American cooking and has a nickname, which is oyster plant. It's not as widely available today, but you'll find it in farmers markets in the fall. It is a somewhat starchy root that is a favorite among the French, Italians, and Spanish. It has a creamy white flesh, and once peeled needs to be immersed in acidulated water (cold water with a little lemon juice) or it will quickly discolor. As for flavor—it is mild and reminds me most of artichoke with a nuttier finish. Not a strong flavor, but very pleasant and a foil for the Serrano ham and the pear in this salad.

Warm Lobster Salad
with Golden Potatoes, Papaya, and Basil

I usually make this salad in the colder months, when I think lobster is at its best. Unfortunately, it is scarcer and more expensive at this time—I don't know if this is due to winter storms keeping the lobstermen on dry land or the market forces. Anyway, during the summer months when lobsters are more plentiful, they molt and trade up to a larger shell; this shell is plumped up with water as they grow into it, so you wind up paying for a lot of water instead of delicious lobster meat. I'm just warning you so you're not fooled by "cheap" summertime lobster. As a chef I learned that lobster, like other crustaceans, benefits from being cooked in very salty water to approximate seawater. And when I can get my hands on fresh seaweed (just ask your fish supplier) I throw that into the pot as well. Steaming is the best technique for conserving as much flavor as possible, but a plunge in well-seasoned boiling water is fine too.

SERVES 6

for the lobster
$\frac{1}{2}$ pound seaweed (optional)
Sea salt, 1 tablespoon per
    quart of water
Three $1\frac{1}{2}$-2-pound lobsters

Cooking Times for Lobster

Boiled:	$\frac{3}{4}$-1 lb.	5–6 minutes
	$1\frac{1}{4}$ lb.	7–8 minutes
	$1\frac{1}{2}$-2 lb.	9–10 minutes
Steamed:	$\frac{3}{4}$-1 lb.	6–8 minutes
	1-$1\frac{1}{4}$ lb.	9–10 minutes
	$1\frac{1}{2}$-2 lb.	10–12 minutes

cook the lobster
Bring 6 quarts of cold water to a rapid boil. Add seaweed (if using) and sea salt. Plunge the live lobsters into the boiling water and cook 9 minutes—do not begin counting the time until the water has returned to a boil. Pull the lobsters from the water and pierce behind the eyes to let any water drain out. When cool enough to handle, remove the

meat from the shell: Twist the tail off the body, cut the tail flipper off, and, using your thumb, push the tail meat out of the shell, starting at the smaller end and working toward the larger opening where the tail meets the body. Try to get the tail out in one piece. Crack the knuckles and claws and remove meat in as large chunks as possible. Slice the tail meat into medallions. Refrigerate the meat until ready to make the salad. This preparation can be done a day ahead.

If you'd rather steam your lobsters, set a colander or a steaming basket over a large pot of boiling salted water, and cook the lobsters, covered, according to the chart on the previous page.

make the dressing
Whisk together all the dressing ingredients and let mellow at room temperature for 30 minutes. Refrigerate after that.

for the dressing
2 teaspoons minced fresh ginger

1 shallot, minced

½ jalapeño, minced

1 teaspoon grated orange zest

3 tablespoons rice vinegar

1 teaspoon sesame oil

2 tablespoons unsweetened coconut milk (optional)

6 tablespoons olive oil

With Luke in the Beard House kitchen

About Lobsters The only really nonedible parts of the lobster are the feathery lungs (they have a great nickname—dead man's fingers! They won't kill you, they're just unpleasant to eat), the brain sac, and the intestinal tract that runs along the outside of the tail. Discard them. Everything else is delicious, including the reddish roe if the lobsters are female and the dark green tomalley, or liver. The tomalley is great spread on toast. I used to eat it in the restaurant kitchen, as a chef's snack. The coral or roe is beautiful when broken up and sprinkled on the salad as a garnish.

for the potatoes

3 medium Yukon Gold
    potatoes, peeled and cut
    into $\frac{1}{2}$-inch cubes

1 bay leaf

1 clove garlic, smashed with
    side of a knife

3 tablespoons butter

1 tablespoon olive oil, for
    browning

Salt and pepper

$\frac{1}{2}$ papaya, peeled, seeded,
    and diced small

10–12 basil leaves, torn

3 tablespoons butter

2 tablespoons cold water

2–3 tablespoons basil oil
    (see Appendix; optional,
    for garnish)

cook the potatoes

Start the potatoes in cold, salted water with the bay leaf and the crushed garlic clove. Bring to a simmer and cook 5–8 minutes, until potatoes are tender. Drain.

assemble the salad

You'll be multitasking here, so get ready. You want the warm lobster and the warm potatoes simultaneously, so that they are ready at the same time. It is important to have your mise en place! (See next page.)

brown the potatoes

Heat a 10-inch nonstick skillet with the butter and olive oil. When butter is foaming, add the potatoes and let them cook, without stirring, until they begin to brown on one side, then stir or flip them to let them brown on the other side. When well browned, season with salt and pepper. Pour the potatoes into a bowl, add the diced papaya, half of the dressing, and the torn basil leaves, and toss to coat and combine.

warm the lobster meat

Heat 3 tablespoons butter and 2 tablespoons cold water in a skillet. Whisk together over medium heat—the butter will form a creamy emulsion with the water, which protects the lobster from drying out when it's heated. Slip the lobster meat into the butter and heat gently until warmed through. High heat toughens lobster, so do this over medium-low flame.

To serve, divide the potatoes among 6 plates and arrange the lobster pieces over the potatoes, making sure each plate gets some tail meat as well as knuckle and claw. Garnish with a drizzle of basil oil if you wish, and some of the reserved dressing.

ON MISE EN PLACE

As soon as I set my first clog-clad foot inside the gleaming, stainless-steel Sauces Kitchen of Johnson & Wales University's Culinary Division, I heard the chef-instructors chant "mise en place" like a mantra, in an obvious effort to indoctrinate us fledgling cooks. Cooking school is a lot like a military academy, and so much of what is taught is really drummed into your brain and seeps into your pores. I still get chills remembering the chef-instructors marching down the row of cooks, inspecting fingernails and adjusting hairnets. In a kinder, gentler way, I want you to absorb the term "mise en place," and even mumble it in your sleep: "Mise en place, mise en place, mise en place . . ."

So what is it? Here's a sound bite that I still remember twenty-odd years later: "*A place for everything, and everything in its place.*" Really, it's a mind-set—a way of approaching your work so you have the best chance of success.

Cooking requires organization and concentration, and your mise en place is the tool to get you there. You want to think your way through the dish and its accompaniments from beginning to end, and prepare for all the steps along the way. It's not just having all of your ingredients for your recipe ready to go—chopped, diced, sliced, whatever the case may be—it's thinking about the entire recipe process, from preheating the oven, to having a rack for resting the roast, to making room in the fridge for a marinade that needs time to rest, and on and on. Think of yourself as a craftsperson, someone who would never start a project with crappy tools, second-rate materials, and an irritated or anxious mentality. Get Zen . . . get your mise en place.

Summer Tomato and Sweet Onion Salad
with Creamy Herb Vinaigrette

I can think of no other vegetable (or fruit, as the botanical purists insist) that arouses such passion as the tomato. There is nothing like biting into a warm, ripe, sun-soaked tomato, held like an apple. It is a pure joy. I took part a few summers ago in an Heirloom Tomato Festival in the Berkshires. What a revelation that was—I had pretty much assumed that there were four or five types of tomatoes—beefsteak, cherry, plum, green, yellow—but in fact there are hundreds of these heirloom varieties. And they can be wildly interesting to behold—tubular, donut shaped, striped, spotted, fuzzy like a peach—you name it.

This salad celebrates the tomato in all its diverse glory. Pick as many different shapes and colors as you can find, and be sure, when you get them home, never to refrigerate your tomatoes; the cold will damage the texture and mute the flavor. Leave them out on the counter.

SERVES 6

2 pounds assorted local or heirloom tomatoes
Salt and pepper
2 Vidalia or other sweet onions, cut into half-inch-thick rings

for the creamy herb vinaigrette
1 egg yolk
¼ cup heavy cream
1 teaspoon Dijon mustard
2 tablespoons red wine vinegar
1 teaspoon lemon juice
1 small clove garlic, mashed with a pinch of salt with the side of a knife
6 tablespoons olive oil
3 tablespoons minced fresh tarragon or chervil
Salt and pepper

Cut the larger tomatoes into ½-inch-thick slices and the cherry tomatoes in half. Other tomatoes can be cut into wedges—you want some visual diversity here. Season with salt and pepper on the plates or platter. Arrange the onion rings over the tomatoes.

make the dressing
Whisk the egg yolk and cream together. Then whisk in the mustard, vinegar, lemon juice, and garlic. While whisking, pour in the olive oil drop by drop to start an emulsion. When all the oil is incorporated, stir in the minced herbs and season with salt and pepper.

make the croutons

Melt the butter in a large skillet—cast-iron or nonstick. Add the bread cubes and stir periodically over medium-low heat until they are a toasty brown. Season with salt and pepper.

To serve, dress the tomato salad generously with the creamy herb vinaigrette and scatter the croutons on top.

for the croutons

3 tablespoons butter

3 slices country rye bread, cut into half-inch cubes

Salt and pepper

❰ weighing your options ❱

A crumble of sharp blue cheese like Stilton, Maytag Blue, or Roquefort is fantastic on this salad.

Seasonal Country Salad with Spiced Walnuts

What is a country salad? In my mind it is a thoughtful blend of greens—Lola Rosa, frisée, red oak leaf, tatsoi, endive, mâche, arugula, and mizuna—combining different tastes and textures, topped with a ripe cheese and an artisanal cured ham, and garnished with seasonal fruit and vegetables. A well-balanced vinaigrette and spiced walnuts make it impossible to resist.

This salad was always a bestseller at Quilty's, the small restaurant in SoHo where I created my contemporary American seasonal cuisine. It was always on the menu—tweaked a bit every few months. It was fun to march around the year with this salad, the seasons reminding me when to change from the last, dark red blood oranges of the winter to the first tender spears of asparagus, from the voluptuous fresh Black Mission figs of the summer to the delicately perfumed Seckel pears of the fall.

The same technique I used at Quilty's can easily be used in your home kitchen. Look around at the markets, and take your cues from the seasons. Making this salad is not so much about a recipe as it is a framework, helping you to build your own best-selling salad for your family.

SERVES 6

for the spiced walnuts
²/₃ cup sugar
1 tablespoon ground star
  anise
2 tablespoons ground
  coriander seed
½ teaspoon cayenne
Salt
2 cups shelled walnut halves

make the spiced walnuts
Preheat oven to 350°F. In a medium bowl, stir together the sugar, spices, and salt. Toast the walnuts lightly on a sheet pan in the oven, for about 4–5 minutes. While the nuts are toasting, heat the spiced sugar in a 10-inch skillet over medium heat. When the sugar just begins to melt around the edges, toss in the warm nuts, straight from the oven. Shake the pan vigorously over the burner until all the nuts are coated in sugar—it will cling in somewhat uneven patches, but

that is the effect I like. Pour the nuts onto a plate or baking sheet to cool—don't be tempted to try one until they have really cooled down, since sugar at this temperature will give you a burned tongue to remember!

make your salad

Toss the salad greens with the spiced walnuts and the vinaigrette and top with a generous slice of ham and 1 ounce of cheese per person, according to the seasons (see Weighing Your Options).

for the salad

1 pound mixed lettuces, washed and dried

¼ cup Aged Sherry–Walnut Vinaigrette (see recipe on page 261)

‹ weighing your options ›

Spring: Grilled Asparagus with Serrano Ham and Maytag Blue Cheese
(to grill asparagus, blanch the asparagus to halfway tender,
brush with a little olive oil, season with salt and pepper,
and grill until lightly brown)

Summer: Fresh Black Mission Figs with Smithfield Ham (see page 48)
and Aged Goat Cheese

Fall: Lightly Roasted Seckel Pears with Pecorino Romano and Prosciutto
(for pear-roasting technique, use the method on page 83)

Winter: Blood Oranges and Fennel with Feta and Prosciutto (see Sources)

Roasted Baby Beets
in Cayenne-Buttermilk Dressing

Without bragging too much, I must say that I have converted quite a few people who were adamantly anti-beet into ardent fans. If your only experience with beets has been from a jar or a can, you have to promise me that you will roast your own and try them as nature intended. They are so sweet and earthy that you immediately feel a connection to the land. Some vegetables are like that—they communicate such a strong sense of place, something ancient and essential.

SERVES 6

for the roasted beets

1½ pounds baby beets, red and gold, unpeeled, with stems trimmed and washed

2 tablespoons butter

2 tablespoons olive oil

2 teaspoons chipotle puree (see page 204; optional)

2 sprigs thyme

2 strips lemon or orange peel

Salt and pepper

roast the beets

Preheat oven to 400°F. Make 2 separate packages from 1-foot-square pieces of double-layer foil. Place half the beets in the center of each square, and to each package add 1 tablespoon of butter, 1 tablespoon of olive oil, 1 teaspoon of chipotle puree (if using), 1 sprig of thyme, 1 strip of peel, and salt and pepper. Close packages tightly and place on a cookie sheet in the oven. Roast for 30 minutes.

while beets are roasting, make the dressing

Whisk together all ingredients and let age 30 minutes in refrigerator before using. Before dressing your salad, whisk the dressing up once more.

After about 30 minutes of roasting, test the beets to see if they are done: Open a package and pierce the beets with a sharp knife—it should pull out easily when they are tender. If the beets aren't ready, close up the foil and continue to roast, checking for doneness every 10 minutes. When tender, open the foil packages to let the steam escape and cool before peeling. The skins will rub right off. Reserve the cooking liquid that collected in the packages—it can be drizzled over the beets along with the buttermilk dressing.

To serve, dress the beets with the buttermilk dressing and arrange on a platter or in a ceramic bowl. This salad is equally good warm or cold.

NOTE: Chipotles are smoked jalapeños, usually preserved in a tomato-vinegar-based sauce called adobo, which is extremely delicious. Chipotles are quite spicy and have a lingering smoky flavor that adds a unique dimension to this dish.

for the dressing

3 tablespoons crème fraîche
(see box on page 29)

¾ cup buttermilk

1 clove garlic, minced

1 teaspoon cayenne

1 tablespoon lemon juice

Salt and pepper

❬ weighing your options ❭

If you have any bits of blue cheese in the fridge, you can add them to this salad, as well as some toasted nuts like almonds, pecans, or walnuts. These beets are also an amazing side dish for fried chicken or anything barbecued.

Steamed Mussels with Toasted Garlic, Saffron, and Basil

Soft-Shell Crab Tempura with Crushed Blackberry and Horseradish Relish

Maine Lobster in Sherry-Ginger Sauce

Almond-Crusted Fried Squid with Thyme

Red Chile–Basted Shrimp in Apple Cider Sauce

Oysters in Gewürztraminer Cream

Sea Scallop Carpaccio with Lychee, Cucumber, and Caviar Vinaigrette

SALMON—FOUR WAYS
Sautéed Fillet of Salmon on French Lentils with Mango and Oil-Cured Olives
Grilled Salmon with Wasabi-Honey Glaze
Paillard of Salmon "Unilateral" with Sel Gris and Nectarine Salsa
Oven-Steamed Fillet of Salmon with Zucchini "Pappardelle"

Seared Sea Scallops with a Cool Cucumber, Sesame, and Dill Sauce

Red-Flannel Salmon Hash with Poached Eggs and Coriander Hollandaise

Monkfish with Cassoulet Beans

Halibut Baked in Parchment with New Potatoes, Braised Leeks, and Truffle Butter

Tuna Tartare

Oven-Roasted Grouper with Cabbage, Apples, and Warm Carrot-Caraway Dressing

Red Snapper Roasted on Fleur de Sel with a Warm Citrus-Chive Dressing

Pancetta-Wrapped Tuna with Red Wine–Braised Onions

Grilled Whole Fish

Oven-Braised Halibut in Wild Mushroom Broth with Baby Herb and Hazelnut Salad

FISH AND SHELLFISH

When I was a kid growing up in Middlebury, Vermont, fresh seafood was hard to come by. The "fish man," Willy Ford, from the Maine coast, would drive into town on Friday afternoons and park his refrigerated truck in the lot of the Knights of Columbus hall. I liked standing with my mom while she visited with the neighbors while keeping an eye out to see who was flush enough to buy the lobster. The fish man in his thick rubber boots would silently weigh out the fish or shellfish as though administering a dose of much-needed medicine—and that's pretty much how we felt about it, too.

Though most Vermonters had a pretty meat-centric diet at that time, there were still riches to be found in the streams, rivers, and lakes. Brookies—small brook trout—make a fabulous breakfast when pulled right out of a sparkling mountain stream and into a cast-iron pan primed with bacon drippings. And Lake Champlain walleye, perch, and landlocked Atlantic salmon were particular local delicacies. But these days there's a full-time fishmonger in Middlebury and more than one sushi bar in Burlington, thirty miles to the north.

My father is a devoted fisherman, but I never caught the bug (sorry, bad fly-fishing pun). He and my brother, Michael, are regulars at Sandy Martin's fishing camp on Martha's Vineyard. There, at a men's-only retreat, they'll enjoy the striped bass, bluefish, and only God knows what else. But it's just fine with Mom, who indulges herself in all the comfort foods that my father can't abide—meatloaf and roast chicken, and their spinoffs, cold meatloaf sandwiches and chicken salad. She's a thrifty lass, my mom is.

I honestly can't think of many leisurely pursuits in my family that don't lead to something good to eat. My parents even risked certain fines, if not imprisonment, in a foreign country (all right, Canada) for the sake of a lobster dinner. The story goes that during one of our summer camping trips to Mabou, Nova Scotia, we went down to Mabou Harbor, formerly the site of a lobster cannery and now just home to area fishermen. I can still recall the smell of the place—it was the ripe stench of intense, commercial fishing, and many tons of fish and lobster guts spilled on the wharf with a good measure of diesel fuel soaked into the soil. At any rate, my father, with his practiced eye, spied a cache of lobster traps piled on the wharf, some with crabs inside. Not one to let such a treat pass his family by, even if just for crabs and not the prized lobsters, he asked a nearby boat owner if he could be hired to take us out and fish—knowing full well that the lobster season was over and catching any was strictly verboten. The fisherman agreed to take my parents out to a couple of his traps, and we kids were left ashore. My father remembers that when they arrived at the traps and hauled them up, they were entirely full of lively, thrashing lobsters. Our fisherman (now a family friend) said, "Well, whadaya think of them crabs?" as he stuffed several large lobsters into my

My father with a good catch

mother's capacious wicker handbag. Once back ashore, he admonished my parents to "make sure you eat them crabs tonight," and we made sure we did. No lobster has ever tasted as sweet as the Mabou Contraband of 1974.

Years later, I moved from Providence, Rhode Island, to Seattle with a freshly minted culinary diploma in hand. I was looking for a good line-cooking job and some adventure far from the terra cognita of the East Coast for really the first time. Soon I found myself working with Pacific species of fish and shellfish, which took some getting used to. It seemed like all the seafood was much larger than its eastern cousins. The real prize out there is the chinook or king salmon, some weighing over a hundred pounds. I was used to the sleeker but comparatively puny Atlantic salmon, in the twelve-to-fourteen-pound range. The style of cooking king salmon was different, too. Most often you would enjoy one of these beauties on somebody's barbecue grill or hot-smoked and packaged up by the Native American tribes of the Pacific Northwest. Never did I see a king salmon lightly poached and served with a delicate lemon-dill sauce at a croquet match.

I took a couple of memorable trips to the Quileute Indian Reservation at La Push, Washington, at the mouth of the Quillayute River on the Olympic Peninsula. The towering coastal sea stacks were unlike anything I had ever seen—spooky sentinels guarding the shore. I could see where the idea of totem poles came from. I went during the off-season, when the dramatic winter storms would rake the coast and intensify the otherworldly feeling. The Quileute Indians operate a marina and a fish hatchery and are skilled at attracting tourists who are keen to have a glimpse of life from a bygone era.

The salmon are still smoked in the traditional way: A large cedar fire is built near the beach, and the salmon are opened up like a book with their backbones removed and then nailed onto red cedar planks. These planks are then driven into the soft soil around the roaring fire at some distance so the fish cooks slowly and absorbs a distinct smoke and piney flavor from the cedar. It's an experience worth the difficult drive from Seattle. I left the reservation elated by my experiences there, but also unsettled by the feeling that I was somehow trespassing on a sacred land that didn't belong to me. And the ugly gashes of clear-cutting, the indiscriminate logging, are reminders of the inevitable clash between commercialism and the natural environment.

When I moved back east and found myself in Manhattan, I was told that I had to visit the Fulton Fish Market—preferably at about four a.m., when the place is in full swing. It is a cook's rite of passage. So I took a buddy and went down to see what the fuss was all about. Well, I can tell you, it's no place for the casual gawker. You need to keep your eyes open and your feet ready to move out of the way as fishhooks are swung in every direction and forklifts dart through small channels between massive crates of seafood. The fishmongers keep their hooks slung around their necks like a doctor does his stethoscope. Seafood is a highly perishable and expensive commodity, and the intensity of the people working at the market really brings that home.

Now, as a chef in New York City, I can get my hands on pretty much anything that swims or lurks on the silty bottom of any ocean. But just because I can doesn't mean I do. I check in often with my suppliers and ask them what is local and in season, because that often translates into plentiful and less expensive. I'd rather buy a local and relatively humble fish like cod than pay for Dover sole to be flown in first class. But, to be fair, when the modern distribution channels are working at peak efficiency you can sometimes get fresher seafood from thousands of miles away than from a nearby but disreputable source. It's critical to forge a good relationship with whoever sells you fish. Ask questions and, if possible, examine the whole fish before it has been filleted.

PURCHASING SEAFOOD

FIN FISH

Whether you're buying whole fish or fillets, certain clues will help you decide if the fish is fresh or not and if it's been well handled. Let's talk about *whole fish* first. These are the qualities you want to see:

1. There should be a sheen to the skin. Sometimes a translucent slime will be apparent—this is a good thing. Fish lose their slime as they age.

2. The scales should be firmly attached to the skin. Missing scales are a sign of improper handling.

3. The fish should have a clean, briny odor. The fish should smell like a clean ocean breeze, not "fishy."

4. The gills should be bright pink or red, not tinged with brown or gray.

5. The eyes should bulge and in most cases be clear, though there are a few species whose eyes are never clear.

6. The flesh should be firm to the touch and almost stiff. The stiffer the better—this means the fish was killed recently and is still in rigor mortis.

For *fillets* the signs are more subtle, but should still be obvious to your trained eye.

1. The grain or "flake" of the fish should be tight, not gaping, which indicates poor handling.

2. There should be translucence, or what I call "glow." The fillet should have discernable light passing through it. If it is opaque, it has probably been frozen.

3. Meatier fish often have blood lines (swordfish, for example), and these should be bright red, not brown or gray, which would indicate the oxidation and blood loss of age.

4. Avoid buying the tail piece. Because of the swimming action, this part will be tougher and more fibrous. Don't worry: the fish shop will make good use of it in a seafood salad or something similar.

SHELLFISH AND CRUSTACEANS

- **Lobster and crab:** These are relatively easy to purchase. You want lively ones right out of a well-maintained tank. Look for a tank that looks clean, with clear, oxygenated water. Female lobsters often have roe (coral), which makes a delicious compound butter or garnish, but if this doesn't appeal to you, buy the males. You can tell the difference by the swimmerettes under the tail; the male's are hard and sharp and the female's are feathery and softer. Likewise with the crabs. The male "key"—sort of like a hinge on the underside of the crab—is long and narrow, and the female's is broader at the base.

- **Mussels and clams:** Like lobster and crabs, these bivalves need to be alive when you cook them. Unfortunately, they don't have any arms or legs to wave around to let you know that they're still with us. But there are signs. The shells should be closed, or gape only a little. If they gape, rap a couple of the mussels or clams together; their shells should close in fifteen to thirty seconds. If they don't, they're dead and must be thrown out. For this reason, I never buy precooked shellfish from a fish store. There's a good chance that the product either expired or was looking close to it when it was cooked—not in itself a health hazard, just inferior eating. Mussels and clams should also feel somewhat heavy for their size. Too heavy, and they may be filled with mud; too light, and the meat inside has probably shriveled.

- **Oysters:** Oysters, too, should be tightly closed and never gape when alive. Look for oysters that are heavy for their size, which indicates they are full of delicious brine or "liquor." Look for oysters that are arranged on ice with the deep side or vault of the shell down to preserve this liquor. If they're all in a jumbled pile, there's a good chance some of the delicious juice has escaped via gravity.

- **Scallops:** Ask for "dry" scallops. These are scallops that have never been soaked in a bleaching solution, which pumps them full of water and destroys their delicate flavor and texture. Scallops are naturally colored ivory, pink, or even a peachy orange. A pure white color with no translucence indicates bleaching.

- **Shrimp:** I've found shrimp to be the most perishable of all the shellfish, and in many cases it is better to buy blast-frozen shrimp than "fresh" shrimp that's been out of the water more than a day. Unless you live within an hour's drive of a shrimping area, even when you buy unfrozen shrimp it's likely to have been frozen and thawed. Fortunately, shrimp freezes pretty well, not losing much flavor or texture in the process. The shell will give you a good clue to freshness—you want a uniform color, either white, pink, or striped. Black spots along the tail are the first sign of deterioration. I usually buy shrimp with the head on. The head will blacken and loosen first, so if it's still firmly attached and has good color, I know I have a lovely shrimp.

These are the most common types of shellfish on the market. For more in-depth writing on sea urchin, octopus, abalone, conch, whelk, periwinkles, and the like, I recommend James Peterson's book *Fish and Shellfish* (Morrow & Co., 1996).

STORING SEAFOOD

One word sums up how to store seafood: Cold! That's the key. The microorganisms that thrive on and in seafood are habituated to cold conditions and are not discouraged from thriving in cool temperatures. You want to store your seafood at just above freezing, so 34–36°F. If you live more than ten minutes away from your fish store, bring along a cooler or ice packs to keep the fish in good condition on the way home. Whole fish will have been scaled and gutted at the store, but give them a good rinse under cold water when you get home anyway. Wrap the fish in damp towels, wrap well in plastic, and place in a colander over a drip pan. Scoop ice over the fish. The ice must have a place to drain into as it melts, or it will leak into the fish and damage it.

Clams, oysters, and mussels are also stored in a colander with ice over them, but not wrapped in plastic—they are alive and need to breathe. Again, they must be separated from the melting ice water, which will drown them. Take a few extra minutes to store your oysters vault down. You've just made a sizeable investment and need to protect it. Lobsters and crabs are prone to wandering around inside your fridge if not kept in a paper (not plastic) bag. Consume your seafood the day that you bought it for the best flavor. But, if well stored, the next day is probably fine. Think of it this way: Your live seafood, such as lobster, crab, oysters, clams, and mussels, are slowly losing weight the longer they don't have anything to eat. They are castaways in your kitchen, and there's no virtue in slim shellfish.

Steamed Mussels
with Toasted Garlic, Saffron, and Basil

Making this dish always reminds me of gathering mussels at low tide on the coast of northern Scotland. My sister and her son live just outside of Edinburgh, and whenever we go over for a visit, they take us on a camping adventure to the Highlands or the Isle of Skye. We cook the fresh-from-the-rocks mussels in a large steel wok—which is a great camping tool, by the way. Just tie it to the strap of your backpack (kind of tricky to fit it inside) and go! You can boil water in it for pasta, steam mussels, sauté freshly picked chanterelles, and prepare any number of haute-survival goodies. Make sure you have a loaf of crusty bread on hand—you won't want to miss any of this deliciously rich broth.

SERVES 6

You'll need a large pot or wok with a tight-fitting lid. Heat the pot over medium-high heat and then add the oil and the garlic slices. Stir until the garlic becomes lightly browned, then pour in the wine, add the saffron, and let the sauce cook, reducing slightly. Add the mussels, stir once, and cover.

Check the mussels after 4 or 5 minutes—you want most of the mussels to be opened before you start pulling them out of the pot. I pull them out in stages to make sure that the early openers are not overcooked. Any stubbornly closed mussels should be discarded, as this is a sign that they were dead on arrival.

Strain the broth into a fine sieve to remove any grit or shell and then return the broth to the pan to reduce by half its original volume. Temper in the crème fraîche (see Chef's Trick on tempering on page 91), and reduce the sauce until it just lightly coats a spoon. Then fold in the basil. Pour the sauce over the mussels, grind lots of fresh black pepper on top, and serve right away.

2 tablespoons olive oil

3 cloves garlic, shaved as thinly as possible

1 cup white wine

Small pinch saffron threads

3 pounds mussels, scrubbed and beards removed

2/3 cup crème fraîche (see box on page 29)

1/2 cup torn basil leaves (cilantro or tarragon works well, too)

Lots of fresh coarsely ground black pepper

Soft-Shell Crab Tempura
with Crushed Blackberry and Horseradish Relish

Why blackberries with crab? Well, I think it has a lot to do with the timing. As a chef, I'm always drawn to cooking what's in season, and blackberries seem to arrive on the seasonal scene about the same time soft-shell crabs do. Blackberries are often not the sweetest of the berries, but you can transform this weakness into a virtue by combining them with peppery horseradish to challenge the rich sweetness of the crab. The tempura coating acts as a delicious faux shell to give the soft shells some crunch. I love crispy seafood—it harkens back to summers on the shore and baskets of fried clams. While the cardamom browned butter is optional, I encourage you to make it—I find this really ties the dish together and is very easy to make.

SERVES 6

for the blackberry and horseradish relish

1 pint blackberries
1 teaspoon lemon zest
1 teaspoon sherry vinegar
2 tablespoons prepared horseradish
1 tablespoon olive oil
Salt and pepper

make the relish

Pick over the fruit for stray leaves or moldy berries. Put them in a medium-size bowl and crush them with your hands. Add the lemon zest, vinegar, horseradish, olive oil, and salt and pepper and taste for seasoning. The relish should be somewhat sweet and tart, with a finishing note of peppery horseradish. Add a small pinch of sugar if you need to increase the sweetness.

for the cardamom browned butter (optional)

3 tablespoons butter
½ teaspoon ground cardamom
1 teaspoon lemon juice
Salt and pepper

prepare the cardamom browned butter (if using)

Put the butter in a small saucepan over medium-low heat. Melt the butter and keep it cooking until the solids turn a hazelnut color. Remove pan from the heat, stir in the cardamom, lemon juice, and salt and pepper and keep in a warm place until ready to use.

make the tempura batter

You want to make the batter at the last minute, because the bubbles in the club soda make a crispy and light batter, and you don't want to let them deflate by making it too early.

Sift the flour and cornstarch into a bowl and slowly whisk in the club soda until a thin batter forms. The batter should coat the back of a spoon and not drip off too quickly. Stir in the chives and sesame seeds.

clean the crabs

It is easiest to clean—a euphemism for kill, I'm afraid—the crabs with a pair of scissors. You hold a crab in one hand and snip off the head (just behind the eyes) first. Then lift up the pointy flaps of what is now its shell and snip out the lungs—they look like gray, feathery gills. Next you pull off the apron and snip that off too. You can ask your fishmonger to show you how to do one, but the crabs should really be cleaned just before cooking.

fry the crabs

Lightly season the crabs with salt and pepper, dredge thoroughly in the batter, and deep-fry (see page 132) until golden brown—about 2 minutes.

Serve with a spoonful of the blackberry relish and a drizzle of the cardamom browned butter, if using. Serve right away to enjoy the maximum crispiness.

for the tempura-crusted soft-shell crabs

1 cup flour

1 cup cornstarch

Enough club soda to make a pancake batter consistency, about 2 cups

2 tablespoons minced chives

2 tablespoons black or white sesame seeds (optional)

6 live soft-shell crabs

Salt and pepper

2 quarts vegetable oil, for frying (light olive, canola, or peanut)

A HOME COOK'S GUIDE
TO DEEP-FRYING

Preparation is the key to successful deep-frying. You'll want to set up a "station" as we do in a professional kitchen. This involves several simple steps:

1. Use a **deep, thick-walled pot** to heat the oil. I use a cast-iron Dutch oven. The oil should only reach halfway up the sides of whatever pot you choose, since oil expands as it heats, and the food you add to the oil will cause displacement, further increasing the oil volume.

2. The next item is a **candy thermometer,** so you'll know when your oil is the proper temperature—in most cases this is 350°F. Blanching is done at a lower temperature—300°F in the case of French fries—with the second crispy cooking done at 350°F. If you don't have a thermometer, you can make an educated guess by dropping a little dribble of batter into the hot oil—it should sizzle vigorously and brown immediately without burning. Wisps of smoke that appear on the surface of the oil mean you've taken it too far and the oil has now begun to break down and become toxic. If this happens, discard the oil and start again. On the other end of the spectrum, oil that is too cool will be soaked up by the food you are frying, creating a greasy and heavy result.

3. A **spider or slotted spoon** for retrieving the fried food. I use a spider, which is like a net with a handle—it grabs less oil when dipping into the pot.

4. **Paper towels** laid out on a tray or cookie sheet for draining the food.

5. **Salt and pepper or whatever final seasoning you are using.** This might be ground cumin, ancho chile powder, curry, minced herbs, and so on. You want them handy, since once the little bit of oil clinging to the food has been absorbed by the towel, the seasonings won't adhere as well.

6. **Your mental mise en place.** Don't get flustered when deep-frying. While it is not as inherently dangerous as skydiving or something like that, you can still get a nasty burn if you're not paying attention. Don't leave your pot on the fire unattended. Do set it on a back burner to avoid accidental bumps, and gently lower the food into the oil—don't get all panicky and drop it in from a great height. The closer your fingers are to the oil when you release the food, the less likely you are to be splashed, which is no fun at all.

Maine Lobster in Sherry-Ginger Sauce

This is basically a glorified version of boiled lobster with butter. But instead of leaving well enough alone, I infuse the butter with a lovely dry sherry and lots of fresh ginger. You don't have to do that much more work to achieve results that are really quite impressive—even the aroma will intoxicate your guests. I prefer to use smaller lobsters—those at 1 to 1¼ pounds. The ratio of shell to meat is high, and this translates into a more pronounced lobster flavor.

SERVES 6

Bring a large pot of water to a strong boil. Add enough salt to approximate seawater (2 teaspoons per quart), and cook the lobsters 3 at a time, 8 minutes for each set of 3. When lobsters are cool enough to handle, remove the claws and crack them with a mallet. Cut the tails in half lengthwise, leaving the meat in the shell. Reserve all the juices that come from the lobster—they will be added to the sauce.

make the sauce

Heat 1 tablespoon of butter in a small saucepan. Sweat the ginger and shallots until softened—about 4 minutes. (For more on sweating, see page 70.) Pour in the dry sherry and the chicken stock and drop in the sachet. Add the reserved lobster juices and simmer the sauce for about 10 minutes, reducing it to half of the original volume. Strain the broth through a sieve, pressing on the solids.

Heat the second tablespoon of butter in a wide skillet, add the lobster tails and claws, pour the sauce over them, then simmer gently to heat the lobster through—about 3 minutes. Remove the lobster pieces, and as you continue to simmer, whisk in the sherry vinegar and the remaining 4 tablespoons of butter, and sprinkle in the minced herbs, salt, and pepper. Pour the sauce over the lobster pieces and serve.

Salt
Six 1–1¼-pound lobsters
2 tablespoons butter, plus 4 tablespoons to finish the sauce
2 teaspoons grated fresh ginger
1 shallot, minced
2 cups dry sherry (Dry Sack or Tio Pepe are both fine brands)
1 cup chicken stock
Sachet of 8 black peppercorns, 12 coriander seeds, 1 strip of orange peel, and a small handful of cilantro stems, tied in cheesecloth
2 tablespoons aged sherry vinegar
1 tablespoon minced cilantro or tarragon
Salt and pepper

‹ weighing your options ›
I serve this dish with plain steamed rice or steamed new potatoes. I like simple sides so that the lobster is the star of the show.

Almond-Crusted Fried Squid with Thyme

This recipe belongs in the category of "building a better mousetrap." Fried squid is on practically every neighborhood restaurant menu, and I love it when it is well done—distinct, crispy rings and crunchy tentacles. But I wanted to do my own version and came up with the idea of dredging the squid in almond flour to give it a rich nutty flavor. The clean, floral notes of fresh thyme with a squeeze of lemon make it just right.

SERVES 6

2 pounds cleaned squid
    bodies and tentacles,
    bodies cut into ½-inch-
    thick rings
1 quart milk
2 cups blanched almond
    flour (see Sources)
2 cups flour
Salt and pepper
2 quarts vegetable oil (light
    olive, canola, or
    peanut)*

*You can recycle the oil by letting it cool, then straining it through a coffee filter.

Review deep-frying technique on page 132.

Soak the squid rings in the milk in the fridge for an hour or so. This tenderizes them, and the liquid clinging to the squid will form a batter when they are dredged in the flour mixture. Thoroughly combine the almond flour and regular flour, and season with salt and pepper.

Heat your oil in a large Dutch oven. When it reaches 350°F, dredge the squid rings and tentacles in batches in the flour mixture and fry until golden, about 3 minutes. Drain on paper towels.

make the chile-roasted almonds (optional)

Heat the butter in a skillet. When it is foamy, add the sliced almonds, stir until lightly browned, then sprinkle on the ancho powder and salt and pepper. Drain on paper towels.

Serve the fried squid with a sprinkle of minced thyme, the lemon wedges, and the chile-roasted almond slices scattered on top, if desired.

for the chile-roasted almonds (optional)

2 tablespoons butter

½ cup sliced almonds

1 tablespoon ancho chile powder

Salt and pepper

for the garnish

2 tablespoons minced thyme

6 lemon wedges

❮ weighing your options ❯

Sometimes, only a creamy, mayonnaise-based sauce will satisfy with fried squid. In this case, I recommend Smoked Chile and Caper Remoulade (see recipe on page 271). It has a nice smoky kick and plenty of bright acidity to complement the fried squid.

Red Chile–Basted Shrimp in Apple Cider Sauce

The fruity tartness of well-made apple cider lends the perfect balance to these red chile-basted shrimp. Since there's still a lot of the Vermonter kicking around in me, I try to use cider from my home state, where just about every village has a cider mill, sending its sweet aroma into the crisp autumn air. It takes talent to blend just the right varieties of apple. You don't want them all sweet—that makes for a monotonous flavor. If I can't find the blend I like, I spike one with a little cider vinegar to get the right edge. Play around with the one you find and adjust it so it suits your tastes.

SERVES 6

for the red chile butter

1 dried New Mexico or
    guajillo chile
2 sticks butter, softened
1 clove garlic, minced
2 tablespoons ancho chile
    powder
1 teaspoon grated lemon zest
1 teaspoon salt and some
    generous grindings of
    fresh black pepper

for the cider sauce

4 tablespoons butter
½ bulb fennel, thinly sliced
1 shallot, thinly sliced
1 teaspoon grated fresh
    ginger

prepare the red chile butter

Toast the chile in a dry pan until it puffs up. Then seed it and grind it fine in a spice mill. Mix together the softened butter, garlic, ancho powder, lemon zest, ground chile, and salt and pepper. Stir the butter with a wooden spoon until it is very well blended. Roll the butter into logs in parchment or wax paper and freeze half of it—this recipe won't require the full amount (see Leftover Alert on the next page for uses for leftover butter). Keep the remainder softened at room temperature.

prepare the cider sauce

Melt 2 tablespoons of butter in a saucepan, add the fennel, shallots, and ginger and sweat until vegetables are soft, about 5 minutes. Add the wine and reduce by half. Pour in the cider, the sachet, and either the chicken stock or fish fumet. (Either stock works well, so go with whatever you have on hand or in the freezer.) Simmer the sauce until it is reduced by ⅔. Remove the sachet and put the sauce in a blender or use a handheld immersion blender to puree. If the sauce is too thick, thin it with a little water. Return the sauce to a clean saucepan over medium heat. Add the cider vinegar and whisk in the remaining 2 tablespoons of butter to finish. Season with salt and pepper. Keep warm.

cook the shrimp

Heat a 10-inch skillet over medium-high heat. Season the shrimp with salt and pepper. Pour the olive oil into the pan, and when it shimmers, lay in the shrimp carefully to avoid getting splashed with hot oil. For this amount of shrimp, you will need to do 2 or 3 batches. You want the shrimp in a single layer in the pan so they get a chance to brown and become crispy.

When the first side of shrimp has cooked 2 minutes, flip the shrimp over and add 2 tablespoons of red chile butter. Baste the shrimp when the butter is melted, tilting the skillet a little toward you, spooning up the butter over the shrimp. Do this many times while the second side of the shrimp is cooking. When shrimp are cooked on both sides, remove from the pan and keep warm while cooking the next batch. Just wipe out the pan with paper towels and you can reuse it, adding another dose of olive oil and red chile butter (about 2 tablespoons each). When ready to serve, gently rewarm the cider sauce, divide the shrimp among 6 shallow bowls, and spoon the sauce over and around them.

‹ weighing your options ›
This recipe works nicely with scallops as well. A simple arugula salad dressed with extra virgin olive oil and lemon juice is a fine accompaniment.

½ cup dry white wine (Alsatian whites are great here—pinot blanc, gewürztraminer, Riesling—and you can drink the rest with your dinner)

2 cups apple cider, locally made if possible

Sachet of 8 black peppercorns, 12 coriander seeds, 1 strip of orange peel, and a small handful of cilantro stems, tied in cheesecloth

1 cup chicken stock or fish fumet (see Appendix, or use organic, low-sodium boxed)

2 tablespoons cider vinegar

Salt and pepper

for the shrimp

2 pounds large shrimp, preferably with the heads on

Salt and pepper

4–6 tablespoons olive oil

‹ leftover alert ›
You can stuff the remaining chile butter under the skin of a roasting chicken, or let it melt on top of a grilled steak. It's also nice to use this butter to sauté corn or mushrooms.

Oysters in Gewürztraminer Cream

Oysters figure prominently in my family's celebrations. These days the cause for celebration is just as likely to be the fact that we were able to scoot up to Vermont for a long weekend. Then my father gets on the phone and orders half a bushel from Rulon Wilcox, an oyster farmer out on Cape Cod. As Baltimore natives, my folks are hard-wired to adore East Coast oysters and blue crabs, and they've passed down that genetic tic to me.

Although purists contend that the only thing you do to a good oyster is gulp it down raw, I love them in all their permutations: oyster roasts, stews, gratins, deep-fried, and in stuffings. One of my favorite cookbooks is *Maryland's Way* (Hammond Harwood House, 1963), which boasts no fewer than two dozen oyster recipes. I came up with my own version of an oyster stew that is shaped by my experiences in Germany and Austria. I thought that the oysters' pronounced brininess would be enhanced by a wine sauce with a lot of character, so after a considerable amount of wine tasting, I decided on gewürztraminer, for its intriguing floral and spice notes. And it works. In fact, this dish has become one of my signatures, having appeared in the press more than any other recipe I've concocted to date.

SERVES 6

for the grapes
1 tablespoon butter
½ cup green or muscat
    grapes
Pinch of sugar

begin by glazing the grapes
Melt the butter in a small saucepan. When it foams, add the grapes and the sugar, and swirl the pan over medium heat until the grapes begin to soften but do not entirely deflate, about 4 minutes.

make the gewürztraminer sauce
Heat the butter in a saucepan over medium-low heat. Add the shallots, ginger, and fennel and sweat the vegetables until soft, about

10 minutes. Pour in the wine and reduce it to half its volume. Add the heavy cream, drop in the sachet, and simmer very gently over low heat until the cream has reduced by half. Turn off the heat and let the flavors just steep for 30 minutes or so, then strain, pressing gently on the solids.

finish the oysters

Heat the strained wine sauce in a wide saucepan. When simmering, add a few spoonfuls of the reserved oyster liquor. The oyster liquor will add brininess, so taste the sauce before adding any more salt. When you have the right balance between the sweetness of the wine sauce and the oyster brine, gently lower the oysters into the sauce and cook them until their edges just curl—about 2 minutes. Divide the oysters among the plates, scatter the sautéed grapes evenly over them, and ladle in the warm gewürztraminer cream. To sop up the sauce, pass around some bread.

Review deep-frying on page 132. Heat the oil, and sprinkle the cut leeks with a little water on your fingertips to help the flour adhere better. Toss the moistened leeks in flour and shake off the excess. Fry until golden brown, drain, and season lightly with salt. Garnish the oysters with the fried leeks and serve.

‹ weighing your options ›

While this dish is quite impressive on its own, if you are having company over that loves food you might want to top the oysters with a fried-leek garnish, which makes a very dramatic restaurant-quality presentation.

for the gewürztraminer sauce

2 tablespoons butter

1 shallot, minced

1 teaspoon grated fresh ginger

½ bulb fennel, minced

1 cup gewürztraminer (ask for a moderately sweet one, without too much residual sugar)

1 cup heavy cream

Sachet of 8 black peppercorns, 12 coriander seeds, 1 strip of orange peel, and a small handful of cilantro stems, tied in cheesecloth

for the oysters

2 dozen freshly shucked oysters, liquor reserved and strained

for the fried-leek garnish

1 quart canola oil, for frying

1 leek, white part cleaned and julienned very fine

3 tablespoons flour, for dusting the leeks

Salt

Sea Scallop Carpaccio
with Lychee, Cucumber, and Caviar Vinaigrette

If you have ever wondered how a chef comes up with a dish for a menu, here's a little insight. For this scallop carpaccio—very thinly sliced raw scallops—I knew I wanted to create a starter that was pure theater, a dish to intrigue and entertain my restaurant guests. My thought process was very stream-of-consciousness. I thought: Scallops are sweet, tender, mild, and white, and so are lychee nuts. It might be fun to pair them together. I like a little crunch with my scallops, but nothing too strong in flavor that might overwhelm the delicate mollusks. I know: What about small-diced cucumber? That will give me some crunch, and it is nice and mild and refreshing. Now I need a little bit of brininess and acidity to keep my taste buds dancing. Okay, how about some caviar, but I'll suspend it in a delicate rice vinegar dressing. Yes, that seems to work out pretty nicely.

While this is a restaurant-style dish, you can easily make it at home without too much drama. Just one last detail: a flute of sparkling wine or champagne to celebrate with.

SERVES 6

1½ pounds dry sea scallops

for the vinaigrette
Salt
1 shallot, minced
¼ cup rice vinegar
1 teaspoon grated fresh
    ginger
1 tablespoon lemon juice
3 tablespoons extra virgin
    olive oil

Preheat the broiler. Remove the adductor muscle from the scallops (this is the small, tablike piece) and slice each scallop crosswise as thin as possible. Arrange the scallop slices in concentric circles on 6 ovenproof plates. Cover each completed plate with plastic wrap and refrigerate until ready to broil.

make the vinaigrette
Lightly salt the minced shallots and whisk together with the remaining vinaigrette ingredients.

make the carpaccios

Remove the plastic wrap from the plates and spread a very thin layer of olive oil over the surface of the scallops. Season lightly with sea salt.

Add the diced cucumber, lychee nuts, caviar, and chives to the vinaigrette. Pass each plate of scallops under the broiler for 10 seconds—this will firm up the texture of the scallops but not entirely cook them. Generously spoon dressing over each carpaccio, smoothing it out to cover the entire surface. Serve at once.

A few drops toasted sesame oil

2 tablespoons extra virgin olive oil, for broiling

Sea salt

1 seedless cucumber, peeled and diced small

½ pound lychee nuts, peeled and pitted

2 ounces caviar, of your choice and budget (see page 142)

1 tablespoon minced chives

‹ weighing your options ›

An interesting variation on this dish is to dress the sliced scallops in a bowl with the rice vinegar dressing, season with sea salt and some freshly ground pepper, and refrigerate for 30 minutes or so. This will create a quick ceviche, which I pair with the Avocado-Sesame Relish on page 77.

CAVIAR

Two things are guaranteed to make any night feel special—champagne and caviar. Like the bubbly stuff, caviar—salted fish roe—comes in many grades and at many price points, but I think its presence alone is enough to bring a touch of celebration and elegance to any cocktail party or dinner fete.

Most of the world's caviar comes from the roe of sturgeon that swim in the Caspian Sea, a cold inland passage located between Russia and Iran. Beluga caviar, from the huge beluga sturgeon, is the most costly and of the highest quality. It is prized for its fat, soft roe and mild taste. The best beluga roe, called triple zero, are light golden gray in color with a creamy texture and almost buttery taste. Osetra caviar is the next in quality, with medium-size gray to brown eggs, and more of a fruity, nutty quality. Sevruga caviar is harvested from the smallest sturgeon, which produces tiny steel gray roe that burst in your mouth, with very intense flavors.

While Russian caviar is certainly the most extravagant, it is also a diminishing resource because of pollution and overfishing in the Caspian Sea. But the good news is you don't need to give caviar up completely. American caviar from sturgeon, salmon, trout, and paddlefish farmed in local waters have great texture and taste, and are environmentally sustainable, not to mention more affordable. For quality producers of farmed American caviar, see Sources.

Whatever caviar you choose, be sure to purchase fresh, unpasteurized caviar and store it properly, as it is very perishable. Some general tips: Keep your caviar cold at all times and don't open it until it is needed. If you have any left over, I recommend forcing yourself to finish it! But if you must store your caviar, it will last two or three days in the fridge. Smooth the surface of the eggs and cover with plastic wrap. Refrigerate it immediately, and turn the tin over each day so the oil reaches all of the eggs.

SALMON—FOUR WAYS

I have a real tender spot for salmon. Salmon, like several other fish species, are anadramous—that is, they live in the ocean but return to rivers to spawn. It's a heroic trip, and if you ever saw these fish hurl themselves up waterfalls, rapids, and even small dams to get back to the exact place of their birth, I think you would be inspired too. It's no wonder that they are such a fatty fish—they expend a lot of calories on their trip back to their birth site. It is better to purchase salmon caught in the open ocean before they reach the rivers, because they stop feeding on their journey home and lose some of their vigor and, hence, flavor. Sadly, once they create the next generation, they expire. All of this of course describes wild salmon, which are still around in reasonable numbers, and I prefer them to farm-raised salmon, mainly because the flavor is more interesting. But I am concerned about the environment, as the impact of fish farming is still not fully understood.

I cook a lot of salmon at home. It's affordable, healthful, easy to find, and can be prepared in many ways. Here are four of my favorite salmon preparations—sautéed, grilled, paillard style, and oven steamed. I hope you'll experiment with each. Once you learn these techniques, you can add your own relishes, sauces, and sides, depending on the style of dinner you are in the mood for.

Sautéed Fillet of Salmon on French Lentils with Mango and Oil-Cured Olives

SERVES 6

for the lentils

1 cup French or green lentils

1 tablespoon olive oil

¼ cup diced pancetta or bacon

½ small white onion, minced

1 clove garlic, minced

1 small carrot, peeled and diced small

1 rib celery, diced small

Sachet of 8 black peppercorns, 1 sprig thyme, 1 bay leaf, and 12 coriander seeds, tied in cheesecloth

Salt and pepper

1 tablespoon sherry vinegar

⅓ cup diced oil-cured or Kalamata olives

1 ripe mango, diced

2 tablespoons butter

1 tablespoon cilantro or torn basil leaves

for the salmon

Olive oil, for sautéing

1½–2 pounds salmon fillet, skin on, cut into 6 portions

Salt and pepper

cook the lentils

Pick through the lentils to remove any debris or stones. Give them a good rinse under cold water. Heat the olive oil in a 4- to 6-quart pot, add the pancetta or bacon, and render until half crispy. Add the onion, garlic, carrot, and celery, stir once, and sweat until vegetables are tender—about 5 minutes. Add the lentils, enough cold water to cover by 1 inch, and the sachet. Add water as necessary while cooking to keep the level about an inch above the lentils. French and green lentils cook fairly quickly, so taste after 20 minutes or so. Once tender, season with salt and pepper. The lentils can be cooked up to this point a day or two in advance. Pour the lentils and their cooking liquid into a shallow container and stir frequently until the lentils cool to room temperature. Then transfer to a container with a lid and store them in their cooking liquid to keep them moist. When ready to serve, use a slotted spoon to transfer as many lentils as you need into a small saucepan. Add a little cooking liquid and warm over medium heat. Stir in the sherry vinegar, olives, mango, and butter. Fold in the cilantro or basil and taste once again for seasoning.

sauté the salmon fillets

Heat a heavy-bottomed skillet over medium-high heat, adding enough olive oil to just coat the bottom. Season the salmon with salt and pepper. When the oil shimmers, lay the fillets in the pan skin side down (if skin is on) and cook 2–3 minutes on each side, depending on thickness. I prefer to leave the skin on the salmon: it's delicious when crispy and is also a beautiful visual contrast with the pink fish.

Ladle or spoon the lentils onto 6 plates, place the fillets on top, and serve. A green salad and crusty bread with butter are all you need with this essentially bistro dish.

Grilled Salmon with Wasabi-Honey Glaze

SERVES 6

make the glaze

In a saucepan, melt together the honey, soy sauce, and ancho powder. Remove from heat, pour into a bowl, and stir in the wasabi. Let this glaze stand several hours before using so the strong flavors meld together.

grill the salmon

Light your grill or heat a grill pan on the stovetop. Brush the salmon fillets lightly on both sides with olive oil, and season with salt and pepper. Grill 2–3 minutes on the first side, then turn the fillets over and begin basting the top side with the wasabi-honey glaze. Glaze the fish repeatedly until a thin layer accumulates. You'll cook the second side 2–3 minutes, depending on thickness and how much you like your salmon cooked. Remove the fillets from the grill and drizzle a little bit of glaze on the fish and around the plate or platter.

for the glaze

1/4 cup honey

2 tablespoons soy sauce

1 teaspoon ancho chile powder

2 tablespoons prepared wasabi, or 1 tablespoon dry wasabi powder mixed into a paste with water

for the salmon

1 1/2–2 pounds salmon fillet, cut into 6 portions, or 6 salmon steaks

2 tablespoons olive oil

Salt and pepper

‹ weighing your options ›

This glaze also works very well with tuna, pompano, and mahi-mahi, or any reasonably fatty, firm-fleshed fish. I serve this dish with steamed rice with scallions and sesame seeds. Just prepare white rice as usual and stir in some minced scallions, lightly toasted sesame seeds, a couple drops of sesame oil, and a squeeze of lemon juice. Steamed baby bok choy or lightly wilted napa cabbage is also very nice. Just wilt the cabbage in a little butter in a saucepan, sprinkle with rice vinegar, and season with a little salt and pepper.

Paillard of Salmon "Unilateral" with Sel Gris and Nectarine Salsa

SERVES 6

for the nectarine salsa

2 ripe nectarines, diced
    small
½ teaspoon grated fresh
    ginger
Juice of ½ lime
½ red onion, thinly sliced
½ jalapeño, seeded and
    minced
1 tablespoon extra virgin
    olive oil
1 tablespoon minced
    cilantro or tarragon
Salt and pepper

for the paillards

3–4 tablespoons olive oil
1½–2 pounds salmon fillet,
    cut into ¼-inch-thick
    slices, slightly on the
    bias
Sel gris, or coarse sea salt
Freshly ground black pepper

prepare the salsa

In a medium bowl, gently mix together all salsa ingredients. Taste for seasoning.

cook the paillards

Heat one or two nonstick pans over medium-high heat with enough olive oil to just coat the bottom of each pan. When the oil shimmers, gently slide the paillards of salmon into the pan, leaving a little space between them. You will be cooking the salmon on one side only—hence "unilateral." The thin slices will cook within 1 minute and become crispy on the bottom. Remove the paillards carefully while supporting them fully with a spatula. Transfer to plates (presenting the uncooked side up) and season with a little sprinkle of sel gris and some freshly ground pepper. Serve with a spoonful of the salsa on each paillard or pass around a bowlful and let friends and family serve themselves.

‹ weighing your options ›

Tuna cut into similar thin paillards and seared on one side is a wonderful alternative to the salmon. The acidity of the nectarine salsa works very well with both fish; you can substitute other high-acid stone fruits like peaches or mango for the nectarines. A green salad with some crunchy garnishes like spiced walnuts (page 116) or garlicky croutons (page 77) is just the right accompaniment to this light fish preparation. Drape a paper-thin slice or two of smoked or cured ham over the greens and you'll have something really special.

Oven-Steamed Fillet of Salmon with Zucchini "Pappardelle"

SERVES 6

Preheat the oven to 400°F.

steam the fish

Oven steaming is an easy way to gently cook fish with no added oil or butter while introducing aromatic flavors like herbs and spices. Using a glass or enamel casserole dish, lay the celery, carrot, and fennel on the bottom, to create a kind of rack that the fish will sit on as it steams. Pour the wine and water into the casserole, and scatter in the lemon zest, coriander seeds, and herbs. Season the fish with salt and pepper and place the fillet on the "rack" of vegetables. Cover the casserole tightly with foil and place it in the hot oven for about 6–8 minutes, or longer if necessary. Immediately remove the foil to let the steam escape to avoid overcooking the fish.

prepare the zucchini

Using a wide skillet, heat the butter with about 1 tablespoon of water to prevent it from browning. Add the shallots, and sauté them for a few minutes, allowing them to wilt. Lay the zucchini ribbons down in the skillet in slightly overlapping layers. Season each layer of zucchini lightly with salt and pepper. Shake the pan around a bit while the bottom layer of zucchini cooks. When it has wilted and the edges are bright green, flip the contents of the pan over with a spatula to let the top pieces cook—this all happens quickly, in 2–3 minutes.

for the salmon

2 ribs celery

1 medium carrot, cut in half lengthwise

2 slices fennel

1 cup white wine

½ cup water

1 strip lemon peel

1 teaspoon coriander seeds

Small handful herbs— cilantro, tarragon, parsley

Salt and pepper

1½–2 pounds salmon fillet, left in 1 whole piece

for the zucchini

3 tablespoons butter

1 tablespoon water

1 shallot, thinly sliced

(continued)

‹ weighing your options ›

This dish is equally good hot or cold. When serving cold, you may want to heighten the seasoning—cold dishes always seem to need a little more salt and lemon for brightness. Other fish that you can substitute successfully are snapper, black sea bass, and halibut.

2 medium zucchini, sliced
　　into long, wide ribbons*
Salt and pepper
½ teaspoon grated lemon
　　zest
1 teaspoon minced thyme
1 small ripe tomato, seeded
　　and diced

for the garnish
Drizzle of extra virgin olive
　　oil
Squeeze of lemon

*You want the zucchini to be quite
thin, almost sheer, so you can
either use a mandoline, to ¹⁄₁₆ inch,
or your chef's knife if you have a
steady hand. See Sources for a good
inexpensive Japanese mandoline.

When all the zucchini has wilted, slide the contents of the pan out onto a platter. Pour the buttery liquid in the pan over the zucchini as the sauce and sprinkle with the zest, thyme, and diced tomatoes. Use your fingers to fold some of the zucchini "noodles" into ribbonlike shapes—you want a little visual texture to the platter. Using a fork and a spoon, flake off big pieces of the salmon and garnish the zucchini noodles with the fish. Dress the whole plate/platter with a drizzle of fruity olive oil and a squeeze of lemon.

Using the mandoline to make thin zucchini slices

‹ leftover alert ›

When I have leftover oven-steamed salmon, I like to turn it into a sort of fish cake/hash (see page 150) for breakfast or brunch the following day. If you don't have any leftover salmon on hand, it is easy enough to poach a fillet in court bouillon and make this from scratch.

Seared Sea Scallops with a Cool Cucumber, Sesame, and Dill Sauce

This dish illustrates how contrasting temperatures—the hot, griddled scallops against the chill of the cucumber sauce—really wake up your palate. You'll want to have friends and family waiting at the table, since the scallops cook quickly and some of the charm of this dish is lost if you don't dig into it right away.

SERVES 6

prepare the cucumber sauce

Pass the diced cucumber through a food mill into a bowl. Stir in the garlic, lime juice, sesame oil, olive oil, and dill. Season to taste with salt and pepper. Refrigerate until ready to use.

prepare the scallops

Heat a heavy-bottomed skillet over medium-high heat. I use one of my well-seasoned cast-iron pans—it gives the scallops a wonderful crust. Combine the coriander seed and ancho powder and sprinkle it on one side of the scallops. Season same side with salt and pepper. Pour enough olive oil into the skillet to coat the bottom with a thin film. When the oil shimmers, carefully place the scallops in the pan spice side down and add 1 tablespoon of butter. Sear scallops for 1 minute, then turn over and cook the second side for 1 minute longer. That should be all it takes—you want the scallop still translucent and creamy on the inside.

Spoon a puddle of the chilled cucumber sauce on each plate and garnish the sauce with a sprinkle of the toasted sesame seeds, if using. Divide the seared scallops among the sauced plates and serve immediately.

for the cucumber sauce

1 seedless cucumber, peeled and diced

1 small clove garlic, mashed to a puree with a little salt

Juice of half a lime

½ teaspoon toasted sesame oil

1 tablespoon extra virgin olive oil

1 tablespoon minced dill

Salt and pepper

for the sea scallops

1 teaspoon ground coriander seed

1 teaspoon ancho chile powder

1½–2 pounds large sea scallops, adductor muscle removed

Salt and pepper

Olive oil

1 tablespoon butter

Toasted white and black sesame seeds, for garnishing (optional)

Red-Flannel Salmon Hash
with Poached Eggs and Coriander Hollandaise

SERVES 4

for the custard
1 tablespoon butter
2 shallots, thinly sliced
1 egg
¼ cup heavy cream
½ teaspoon chipotle puree
(see page 204)
1 tablespoon minced fresh
cilantro, thyme, or
parsley
Salt and freshly ground
black pepper

for the hash
8 ounces oven-steamed
salmon, or an 8-ounce
fillet of raw salmon
poached in 2 cups court
bouillon (see Appendix)
1 medium-size red beet,
roasted until tender,
peeled, and cut into
½-inch dice
1 large russet potato, cooked
until tender, peeled, and
cut into
½-inch dice
½ cup panko (Japanese
bread crumbs), or fresh
bread crumbs
2–3 tablespoons butter,
for sautéing

make the custard
In a sauté pan, melt the butter over medium heat and sauté the shallots in the butter until soft, about 4 minutes. Spoon the shallots out of the pan and into a mixing bowl. Crack the egg into the shallots and whisk in the cream, chipotle puree, herbs, and salt and pepper.

make the hash
Break up the salmon into large chunks. Fold the salmon in with the beets and potatoes in a medium-size bowl and pour the custard over the top, then toss gently with half of the panko or fresh bread crumbs. Try not to break up the salmon chunks. Form the salmon hash into 4 equal-size cakes no thicker than 1 inch, and sprinkle each cake with the remaining bread crumbs. Let the cakes rest in the fridge for 1 hour to set.

Heat the butter in a deep heavy-bottomed skillet until shimmering and sauté the salmon cakes for 4 minutes on each side, until they develop a nice brown crust and are warm inside. As they are cooked, keep them warm in a 200°F oven.

make the coriander hollandaise
In the top of a double boiler, whisk the egg yolks with the lemon juice and water until the liquid forms pale ribbons; this takes about 5 minutes. Whisk in the clarified butter until the mixture thickens. Season with salt and pepper and ground coriander seed and fold in the cilantro leaves.

poach the eggs
Use a heavy saucepan, about 10 inches in diameter with sides at least 2 inches deep. Add water to a depth of 1 inch and bring to a simmer.

Add a small amount of white vinegar to the poaching water for the eggs. (White vinegar helps the whites to coagulate.) Stir the water a little bit to create a vortex and crack an egg into the center. This helps the white stay centered around the yolk. Repeat for each egg. (You can also use a commercial poaching dish.) Poach the eggs to the desired degree of doneness.

To serve, gently place a poached egg on each salmon cake. Drizzle with hollandaise and serve immediately.

for the coriander hollandaise
2 egg yolks
2 tablespoons lemon juice
1 tablespoon water
1 cup clarified butter (see Chef's Trick)
Salt and pepper to taste
1 teaspoon ground coriander seed
3 tablespoons minced fresh cilantro

for poached eggs
White vinegar
4 large eggs

Chef's Trick: How to Clarify Butter Cut 1 pound of butter into 1-inch pieces and place in a heavy-bottom saucepan over low heat. Simmer butter very slowly, skimming off any white foam that rises to the top. After 15 minutes or so, the butter solids will sink to the bottom of the pan. Remove the pan from the heat and let stand for a few minutes. Carefully ladle the clarified butter into a clean jar or crock. The clarified butter will keep, if well covered in the fridge, for up to 4 weeks. Yield: about ¾ pound of clarified butter.

Monkfish with Cassoulet Beans

Some fish beg to be treated like meat—and monkfish is one of them. It has a dense, firm, sweet flesh that has a real affinity for rich and hearty flavors. One of its best partners, in fact, is garlic, and nothing to my mind is as wonderfully garlic-laden as cassoulet. Cassoulet is basically a French white bean casserole flavored with lots of garlic and herbs, with duck or goose confit, cured pork, and smoked meats nestled in. While the cassoulet is cooking in a slow oven, a crust forms on the beans. This crust is broken with the back of a spoon and resubmerged repeatedly during the cooking process, thereby creating an entire dish of the best crusty part. It's brilliant! So I appropriated a version of those beans for this recipe. Since cassoulet is a long, involved process, I've streamlined it quite a bit while not cheating on flavor. This dish is a lovely undertaking on a cold winter afternoon.

for the cassoulet beans

3 tablespoons olive oil

2 cloves garlic, crushed with the side of a knife

2 links smoked sausage (I use a good, imported Spanish chorizo), diced

2 links garlic sausage (I like the French-style *saucisson à l'ail*), diced

2 cups cooked white beans, Great Northern or cannellini, with 1 cup of cooking liquid (see bean-cooking method on page 80)

1 bay leaf

1 strip orange peel

SERVES 6

Preheat oven to 375°F.

prepare the cassoulet beans

Heat 3 tablespoons olive oil in a casserole dish. Add the crushed garlic cloves and toast until golden brown. Remove the garlic and reserve. Add the sausages and render out most of the fat. Remove the sausages and reserve. Tip out most of the fat, return the sausages and garlic to the casserole, add the beans and their cooking liquid, the bay leaf, and the orange peel, and place the casserole in the oven. Meanwhile, prepare the bread crumb crust.

for the crust

Heat a wide skillet over medium heat with ¼ cup of olive oil. Stir the bread crumbs into the warm oil and keep stirring until they are golden brown. Sprinkle on the ancho powder and the minced herbs. Season lightly with salt and pepper.

After the beans have cooked in the oven for about 30 minutes, cover the surface evenly with the bread crumbs and continue to bake another 30 minutes. The beans should be moist, but without any visible liquid around the edge of the casserole.

sauté the monkfish

Heat a large skillet over medium-high heat. Add enough olive oil to coat the bottom of the pan. Season the slices of fish with salt and pepper and gently lay them in the pan. Sauté each side for 2 minutes. Monkfish is best when it is cooked to medium: too rare and it is tough; too well done and it is dry. When all the fish has been cooked, deglaze the pan with the white wine, scraping up all the stuck-on juices. Add a squeeze of lemon juice to make a quick pan sauce.

To serve, divide the fish among 6 plates with a generous spoonful of the beans, making sure to get some crust with every portion, as well as a drizzle of the lemony pan sauce.

for the red chile and herb crust
¼ cup olive oil
1 cup fresh bread crumbs (see Chef's Trick)
2 teaspoons ancho chile powder
1 teaspoon minced fresh thyme*
1 teaspoon minced parsley*
½ teaspoon minced fresh rosemary*
Salt and pepper

for the fish
2 pounds monkfish, cleaned and sliced into ½-inch-thick medallions
Olive oil, for sautéing fish (see box on page 78)
Salt and pepper
½ cup white wine, for deglazing the fish pan
Fresh lemon juice

*See box on page 173 for substitutions.

Chef's Trick Fresh bread crumbs are preferable to dry since they are still light and fluffy and won't act like a sponge and soak up every last bit of moisture around them. I either trim the crusts off a loaf of white bread and cut the bread into a very fine dice, or tear off large-ish chunks of a country-style bread (crusts removed) and pulse the bread in a food processor with the blade attachment. This will result in finer cumbs than the hand-cutting.

❮ weighing your options ❯
I think the Cumin-Cured Cherry Tomatoes on page 276 are excellent with this dish. I also serve a little steamed or sautéed spinach: the pleasant astringency of the spinach is the perfect foil for the creamy, garlicky beans.

Halibut Baked in Parchment
with New Potatoes, Braised Leeks, and Truffle Butter

Cooking in parchment is an ancient technique that is due for a revival. It's an ideal way to cook fish: all the flavors and moisture are sealed inside what is essentially a paper bag. It's very dramatic to present the puffed-up "papillotes" at the table, where the aromas of the fish and its truffle-laced garnishes intoxicate your guests as soon as the packages are cut open. If you can't find parchment, you can substitute simpler aluminum foil. I use white truffle oil to season the butter, which is thankfully a very fragrant and affordable truffle product—a little goes a long way. This recipe is just several very easy steps strung together, so don't be intimidated by the unfamiliarity of it.

SERVES 6

for the braised leeks

2 tablespoons butter
2 leeks, white part thinly
    sliced and washed
    several times
½ cup white wine
Pinch of sugar
½ teaspoon ground
    coriander seed
Salt and pepper

for the truffle butter

6 tablespoons butter,
    softened
1 small clove garlic, mashed
    with salt
1 tablespoon white truffle oil
    (see box on page 156)
½ teaspoon grated lemon
    zest
Salt and pepper

prepare the leeks

Melt the butter in a small saucepan over medium-low heat. Sweat the leeks until softened, add the wine, pinch of sugar, coriander seed, and salt and pepper and cover. Braise the leeks until they are very tender, and until the wine, sugar, salt, and pepper have reduced to a syrup—about 10 minutes. Cool.

prepare the truffle butter

In a medium bowl, stir together the softened butter, garlic, truffle oil, and zest. Season to taste with salt and pepper.

cook the potatoes

Preheat the oven to 400°F. Toss the potato slices with olive oil and salt and pepper in a bowl. Lay the slices out in a single layer on a baking sheet or two. Bake 6–8 minutes, until the potatoes are completely tender and a little browned on the bottom. Keep the oven on.

assemble the parchment packages
Fold each rectangle in half and start by laying 4 or 5 slices of potato on one side of the fold. Plop a spoonful of the leeks on top of the potato, a tablespoon of truffle butter on top of the leeks, and finish with a fillet of halibut that you've seasoned with salt and pepper. Fold the second side over the fish and crimp the edges together by making a series of folds all the way around. Press the folds well to prevent any steam from escaping. Place the packages on a baking sheet and into the preheated 400°F oven. Bake 8–10 minutes, until the packages are golden brown and puffed up.

Serve on prewarmed plates and cut packages open at the table. I pass around a pair of sewing scissors.

NOTE: These packages can be made hours ahead and refrigerated until ready to pop into the oven.

for the potatoes
3/4 pound small Yukon Gold potatoes, scrubbed and cut into 1/4-inch-thick slices
4 tablespoons olive oil
Salt and pepper

for the halibut
Six 10-by-14-inch (or thereabouts) rectangles of parchment paper or aluminum foil
Six 5-ounce fillets of halibut, skinless
Salt and pepper

‹ weighing your options ›
If you can't find halibut or you prefer another fish, I also make this recipe with red snapper or black sea bass.

TRUFFLE OIL

Truffle oil comes in two varieties—white from the Italian truffle, *Tuber magnatum*, and black, from the French, *Tuber melanosporum*—but the white is far more common and the one that I refer to most in this book. It is made by infusing the incredibly aromatic and earthy flavor of white truffles into a high-quality olive oil.

I recommend buying your white truffle oil in the smallest quantity you can—and it is generally sold in tiny bottles—just like expensive perfume. And the analogy holds up even further—a little truffle oil/perfume is an intriguing finishing touch, but too much of either is overwhelming and even cloying.

Since you'll use just a little at a time, even a small bottle will last quite a while if stored in the fridge. Storing the oil this way will cause it to solidify from the cold, but it will quickly turn back to liquid when left out at room temperature for ten minutes or so. And storing in the fridge will give the open bottle a shelf life of about six months. After that, the oil will steadily lose its flavor and fragrance. If you are storing an unopened bottle, just keep it in a dry, cool, and dark place—like the back of your pantry—definitely not in a cupboard over your stove, where the heat will destroy its nuances.

I use truffle oil as a finishing touch for risottos, for a boost to any mushroom sauces, and to drizzle into a white bean soup. It is best when used with a rather uncomplicated base like starches; polenta and creamy mashed potatoes are really enhanced by a drop or two. It is also great whisked into a vinaigrette of lemon juice, olive oil, and chives. This is a very simple and fabulous dressing for sautéed scallops or steamed lobster.

❮ weighing your options ❯

The recipe opposite is for a basic tartare, but for a spicier version you can add ½ teaspoon of chipotle puree (see page 204) and ½ teaspoon of Dijon mustard to it, substituting minced cilantro for the chives. Another variation is to substitute 1 tablespoon of toasted sesame oil for 1 tablespoon of the olive oil, and add ½ teaspoon of grated fresh ginger and a splash of rice vinegar for an Asian-inspired flavor. If you can get your hands on fresh shiso, which is a Japanese mint, it is fantastic in place of the chives. And although all you really need for eating any of these tartares is a large spoon, it's also nice to perch a spoonful on My Homemade Potato Chips (see page 57).

Tuna Tartare

Tuna tartare has become a menu cliché—for good reason. Tuna tartare (or any tartare, for that matter) is particularly delicious because, since it is diced small, you get great texture and a lot of surface area for the fish to soak up your savory condiments. I've never figured out if it is the tuna I love, or the stuff that goes with it. Ask for bigeye or bluefin tuna if they are available—they have a higher fat content than yellowfin and hence a fuller flavor, but are more expensive and harder to find. Yellowfin is sort of the default high-grade tuna. It's still very good, but not premium. Tell your fishmonger that you're making tartare, and he'll pick out a top piece for you.

SERVES 6

You want to keep the tuna very cold while working with it, so have a large bowl of ice sitting under your work bowl. Also, your bowls should be stainless steel or glass. Plastic won't conduct the cold efficiently enough.

Begin by slicing the tuna, making 1/4-inch-thick slices, then long 1/4-inch-thick strips, then cut crosswise into 1/4-inch dice—just like dicing vegetables. Don't chop the tuna, as this will mash the texture and cause friction, which will heat it up. When you have some tuna diced, deposit it into the top bowl.

When all the fish is diced, fold in the capers, shallot, olive oil, and chives and season with salt and pepper. The tartare should be aggressively seasoned. Taste it several times while adding salt slowly. You can also substitute salmon, Spanish mackerel, or yellowtail (also called hamachi).

1/2 pound of sashimi-grade tuna from the head of the loin

2 tablespoons capers, lightly drained so some brine is still on them

1 shallot, minced

2 tablespoons extra virgin olive oil

Minced chives, to taste (about 1 tablespoon)

Salt and pepper

Oven-Roasted Grouper with Cabbage, Apples, and Warm Carrot-Caraway Dressing

Baking fish is so easy—it takes hardly any time or effort at all—and many types of firm-fleshed fish do well when prepared that way. There is both red and black grouper on the market, but I find the red variety far superior in both flavor and texture. This is real home cooking: simple, clear flavors and a minimum of fuss. Once you've put the fish into the oven, you have time to quickly sauté the cabbage and apples on the stovetop and finish the carrot-caraway vinaigrette, just as long as you have everything prepped in advance. Have your apples cut, your cabbage sliced, and your carrot juice reduced before you put the fish into the oven.

for the grouper
1½–2 pounds skinless
    grouper fillet, cut into
    6 portions
Salt and pepper
3 tablespoons butter
½ cup white wine
1 bay leaf
1 strip orange peel
1 sprig thyme

for the cabbage and apples
2 tablespoons butter
½ teaspoon grated fresh
    ginger
1 teaspoon curry powder
2 firm apples, such as
    Granny Smith, Golden
    Delicious, or Gala, with
    peels, cut into thin slices

Preheat oven to 400°F.

prepare the fish for the oven
Season the fillets on both sides with salt and pepper and place in a glass or enamel casserole. Dot the fish with the butter, sprinkle evenly with the wine, and tuck in the bay leaf, orange zest, and thyme. Cover tightly with foil and bake 12–15 minutes.

prepare the cabbage and apples
While the fish is in the oven, heat a large skillet over medium heat. Add the butter, and when it foams add the ginger and curry, stirring together for 1 minute. Lay the apple sections into the pan and brown them, then add the cabbage. Let the cabbage wilt down before stirring it together with the apples. Sprinkle on the cider vinegar, season with salt and pepper, and fold in the cilantro, if using.

prepare the carrot-caraway vinaigrette

Reduce the carrot juice by half in a small saucepan. Let the reduced juice cool, and stir in the vinegar, orange juice, caraway seeds, and oil. Season to taste with salt and pepper. Don't be concerned that the vinaigrette will look "broken," meaning the oil and the juice base are separate. Once it is shaken together, it will look a little like a Georges Seurat painting when drizzled on the plate.

When the fish is done (the grouper will flake easily when pressed on the corner of a fillet), remove the foil immediately to prevent over-cooking, then remove the fish from the casserole to a platter. Set the casserole on the stovetop over medium heat, and reduce the juices to 4–5 tablespoons. Stir one or two spoonfuls into the vinaigrette for more depth of flavor, if desired.

To serve, place equal portions of the fish and cabbage on 6 plates and drizzle the vinaigrette over the top.

1 small head napa or savoy
     cabbage
2 tablespoons cider vinegar
Salt and pepper
1 tablespoon minced
     cilantro (optional)

for the carrot-caraway vinaigrette

½ cup carrot juice, fresh
     pressed or good-quality
     store-bought
2 tablespoons rice vinegar
1 tablespoon orange juice
1 teaspoon caraway seeds
3 tablespoons canola or
     other neutral oil
Salt and pepper

Red Snapper Roasted on Fleur de Sel with a Warm Citrus-Chive Dressing

Roasting fish on top of sea salt and herbs, even for the few minutes needed to cook a fillet, infuses the flesh with a wonderful perfume. As for the dressing, you can top the fish with any sort of herb and citrus combination. I chose a citrus-chive vinaigrette for this recipe, and I recommend serving it warm, awakening the oniony note of the chives and mellowing the bright acidity of the citrus—sort of a civilizing effect for this elegant dish.

SERVES 6

Preheat the oven to 400°F.

for the citrus-chive vinaigrette

2 lemons, 2 limes, and 2 oranges
½ bulb fennel, thinly sliced
A very small pinch of saffron (optional)
¼ cup extra virgin olive oil
2 tablespoons minced chives
Salt and pepper to taste

prepare the vinaigrette

Using a sharp paring knife, trim the zest and all the white pith from the citrus fruits. Be scrupulous in removing the pith, which will give a bitter taste to your dressing if still attached to the sections. (Reserve the zest for your martini; you won't need it here.) Work over a small bowl to catch the juices as you remove the sections (also referred to as "supremes") from between the membranes. Remove any seeds. Add the remaining ingredients to the supremes and their juice and whisk together.

When ready to serve, heat a dry stainless steel saucepan over medium-high heat. Pour in the vinaigrette and stir it once or twice—you don't want it hot, just warm enough to release the aromatic chive and citrus flavors.

‹ weighing your options ›

Since this dish is such a simple and light preparation, I serve it with either a gussied-up boxed couscous (follow directions on the box and add 2 tablespoons of lightly toasted ground coriander seed and some freshly minced herbs), or my Macadamia Nut Couscous, page 243.

roast the snapper

Spread the sea salt evenly over a baking sheet that has a rim. Strew the herbs over the salt and arrange the fillets (flesh side down, as the skin sticks too much) on the salt; leave an inch or so of space between fillets. Roast the fish for 6–8 minutes or until the fish begins to flake on an edge when pressed firmly. Snapper is at its best when it's slightly underdone and has a pearly translucence in the center.

To serve, use a towel to gently brush off the herbs and salt that may cling to the fillets. Serve with the warmed vinaigrette drizzled over and around the fish.

for the roasted snapper

2 cups fleur de sel or coarse
    sea salt
2 sprigs thyme
1 branch rosemary
2 sprigs parsley
2 pounds red snapper (see
    box below for varieties),
    cut into 6 portions

Red Snapper There are hundreds of species of snapper, and close to a dozen that are consistently caught and brought to market. Most are good eating, but the true prize is the so-called American red *(Lutjanus campechanus)*. This fish is found from Virginia to Florida and even farther south. Another great choice is the Hawaiian snapper, also known as onaga, which is prized as sashimi. In order to be sure that you are getting what you paid for, ask to see the whole fish before it is filleted. The skin should be light pink all over, not just streaked pink, not orange, and not bright red. Whole fish can also display signs of freshness: bright, bulging eyes; dark-red gills; and a glossy sheen. But the only way to really know what you are buying is to build a relationship with your fishmonger—and as with most worthwhile relationships, this will take time. As you ask questions and give feedback, you'll become a regular customer who is likely to get the pick of the catch.

Pancetta-Wrapped Tuna
with Red Wine–Braised Onions

I always think of tuna as the beef of the sea, not chicken of the sea, as a well-known canned tuna brand is called. Tuna's deep ruby color, dense texture, and full flavor are reminiscent of a good steak, and tuna can handle robust preparations just as well. But generally it is quite lean and will become very dry and dull if overcooked. By wrapping it in pancetta—Italian pork belly cured with spices—you are adding a thin layer of fat to "baste" the fish as it cooks.

SERVES 6

**for the red wine–
braised onions**

3 tablespoons butter

3 red onions, quartered,
    unpeeled, and with stem
    attached*

2 tablespoons honey

2 cups red wine (a hearty
    red like a Côte-du-
    Rhône, or a zinfandel)

¼ cup red wine vinegar

Salt and pepper

*Leaving the stem on prevents the onion's layers from falling apart. It also makes a nice presentation. But you can always snip off the end if you prefer.

braise the onions

Heat a large skillet with the butter. Add the quartered onions with their cut sides down in a single layer; use 2 pans if necessary. Brown the onions on both sides over medium-low heat. Pour the honey, wine, and vinegar over the onions, season with salt and pepper, bring to a simmer, and partially cover. Cook the onions until they are very tender, about 30 minutes, and the wine has reduced to a thick, syrupy sauce over them.

prepare the tuna

You can either go for the dramatic presentation of serving the whole, beautifully browned tuna loin at the table with full carving regalia, or precut the tuna into portions. In either case, wrap the portions or whole loin with the pancetta; it will adhere easily to the moist fish. One thin layer will do.

Season the wrapped tuna fairly liberally with salt and pepper. Heat a heavy-bottomed skillet (I use cast iron for an especially good crust) over medium-high heat. Add the olive oil, and when it shimmers lay the tuna down in the pan. After the first side has browned (about 2 minutes), add the butter and the herbs and orange peel. Using a spatula, turn the fish over, basting frequently with a spoon. (Basting prevents overdrying of the crust and adds an herby nuance.) Each side of the tuna will take 1–2 minutes, depending on thickness. I heartily recommend cooking the tuna to rare or medium rare to really appreciate its flavor and texture.

Let the tuna rest for a few minutes before slicing—this allows the blood to return to the center and create a lovely, rosy interior. (For more on resting, see page 190.) Rewarm the braised onions and serve alongside the tuna with a little vessel of coarse sea salt passed around. Sel gris is my favorite, for its crunch.

for the pancetta-wrapped tuna

2–3 pounds tuna loin

½ pound thinly sliced pancetta, or lightly smoked bacon

Salt and pepper

3 tablespoons olive oil

2 tablespoons butter

1 sprig thyme*

1 small branch rosemary*

1 strip orange peel

*If you'd rather use dried herbs, see box on page 173.

< weighing your options >
Any leftover tuna is great cold. As an addition to a salad, it can be thinly sliced and used in lieu of the salmon carpaccio on page 104 or dressed with a classic green sauce (ravigote), as on page 277. Or you can layer it with the onions and make a great sandwich.

Grilled Whole Fish

Despite my formal culinary training, I was for many years quite intimidated by the idea of cooking a whole fish. I thought disaster would surely ensue: I would misjudge the doneness and serve my guests a raw and gummy fish that was impossible to bone, or conversely embarrass myself by overcooking a once-noble specimen—the greater faux pas in the culinary world. But I faced my fears and have learned that there isn't just one incredibly brief "moment" when the fish is done. You have at least a minute, maybe two, to hem and haw, consult your friends, and let them share some of the responsibility!

If you make a few diagonal cuts into each side of the fish, you can speed up the cooking time and take advantage of the slits to tuck in some extra flavor, such as herbs and citrus slices. I don't generally marinate fish before I grill it. I find it makes the skin stick to the grill, and I love to serve the fish with its lovely, crispy skin intact.

One of the best things about this dish is that there really isn't a formal recipe to follow—it's more a method (and quite a simple one at that) that you can modify with different herbs, citrus, and the like, depending on what you have on hand. Enjoy!

While cooking and filleting whole fish may seem like a lot of work, it all makes sense as you go along with each step. And the reward in terms of the flavor you get from cooking on the bone is well worth it. When I'm enjoying a simple grilled fish with close friends and family, I just place the fish in the center of the table and let people fillet as they go, pulling off succulent morsels of moist fish and hoping that the more intrepid among us will be chivalrous!

SERVES 6

Make sure your grill is quite hot; not enough heat will cause the fish to dry out before it has cooked thoroughly. Make 3 diagonal slices about ½-inch deep on each side of the fish. Rub the outside liberally with olive oil and season the fish inside and out with salt and pepper. Tuck some herbs and citrus slices into the slits you've made. Place the fish on the hottest part of the grill, and don't turn it over for about 5 minutes. Once the fish has cooked 5 minutes per side, slide the tip of a paring knife into the back of the fish close to the head—this should be the thickest part. See if the flesh pulls easily away from the backbone. If it does, it's ready; if it doesn't, leave the fish on the grill a minute or two longer.

When it's done, let the fish cool a minute to firm up. To fillet it, first remove the head and tail and then run a small knife along the backbone to free up the top fillet. Using the knife and the support of a soup spoon, gently lift the flesh free of the skeleton. If the fish is properly cooked, this will happen easily; if not, you may have to return it to the grill or a hot oven until the flesh releases—all in all, not a tragedy. Once the top fillet is free, peel the skeleton from the bottom piece.

Fish cooked this way is best served with just a drizzle of good olive oil and a squeeze of lemon.

Three 2-pound fish—
   snapper, pompano,
   striped bass, daurade,
   trout, arctic char, and
   coho salmon are all
   good candidates
Olive oil, for brushing on
   the fish
Salt and pepper
Herbs like tarragon, parsley,
   thyme, cilantro
Slices of lemon or orange

‹ weighing your options ›

If you are using a richer, more full-flavored fish like Spanish mackerel, trout, or arctic char, you can stuff it with hearty ingredients like browned onions, diced cooked potatoes, and sautéed chorizo, held in place with a couple of toothpicks at the belly. This is a great fisherman's breakfast, or a savory supper.

Oven-Braised Halibut in Wild Mushroom Broth with Baby Herb and Hazelnut Salad

There are both Atlantic and Pacific species of halibut, and I prefer the former, with its firmer texture and more delicate flavor. Either a steak or a fillet can be oven braised; just be sure to ask for thick pieces—at least an inch. Fillets tend to taper down toward the tail and become somewhat fibrous, so ask for a cut from the midsection or toward the head. Use any combination of wild mushrooms in season, like morels, chanterelles, porcini, or hen-of-the-woods. Or, if wild ones are hard to find, good cultivated mushrooms like shiitake, oyster, and crimini are also great with this dish. A trick of the trade when the pickings are slim is to fortify the braising liquid with a little dried porcini.

The baby herb and hazelnut salad is enlivened with a little lemon and sherry vinegar and simply tossed with hazelnut oil and sea salt. Simple and elegant and above all—delicious!

SERVES 6

Preheat oven to 400°F.

for the wild mushroom broth

¼ cup dried porcini
    mushrooms (optional)
1 cup chicken stock
¾ pound assorted wild or
    cultivated mushrooms,
    trimmed, cleaned, and
    sliced
3 tablespoons olive oil
2 shallots, thinly sliced
2 tablespoons butter
Salt and pepper
½ cup white wine
¼ cup heavy cream

for the halibut

2 pounds halibut, cut into
    steaks or fillets

make the mushroom broth

Steep the dried porcini, if using, in simmering chicken stock for a minute or two. Turn off the heat and let the porcini soften for up for 10 minutes or so.

Meanwhile, prepare the mushrooms by brushing them free of debris and cutting them into ¼-inch-thick slices. Heat a large skillet with the olive oil. When it shimmers, add the mushrooms and let them brown on the bottom. Strew the sliced shallots over them, add the butter, and give a good flip to the pan (that is, if you have this skill—otherwise, stir contents once with a large spoon). Let the mushrooms brown on the second side before seasoning lightly with salt and pepper. Pour in the wine to deglaze the pan, using a spoon to scrape up any stuck-on juices. Strain the porcinis out of the chicken stock. Add the stock to the mushrooms. Mince the porcini and toss them in as well. This broth is now ready to be used as the braising medium.

prepare the fish

Season the halibut on both sides with the ancho powder, if using, salt and pepper, and minced thyme. Heat a large skillet with olive oil, and when it shimmers give a light browning to each side of the fish—no more than 30 seconds per side. Transfer the fish to the pan that holds the heated mushroom broth, nestling it into the mushrooms and spooning a bit of the sauce on top of each piece. Cover the skillet with a lid or foil and place into the hot oven. If the fish and the broth were hot going into the oven, it should be cooked within 8 minutes. Halibut is a lean fish, so you'll want to leave a little pearly translucence in the center—otherwise it can get dry.

Gently lift the cooked fish out of the pan and keep it warm (tenting it with foil on a warm plate is one way) while you finish the sauce.

Place the mushroom broth on the stove at a simmer. Whisk in the heavy cream and reduce the sauce until it lightly coats a spoon. Taste for seasoning and spoon the sauce over and around the fish.

while your sauce is reducing, make the garnishing salad

Toss the washed and dried herbs and the toasted hazelnuts in a generous-size bowl. Drizzle the herbs with the oil and give them a light toss (this will protect the herbs from the acidity of the lemon and vinegar, at least for a while). Add the lemon juice, orange zest, vinegar, and salt and pepper, and mix gently with your hands so as not to bruise the herbs. Take a pinch of the salad and place it next to the fish on the plate, or pass it around the table as a condiment.

2 teaspoons ancho chile powder (optional, for a lovely russet color and hint of heat)
Salt and pepper
1 teaspoon minced thyme
Olive oil, for sautéing

for the herb and hazelnut salad

1½ cups chopped mixed herbs—any combination of parsley, tarragon, chervil, cilantro, and/or watercress (leaves only, no stems), washed and dried
⅓ cup lightly toasted, chopped hazelnuts
2 tablespoons hazelnut oil, or a fruity olive oil
1 tablespoon lemon juice
½ teaspoon grated orange zest
1 tablespoon sherry vinegar
Sea salt and pepper

Chef's Trick This may sound a little unorthodox at first, but bear with me. I sometimes use a thinned-out version of one of my homemade soups as the braising liquid for this dish. When I have a cup or so of soup in the freezer, it is really the perfect solution. Just thin down the soup with a little water and a dash of white wine and add it to the pan after you have lightly browned the fish, and proceed as if it were the mushroom broth. Ideal soups for this purpose are Cream of Fennel (page 90), Sweet Corn (page 73), Curried Cauliflower (page 72), and, surprisingly, even the Lentil Soup (page 84), for a heartier dish.

Simple Roast Chicken

Grilled Chicken in Marjoram Marinade

Summer Jambalaya with Poussin, Shrimp, Spicy Sausage, and Sweet Corn

Pan-Roasted Chicken Thighs with Calvados Cream and Onion-Sage Confit

Grilled Quail with Warm Muscat Grape, Black Olive, and Pine Nut Relish

Pancetta-Wrapped Duck Breast with Verjuice and Green Peppercorn Sauce

Duck Simmered in Coconut Curry

Spatchcocked Squab with Star Anise, Ginger, and Soy

Fried Rabbit with Whole-Grain Mustard Sauce

Rabbit Sausage

Pork Chops Smothered in Lentils

Medallions of Pork Breaded in Crushed Gingersnaps with Apples and Sage

Chipotle Barbecued Pork with Peach-Radish Salsa

Brined Pork Roast "Wild Boar" Style

Garlic-Studded Leg of Lamb in Red Chile and Cumin Crust

Spiced Lamb Meatballs in Eggplant "Leaves"

Beef Tenderloin with Marrow Toasts and Spiced Tomato Chutney

Beef Short Ribs Braised in Amarone with Dried Cherries and Black Olives

Grilled Flank Steak in a Smoked Chile and Lime Marinade

Pan-Roasted New York Strip Steak with Balsamic Vinegar

Venison with Fox Grape Poivrade

MEAT AND POULTRY

I confronted my feelings about eating meat at a pretty tender age. Back in the 1970s, my parents needed their acreage to pay for itself to some degree, and had a few white-faced Herefords on the land. When male calves were born, they were naturally classified as "vealers." The animals were raised humanely; the calves weren't separated from their mother, but instead drank milk straight from the source and roamed around the meadows, nipping grasses at will. But their lives were short, and we kids unwisely named them like pets and became emotionally attached. By four or five months, the vealers were big enough to be hauled away by a packing company. When a large truck backed up to the barn and the calves were led onto it, I had only a vague idea of what was going on. My parents weren't coy about it, though. When the meat was returned to us in brown-paper bundles, we were frankly told where it came from. I worked my way through my feelings of loss and sadness.

Now, as an adult, I seek out the people who raise meat and poultry in good conscience. In recent years, the marketplace has reacted to the growing demand for responsibly raised meat. Good producers are concerned not only for the animals but for the environment and, ultimately, for all of us. We can't always eat as locally as we would like, but the opportunities are ever expanding. I've included a few Web sites in the Sources section to help you look into what is available close to home, or at least what has been thoughtfully raised somewhere else.

Serving a fragrant roast leg of lamb or a platter full of grilled quail to friends and family is a cultural event rich in meaning. Setting the deeply browned roast or crispy-skinned birds on the table is an act

My family's farmland in winter

that confers status on the host and honor on the guests. Perhaps this sounds too anthropological, but I feel that providing and sharing a meal is a profound gesture. Good food nourishes relationships as much as bodies and has given rise to countless rituals of the table. Esteem for the animals we eat can be expressed in simple gestures— handling the meat with care, using the proper tools, and seasoning and cooking with attention and enjoyment. I find that when I sharpen my knives with great care, it not only makes the task of slicing easier and more efficient, it also ensures that the knife's blade moves cleanly through the meat, causing as little damage as possible. There's something unpleasant and uncomfortable about hacking away with a blunt instrument on a once-vital creature.

When I go home to Vermont for visits, I am aware that there are plenty of people who hunt game for the necessary protein as much as for sport. These hunters often count on hanging a couple of deer each season, then cutting them up and putting the meat in the freezer for the long winter. Even "roadkill" deer or the occasional moose are most often taken care of not by the game warden but by a passing motorist with a pickup truck and tolerable knife skills.

My sister, Liza, lives in Scotland and has found that the Scots have a similar sensibility: Waste not, want not. On our first visit to her fifteenth-century stone cottage in the shadow of the laird's manor house, her then husband presented me with a haunch of venison that had met its fate on one of East Lothian's impossibly twisty roads. To make things even more Gothic, that evening, as I was preparing venison stew with local chanterelles, a dramatic storm knocked out the power and I finished cooking over Liza's wood-burning stove with the help of candlelight and the occasional flash of lightning. Did I hear hounds barking?

On a separate trip, we went camping on the Isle of Skye, and when eating only what we caught in the pristine glens and sleeping on the hard ground got to be too much, we treated ourselves to dinner at the posh Inn of the Four Chimneys. Michael ordered the wild duck, which was authenticated by the buckshot that he picked out of his teeth as he ate. Ah, the joys of the simple life.

I feel bad that so many of us are squeamish about knowing where the meat we consume comes from. I realize from running a restaurant that I have to be careful about using terms like "baby chicken" or "baby goat." (But "baby vegetables" are okay.) I was once asked to propose a few cooking shows for the fledgling TV Food Network. I wanted to do a show on game birds and their marinades (quail, squab, and so on). But I was told by a producer, completely without irony, "We're not doing little birds right now." What a shame, since little birds are among the most delicious things you can eat.

On the topic of eating birds, a very healthy-sized flock of wild turkeys lives on our Vermont property. Quite a few years ago they made their presence known by wandering onto the lawn and peeking into the windows in a rather comical way. If you've never seen a wild turkey, I'll try to describe them to you. They are fast runners and can even fly a few panicky, vertical feet into a tree when they are spooked. They're long-necked and skinny—not at all like the snowy-plumed breeds that are plumped up for our holiday feasts. All in all, the wild turkey is not a glamorous bird—the average chicken is much more fetching. (We have to wonder why Benjamin Franklin wanted turkeys to be our national bird.) So as these curious creatures were gawking at us, my father was aiming his telephoto lens at them, snapping away, until finally he said, "Oh, the hell with it," and traded his camera for his rifle. Nowadays, turkeys don't come close to the house anymore.

That was my family's first experience with a whole bird, but not its last. In the country, you learn by doing, and my parents thought it would be wonderful to celebrate Christmas with a local, fresh goose. They asked a neighbor to raise one to their specifications, and when it was ready, my father brought the ill-tempered beast home (geese are very cranky birds). After dispatching the goose, he realized he had quite a chore on his hands—plucking the darn thing. Our house proved not to be the ideal venue for this operation. The very tall ceilings (twenty-five feet over the main rooms, supported by a single ridgepole harvested from an old barn and buttressed by massive rafters) create an awful lot of air volume, producing thermals and other air currents within the house. Plucking the bird took hours, and once the lighter-than-air downy feathers were exposed, the house looked like the aftermath of a pillow fight staged by Cecil B. DeMille. My mother recalls finding feathers in the oddest places for years to come. But the feast was worth the trouble. My mother did an amazing job cooking the goose. It was memorable.

My father bringing home wild turkey

ON HERBS
FRESH VERSUS DRIED

I cook with a lot of fresh herbs; they really add character and interest to a dish, and it's just a matter of pulling a few leaves or needles off the stem and rubbing them through your fingers to release their oils, or running a knife quickly through them before adding them to your recipe. But don't worry if you can't get your hands on all the fresh herbs a recipe might call for—just use what you have on hand. Even dried herbs can be good if they haven't been sitting in your cupboard since the Carter administration. (Store-bought dried herbs will last no longer than a year, so replace them accordingly.)

As a general rule, dried herbs are stronger than their fresh counterparts. This is because drying concentrates the essential oils that give each herb its characteristic flavor. As a rule of thumb, every tablespoon of fresh herbs equals a teaspoon of dried herbs, basically one-third the amount of dried to fresh. A chef's trick to release the most flavor from your dried herbs is to crumble them between your fingertips as you add them to your dish. This is also a way of checking for freshness. If after you've crumbled the herb you can detect no aroma at all, the herb has lost its flavor and it's time to throw out the old and buy new.

Since fresh herbs are an investment (many cost several dollars per bunch), you'll want to take good care of them so they'll keep as long as possible. I treat fresh herbs as I would cut flowers: snip off the bottom quarter inch of the stems and place the herbs stem side down in a glass or jar with enough water to cover the stems, leaving the leaves exposed. Then loosely cover the leaves with plastic wrap and store the whole assembly in the fridge. Change the water every other day, and the herbs should last ten days.

Simple Roast Chicken

Before I became a mother, I used to make my husband pretty much fend for himself while I was working five nights a week at a restaurant. All that has changed. I want to make sure Luke and Michael have some good meals together, so I've taken to giving small cooking classes to the two of them when I'm home. By teaching Michael a few of the basics, I feel less guilty about not being around every night to cook a good, healthy meal for Luke—I know his dad can. We've found that a well-seasoned chicken slid into a hot oven becomes, with almost no effort, one of the most satisfying dinners we make. The first trick is to buy a well-raised bird that has been allowed to roam around and build up some muscle and flavor. The so-called free-range birds are good, but locally raised, organic birds are even better. Yes, they are a little more expensive than the commercially raised chickens, but the difference in flavor is well worth it.

The next family secret is to make a compound butter; a softened butter blended with flavorings, the combinations and possibilities of which are endless. (I've given a few examples following the recipe. They can be made ahead and frozen so they are always on hand.) Just stuff the butter under the skin of the breast right on top of the meat and then rub some all over the bird. Another avenue of flavor is cavity "stuffing." This can be as simple as a half a lemon you have in the fridge getting dry or a sprig of herbs or a few mushroom stems—anything that will release some extra flavor and aroma. Chicken is a perfect vehicle for experimentation.

The last family secret is my key to knowing when your chicken is done. It may sound silly, but it's true: I know my chicken is done when it smells like chicken—the delicious aroma fills my kitchen. Try it. It's foolproof.

SERVES 4–6

Preheat oven to 400°F.

prepare the compound butter

In a bowl, beat the softened butter with a spoon until smooth. Stir in the lemon zest, herbs, garlic, and pepper. Take half of the butter and roll it into a 1-inch-thick cylinder, wrap in foil, label, and pop it in the freezer for future use.

clean and roast the chicken

Rinse the whole bird under cold water and pat dry, inside and out. Season inside the cavity with salt, pepper, and coriander seed, if using. Place the bird on your work surface so the cavity is facing you. Slide your forefinger gently under the skin of the breast to loosen it from the meat. When you have made a pocket on both sides of the breast, carefully stuff 2 tablespoons of the compound butter under the skin of each side, pressing it toward the front as you go. You don't want to tear the skin, so work slowly and gently. Rub the rest of the butter all over the bird, including the thighs and legs. Season liberally with salt, pepper, and coriander seed. I keep a separate peppermill just for coriander seed, which I think works so well with poultry—it has a fragrance reminiscent of citrus and sage.

Place the bird in a roasting pan that is not much bigger than the bird itself; you don't want the melting butter to burn, which will happen if there is too much exposed surface area. I usually use my 9-by-11-inch glass Pyrex dish.

I find that when I put the bird right in a hot oven with all this butter under the skin there is no need for basting or turning, but you can baste and turn the chicken if you like. I also don't truss the bird for family. It looks less than elegant splayed open, but the hot air circulates nicely around it and crisps the skin in the leg folds as well as the breast. If I am entertaining and want to carve the bird at the table, I truss.

Once the bird is in the hot oven, expect it to take 1 hour and 20 minutes or so. To test, pierce the thickest part of the thigh; if the juices run clear, it's done. Another sign that your bird is done is that the leg joint will be loose and wobbly when you tug on it.

Before carving, it's important to rest the bird on a platter for 10–15 minutes. If you try to carve a hot chicken, you'll let all the

for the lemon and herb compound butter

1 stick butter, softened

Zest of 1 lemon (save the naked lemon to stuff into the cavity)

½ cup minced herbs—any combination of parsley, tarragon, chervil, cilantro, basil, sage, and rosemary (keep the stripped herb stems for the cavity)

2 cloves garlic, mashed to a paste with 1 teaspoon salt

Freshly ground black pepper

for the chicken

1 chicken (approximately 4½ pounds)

Salt and pepper

1 teaspoon freshly ground coriander seed (optional)

for the sauce (optional)

1 tablespoon flour
1 cup chicken stock (see
    Appendix, or use
    organic, low-sodium
    boxed), or water

juices escape, and the meat will be dry and stringy instead of sleek and moist. Return any juices that accumulate on the platter back to the roasting pan.

At this point you have a few options for saucing the bird. Usually, I just spoon the pan drippings over the chicken for flavor and moisture, but if you want to make a sauce or gravy, you'll need to skim off the fat, leaving 1 or 2 tablespoons behind. Sprinkle the pan juices with a tablespoon of flour, scraping up the brown bits, add maybe a cup or so of water or chicken stock, and bring it up to a boil for a couple of minutes, then strain the sauce through a sieve. Making the gravy this way is really not much trouble and leaves you with a smooth and thickened sauce.

The chicken is done.

‹ leftover alert ›

As for leftovers, they run the gamut from shredded chicken salad to a soup garnish to cold chicken sandwiches with mayo, lettuce, and tomato. Most often, the poor bird is just picked clean in the middle of the night by a hungry and sleepless mom or dad.

‹ weighing your options ›

Simple Roast Chicken can be served with so many different side dishes. Depending on the season, I like to serve it with Squash Roasted in Foil Packages (summer/spring, see page 235), Baby Brussels Sprouts with Bacon, Chestnuts, and Pomegranate Seeds (fall/winter, see page 242), or Sweet Corn and Fava Bean Succotash (summer, page 230).

COMPOUND BUTTERS

Compound butters can also be used to top a steak, to dress a vegetable, or to toss with a simple bowl of pasta. For each stick of unsalted butter, fold in about 3 tablespoons of the combined ingredients.

- sun-dried tomato, ginger, and dried currants
- olive, caper, and lightly toasted pine nuts
- saffron, garlic, and fennel seed—bloom a pinch of saffron in a tablespoon of white wine and lightly toast and grind the fennel seed
- dried fig, prosciutto or Serrano ham, and honey—mince the figs, and cut the ham into thin strips
- truffles and Madeira—minced frozen or canned truffles work nicely and aren't very expensive; just reduce the Madeira by boiling it down to a syrup before stirring it into the butter

Grilled Chicken in Marjoram Marinade

I'm always on the lookout for lesser-known herbs and spices. Marjoram is similar in appearance to oregano, and in fact they are both members of the larger mint family. You'll often see marjoram called "sweet marjoram," but it's the same thing. The cumin in this recipe really explodes in flavor once toasted on a hot grill, so there's no need to toast the seeds before grinding them up. You can use boneless breasts, thighs, or half chickens—whatever you have or that is available in the market. If you're cutting up a whole bird, I recommend boning the thighs so they will cook at the same rate as the breasts. The drumsticks and wings I keep for making chicken stock or soup.

SERVES 4

for the marinade

1 cup picked marjoram leaves or half oregano and half parsley

1 clove garlic

1 teaspoon Dijon mustard

2 tablespoons rice vinegar

2 tablespoons crushed, not finely ground, cumin seed

1/3 cup olive oil

Salt and freshly ground black pepper

prepare the marinade

Put the herbs and garlic in the bowl of your food processor. Pulse to chop fine. Add the mustard, vinegar, and cumin seeds and pulse once or twice to combine. Scrape down the sides of the bowl. With the machine running, drizzle in the olive oil to make a pesto-like consistency. Season lightly with salt and pepper.

prepare the chicken

Rinse the chicken pieces under cold water and pat dry with paper towels. Coat the chicken with the marinade and let it sit in the fridge for 2–4 hours. (Marinating the chicken in a large ziploc bag is a good trick.)

When ready to cook, light your grill or heat your grill pan. (You can also broil the chicken.) Season the pieces well with salt and freshly ground black pepper. Lay the chicken on the grill skin side down and cook over medium heat to ensure that the skin will render its fat and not just char. Turn over after 5 minutes and cook the second side of the breasts and thighs. Let the chicken rest 3–5 minutes before serving.

for the chicken
1 chicken (approximately
    4 pounds), cut into
    2 boneless breasts and
    2 boneless thighs
Salt and pepper

‹ weighing your options ›
I love a slightly tart fresh relish with grilled poultry or meats.
Try the Tomato, Basil, and Caper Salsa on page 267.
For a hearty supper, this dish pairs well with Roasted
Cauliflower Gratin, page 240, or Macadamia
Nut Couscous, page 243.

Summer Jambalaya with Poussin, Shrimp, Spicy Sausage, and Sweet Corn

Jambalaya is a Creole rice dish inspired by the Spanish paella. I like to use poussins (three-week-old chickens) here because they are small (about a pound each) and tender and really absorb the wonderfully savory flavor from their neighboring ingredients. If poussins are hard to find, you can substitute a larger bird cut into serving pieces, or two Cornish hens. As for the rice, I use a short-grained variety like arborio or carnaroli (risotto rice), because they can soak up a lot of liquid without turning soggy. There's a lot of "putting in and taking out" in the first steps of this dish, but once everything has been cooked in order and reassembled, it's just a matter of putting the lid on and letting the heavy pot do the work.

SERVES 4–6

3 poussins, cut in quarters, or one 3½-pound chicken, preferably organic, cut into 8 pieces

Salt and freshly ground black pepper

3 tablespoons olive oil

½ pound spicy sausage, like chorizo, cut into ½-inch slices

8–12 large shrimp, peeled and deveined

1 sweet onion, cut in medium dice

1 poblano pepper, seeded and diced small

Season the poussin pieces with salt and pepper. Using a nonreactive casserole dish with a lid, heat the olive oil until shimmering, and then brown the chicken on all sides—this takes about 10 minutes. Remove the chicken to a large bowl or platter. Add the sausage and shrimp to the casserole, sautéing until lightly browned, then transfer them to the bowl or platter as well. Add the onion, poblano, and fennel and sauté 2 minutes, stirring frequently, then remove these vegetables to the bowl or platter and toss the mushrooms and corn into the casserole and sauté them for 2 minutes. Sprinkle in the saffron, paprika, and oregano and stir well.

Add the rice at this point, making sure it makes contact with the bottom of the casserole so it can toast for 4 minutes. Stir once or twice during this 4-minute period. (Toasting the rice adds a little flavor and helps regulate the rate at which it absorbs the liquid.)

Pour in the stock, bring it to a boil, then drop in the bay leaf.

Return the sautéed vegetables, sausage, shrimp, and browned

chicken to the casserole and nestle them evenly into the rice. Bring the entire mixture—the jambalaya—up to a boil, reduce to a simmer, cover, and cook for 25 minutes. Set the lid ajar and let dish stand off the heat for 10 minutes before serving. Tear the basil leaves over the dish and serve with the lemon wedges.

½ small bulb fennel, diced small
¼ pound chanterelles or shiitake mushrooms
2 ears sweet corn, kernels cut from the cobs
¼ teaspoon saffron
1 teaspoon sweet paprika
1 pinch oregano leaves, minced (you can substitute marjoram, thyme, or cilantro)
1½ cups short-grained rice
3 cups chicken stock
1 bay leaf
½ cup basil leaves
Lemon wedges

‹ leftover alert ›

Reheating rice dishes is never ideal—the rice always seems to become extremely mushy. But I find that any leftover jambalaya makes a wonderful soup. Just pick the chicken off the bone and add enough chicken stock to make it brothy. Now the focus of the dish is not so much the rice and you won't notice its textural deficiencies.

Pan-Roasted Chicken Thighs
with Calvados Cream and Onion-Sage Confit

Chicken thighs are often considered the poor cousin to the exalted breast, but they shouldn't be. Particularly when cooked on the bone, they have a rich flavor and juiciness that the leaner breast can only envy. It's fun to use this humble cut and elevate it to a higher status with the help of apple brandy and voluptuous crème fraîche. Calvados is the justly famous brandy from Normandy, and I wouldn't substitute any other apple liquor here. Calvados has a refinement like none other.

SERVES 4–6

for the chicken

8–12 chicken thighs, bone-in

Salt and pepper

1 teaspoon freshly ground coriander seed (optional)

2 tablespoons butter

for the calvados cream sauce

1 shallot, thinly sliced

1 tablespoon minced fresh lemongrass root (optional)

6–8 small crimini or white mushrooms, brushed clean and sliced

½ cup Calvados

prepare the chicken

Rinse the chicken under cold water and pat dry with paper towels. Season well with salt, pepper, and coriander if using. Find a large skillet that will accommodate the thighs with at least ¼ inch of room between them—but not too much extra space, either. Use 2 pans if necessary. Melt the butter over medium-high heat and brown the thighs on both sides; this will take about 8 minutes. Transfer the thighs to a plate while making the sauce. Reserve the fat in the pan.

make the calvados cream sauce

Using the butter and chicken fat that remains in the pan, sauté the shallots, lemongrass (if using), and mushrooms until tender, about 2 minutes. Pull the pan away from the heat before pouring in the Calvados. You don't want to get the bottle of Calvados anywhere near an open flame. This is a high-proof alcohol and will ignite easily—not a problem when it happens in the pan, but a big problem when it happens in your hand. Measure out what you need and pour it in gently off the heat, then return the pan to the stovetop. When the alcohol is warm enough, it may spontaneously ignite, but this is fine, just let it burn off. If it doesn't ignite, it will burn off by boiling down.

Pour in the cider and chicken stock and temper in the crème fraîche. (Tempering is necessary when using cream. See Chef's Trick on page 91 for details.)

Return the chicken to the pan and reduce heat to a simmer. Lightly tent the pan with foil, which will allow some evaporation to thicken the sauce but will trap enough heat in the pan so the chicken can cook evenly.

Simmer the chicken for 15–20 minutes. When you think it's ready, pull out a thigh and pierce it in the thickest part. If the juices run clear, it's done. Remove all the thighs and reduce the sauce a bit more, until it lightly coats a spoon. Season with salt, pepper, and nutmeg, to taste. Serve the chicken with the sauce spooned over it and some warm Onion-Sage Confit.

½ cup dry hard cider or regular sweet cider
½ cup chicken stock
⅓ cup crème fraîche or heavy cream
Salt and pepper
Freshly grated nutmeg

for the onion-sage confit, see page 285.

‹ weighing your options ›
If you decide to not use the Onion-Sage Confit, the dish could benefit from a tablespoon of a fresh herb like minced thyme or cilantro, folded into the sauce during the final reduction. You can serve this with the plain steamed rice, Wild Leek Risotto, page 246, or Celery Root Puree, page 232.

Grilled Quail with Warm Muscat Grape, Black Olive, and Pine Nut Relish

For such a diminutive bird, quail has a surprisingly big flavor. They weigh only about 7 ounces each, so one makes a nice first course or lunch salad entrée, and two are perfect as a main course. When grilling, I spatchcock the quail (see page 192 for this technique) and marinate them for an hour or so. When roasting, I stuff them like tiny turkeys. For the stuffing, I use whatever is on hand—toasted peasant bread moistened with a little stock and freshened with herbs, or leftover polenta or grits with extra cheese folded in, or a ripe piece of fruit (fig, apricot, plum) wrapped in a thin slice of cured ham—anything small and flavorful. I never leave a seasoning opportunity like a bird's cavity unexploited, even if all I have around is a slice of orange or lemon and a few sprigs of herb. The easy-to-make grape relish is evocative of the vintner's harvest. Muscat grapes are a lovely fragrant variety that is used in the dessert wine Beaumes de Venise.

You'll realize when you eat quail that it is really just high-end finger food. There's just too much wonderful meat clinging to the little bones that can't be accessed with a knife and fork. So have plenty of napkins and that old-fashioned courtesy, a finger bowl, ready—warm water with a slice or two of lemon squeezed into it. Both the quail and the relish are delicious cold, but they rarely make it to the next day uneaten.

SERVES 4–6

for the marinade

2 cloves garlic, thinly sliced

1 branch rosemary, leaves minced

1 New Mexico chile, toasted in a dry pan, seeded, and torn into small pieces*

Zest and juice of 1 orange

⅓ cup olive oil

*1 teaspoon dried red chile flakes can be substituted for the New Mexico chile.

marinade the quail

Stir together all the marinade ingredients. Rinse the quail under cold water and pat dry with paper towels. Place the quail in a single layer in a nonreactive pan (glass, ceramic, enamel, or stainless steel) and pour the marinade over them. Refrigerate for an hour or two, but not longer, or the acidity will start to chemically cook the quail and toughen it.

Light your grill or broiler, or heat your grill pan. Brush the large pieces of the marinade off the quail and season with salt, pepper, and ground coriander seed, if using. Cook on the hottest spot for 3 minutes per side. The quail should remain a little pink inside for best flavor. Rest the birds for 4 minutes.

while quail is resting, prepare the muscat grape relish
Heat a large, heavy skillet over medium-high heat. Add the butter, and when it foams add the grapes, shallots, and sugar. Stir together a few times until the grapes begin to deflate a little and get glossy from the sugar. Add the pine nuts and olives and heat through for 1 minute. Pour in the balsamic vinegar and let it reduce lightly, for about 1 minute. Take relish off the heat and stir in the olive oil. Season with salt and pepper and serve over or around the quail.

‹ weighing your options ›
This grilled quail is wonderful served on top of the Greek Salad on page 102, in place of the grilled shrimp. Also, try other seasonal fruit in place of the grapes: apricots in spring, peaches or nectarines in summer, pears or apples in fall, and tropical fruits like papayas and mangos in the winter months. If using tropical fruits, instead of the pine nuts use toasted macadamia nuts, and replace the balsamic vinegar with citrus juices.

for the quail
8–12 whole quail (you can use semiboneless quail too, if they're easier to find)
Salt and pepper
1 teaspoon freshly ground coriander seed

for the muscat grape relish
2 tablespoons butter
1 bunch muscat or red flame grapes, grapes cut in half (enough to yield 1 cup sliced grapes)
2 shallots, minced or thinly sliced
Pinch of sugar
¼ cup pine nuts, lightly toasted
¼ cup pitted oil-cured or Gaeta olives, cut into slivers
⅓ cup balsamic vinegar
3 tablespoons extra virgin olive oil
Salt and pepper

Pancetta-Wrapped Duck Breast
with Verjuice and Green Peppercorn Sauce

Duck is sort of the pig of the poultry world. What I mean by that is that you can eat every part of the duck but the "quack," just as you can every part of the pig but the "oink." Everything has its use, from the sublime foie gras of Moulard ducks (a Muscovy and Pekin cross) to the humble "cracklins" made by slowly rendering the skin. But sometimes you just want to eat a tender, medium-rare duck breast without a lot of fussing around with the other parts. If that's the case, this is your dish. I remove the skin and replace it with a thin wrapping of pancetta, which mimics the fat and flavor of the fatty skin but renders much more easily. I've found that I can grill the duck breast this way, whereas the fat in its own skin creates awful flare-ups.

As for the verjuice, this is an unripe, unfermented wine grape juice. It has a bright acidity that is great with the rich duck, but is not quite as tart as a fruit-based vinegar. A good fruit vinegar, like apple cider vinegar, is a fine substitute for the verjuice if the latter is hard to find. The little punctuation marks from the green peppercorns make this an exciting dish!

SERVES 6

for the duck

6 boneless duck breasts, preferably the Long Island breed, which have smaller breasts and are not as dense as Muscovy ducks

¼ pound thinly sliced pancetta, or lightly smoked bacon

Salt and pepper

prepare the duck breasts

Rinse the duck breasts under cold water and pat dry on paper towels. Remove the skin by gently sliding your fingers between the skin and the breast; it should pull away easily to start with, but when the skin sticks about a third of the way in, use the tip of a small knife to make little shallow nicks to the connective tissue as you gently pull on the skin. Avoid nicking the flesh.

Unfurl the pancetta slices that are coiled into rings. Lay 2 slices out on your work surface and place a breast across the middle of them. Pull up the pancetta to wrap around and cover most of the duck. (You don't need to cover the whole breast.) Simply press the pancetta onto the breast—it will adhere without toothpicks. Repeat with the other duck breasts.

Stir together all the marinade ingredients. Place duck in a nonreactive pan or dish, pour the marinade over it, and set aside for an hour or two in the fridge.

while the duck is marinating, make the verjuice sauce

Melt the butter in a saucepan and sweat the shallot until soft, about 3 minutes. Pour in the verjuice or vinegar and reduce by half its volume. Add the stock and the herb sprigs and simmer gently until the sauce lightly coats a spoon, about 20 minutes. Stir in the rinsed peppercorns and season to taste with salt and pepper. Keep warm while cooking the duck.

cook the duck

You can either grill or pan-roast the duck. If you choose to pan-roast, I'd suggest deglazing the pan that you roast the duck in with the verjuice sauce to pick up some extra flavor. Also, pour in any juices that accumulate on the platter where the duck is resting.

If you are grilling, light the grill, or heat a heavy skillet. Brush the marinade off the duck and season well with salt and pepper. Cook each side 3 minutes for medium rare, a minute longer per side for medium. Duck really needs to rest, so let it sit for 4 or 5 minutes before slicing.

Duck is at its succulent best when thinly sliced at a slight angle. Once the duck is sliced and arranged on plates or a platter, spoon the warm sauce over it and distribute the peppercorns as evenly as you can.

for the marinade

3 tablespoons olive oil

1 tablespoon grated fresh ginger

1 tablespoon coriander seed, crushed

3 pieces star anise, crushed

1 stick cinnamon, broken up

2 strips orange peel

2–3 drops toasted sesame oil (optional)

for the verjuice and green peppercorn sauce

2 tablespoons butter

1 shallot, minced

1 cup verjuice, or ½ cup fruit vinegar

2 cups Rich Chicken Stock (see Appendix)

1 sprig each thyme and rosemary

2 tablespoons green peppercorns in brine, rinsed

Salt and pepper

‹ weighing your options ›

I think grains, seeds, and nuts are wonderful accompaniments to any duck dish—probably because this is what a duck would eat if left to its own devices. So creamy polenta, wild rice, or, for something a bit more elaborate, my Quinoa Salad with Pine Nuts, Dried Cherries, and Basil, on page 248, are all good choices. In the cooler months, roasted root vegetables like turnips, parsnips, beets, and celery root in any combination are a nice accompaniment.

In the spring and summer, I like to pair this duck with a bitter greens salad: simply toss together frisée, baby red mustard greens, and arugula (or any combination of this type of green) in the Aged Sherry–Walnut Vinaigrette on page 261 and scatter with toasted walnuts or hazelnuts.

Duck Simmered in Coconut Curry

Sometimes when a meat is rich, you want to pair it with a lean, bright flavor for contrast, as in the preceding recipe. Other times, the only thing to do is up the ante and pair rich with richer—indulgent, but fun. With its silky, unctuous coconut milk and intense spices, this curry is a treat that only gets better for two to three days after you've made it, so if you feel so inclined, double the recipe. If you must lighten it up, use a whole-milk yogurt in place of the coconut milk, but not lowfat yogurt, which will curdle. However, I recommend that you just surrender to the full pleasure of this dish at least once.

SERVES 6

for the spice rub

3 tablespoons minced ginger
6 cloves garlic, mashed to a
 paste with 1 teaspoon
 salt
2 fresh red chiles, chopped*
2 tablespoons ground
 coriander seed
Zest of 1 small lemon
2 teaspoons turmeric powder
 (optional)

for the duck

Two 4–5-pound ducks
2 tablespoons olive oil
1 tablespoon butter
Salt and pepper
1 yellow onion, diced fine

*For the chiles, choose the small, thin, mean-looking ones like Thai bird chiles, chile de árbol, or red serrano, minced with seeds intact (the coconut milk will moderate the heat).

prepare the ducks

Mix together all the ingredients for the spice rub in a small bowl.

Bone the duck breasts and thighs and remove the skin. Keep the carcass (including drumsticks and wings) for stock or soup and the skin for cracklings (see Chef's Trick on next page). Cut the boneless breasts and legs into approximately 1-inch pieces. Spread the spice rub liberally over all the duck pieces. Marinate the duck for 1–2 hours in the fridge.

cook the duck

Heat the olive oil and butter in a skillet large enough to accommodate all the duck pieces in a single layer but without much room leftover. Season the marinated duck well with salt and freshly ground black pepper. Sear the pieces (you don't need to remove the marinade) on both sides until golden brown. Tip out all but 2 tablespoons of fat from the pan. Scatter the diced onion over the duck and cook 2–3 minutes over moderate heat.

make the coconut curry sauce

When the onions have wilted a little, pour in the coconut milk and chicken stock or water. Partially cover the skillet with a lid or foil and simmer gently for 20 minutes. Toss the diced sweet potato into the curry and simmer 20–30 minutes longer, until the duck is tender. If the sauce is not thick enough to coat a spoon, remove the duck to a warm plate and simmer the sauce to reduce it. Ideally, you could wait a day to serve this so all the flavors could meld, but it's awfully good eaten right away. Fold in the whole cilantro and mint leaves, squeeze in the juice of 1 lime, and taste again for seasoning.

for the coconut curry sauce

Two 12-ounce cans unsweetened coconut milk

1 cup chicken stock, or 1 cup cold water

1 large or 2 small sweet potatoes, peeled and diced into ½-inch cubes

Small handful cilantro leaves

Large pinch mint leaves

Juice of 1 lime

❮ weighing your options ❯

This curry is quite rich, so I serve it with light sides like Orange and Radish Salad with Mint (page 229) or Sesame-Roasted Green Beans (page 237), and a heaping bowl of simply steamed rice.

Chef's Trick: Cracklings are great as a crunchy, salty treat on salads or for garnishing this curry. Heat the oven to 350°F and roast the whole pieces of skin on a rack placed over a baking sheet that has a rim to catch the fat as it renders. When the skin is golden brown, drain on paper towels and season with salt. Cool and cut into strips. These cracklings will keep 2–3 days if stored at room temperature in an airtight container.

RESTING

Unfortunately, this kind of resting has nothing to do with you or me taking a well-deserved nap. Cooking drives the natural juices of any kind of flesh to the surface, and resting allows these juices to retract and redistribute themselves throughout, for a juicier taste and texture. Also, since the muscles naturally (and understandably) contract on contact with heat, resting gives the fibers a chance to relax and elongate, making the meat more tender than if you set into it right away. There will always be some juices lost during cooking, but resting the meat before it is sliced into ensures that the loss will be minimal.

During resting, there will also be some carryover cooking caused by the continued climb in temperature that happens even after meat is removed from the heat source. The amount of carryover depends on a number of things, but generally, the larger the cut of meat and the hotter its internal temperature when removed from the heat, the greater the carryover. Conversely, if you cook a small, thin fillet to a rare or medium-rare temperature, the increased cooking while resting will be negligible.

After many years of cooking, resting for me is now an unconscious automatic reflex. I use those extra minutes to finish a sauce, reseason a condiment, or light some candles for a more celebratory meal.

MARINADES AND RUBS

In these days of relative bounty, we aren't forced to employ an arsenal of tools to subdue tough cuts of meat into something palatable. Marinades and rubs are part of this time-honored array, along with pounding, larding, barding, and just plain cooking it until it falls apart. Now, with affordable prime cuts on the market, we're most likely to use a marinade to enhance flavor and offer some protection against a hot grill or oven. I use marinades a lot—I like to find flavor combinations that either harmonize with existing flavors or create a strong contrast for some excitement. The "wild boar" marinade for the pork on page 206 fulfills both of these goals: the juniper, rosemary, and thyme are natural complements for pork, and the red chile and lemongrass are more dramatic twists. There are of course still times when you want and need a relatively high-acid marinade to start to break down the muscle fibers for a more tender chew, as in the case of the Grilled Flank Steak in Smoked Chile and Lime Marinade on page 218.

There are both **cooked marinades** and **uncooked marinades.** The former is usually a wine-and-vinegar-based solution simmered with aromatics, cooled, then poured over a piece of game to tenderize and flavor the meat. Historically this kind of marinade was employed to mitigate some of the "gaminess." But these days, farm-raised game is much milder in flavor, and gaminess is not usually evident. Uncooked marinades tend to be high in oil content and lower in acidity to keep food moist on the grill or in the oven and to act as a vehicle for other flavors, such as the ground spices and fresh herbs in the Grilled Chicken in Marjoram Marinade on page 178.

A **rub** is a type of marinade that is a fairly dry paste—usually spices and herbs that are bound together with a little oil. An example is the cumin and red chile rub for the lamb on page 208. A rub can be massaged into the meat and left to marinate for a few hours or patted on just before cooking to form a fragrant crust. Either way, rubs tend to be strongly flavored and assertive. Alternately, a rub can be a form of dry cure, with a good amount of salt and sugar along with the spices. The rub is applied to the meat and left for several hours or overnight to lightly cure.

Spatchcocked Squab
with Star Anise, Ginger, and Soy

Domesticated squab are young pigeons—not the kind that populate city parks but birds that are corn-fed and housed in relative luxury. Because squab are sensitive to changes in their diet and to crowded conditions that don't seem to bother factory-raised chickens, they are more expensive to raise and thus to purchase. I would not consider squab an everyday sort of meal—it's a treat. Nothing can compare to its rich, complex, and tender meat. The meat is all dark, like duck but with a finer grain. Squab tastes best cooked to medium rare, or at most medium. Once past that point, the flesh toughens and takes on a faintly liver-like aroma and flavor.

Spatchcocking is the term chefs use to describe removing the backbone, cracking the sternum, and pressing the bird down so that it lies flat on the grill or pan for even and quick cooking. If you want to bone the breasts after cooking, the rib bones pull away easily at that point, but it's important that the flesh has contact with the bone during cooking to render more flavor. I fear I am a horrible taskmaster when I run my professional kitchen. I ask my already harried cooks to roast the squabs whole (for maximum flavor) to order, then carve the meat off the still-hot bird for plating. You have to possess asbestos fingers to do this even after the squab has rested. But the difference in flavor is worth it, and there is a deep satisfaction in knowing that nothing you make is prefabricated, that all of your skills as a cook have to operate at top form and top speed: seasoning, searing, roasting, resting, carving—they all have to come together at just the right moment while doing about twelve other things at the same time. This is why line cooking is addictive—it's like mastering the choreography of a vigorous and beautiful dance. But it's also fun to perform at home, where there is far less pressure.

SERVES 4

make the marinade

Stir together all the marinade ingredients in a bowl until the honey dissolves. Let the marinade mellow at room temperature while you are preparing the squab. Pour off about ⅓ of the marinade and reserve for drizzling over the grilled squab.

spatchcock the squab

Remove the backbone with a pair of poultry shears or a sturdy chef's knife. Save the backbone for stock. With the bird flat on the cutting board, skin side down, crack the sternum with the heel of the knife and press the bird as flat as possible. Make two small incisions at the bottom of each breast and tuck the end of the drumsticks through each slit. If this operation seems too complicated, skip it—but it makes for a neater look. Cut off wing tips and save for a poultry stock. Now the bird is ready to marinate.

prepare the squab

Pour the marinade (minus the third you set aside earlier) over the squab and marinate 1–2 hours in the refrigerator. It is a strong marinade and will do its work quickly.

cook the squab

Light your grill or broiler or heat your grill pan(s). Remove the squab from the marinade, brush off any solids (like pieces of star anise), and pat dry on paper towels. (A dry bird will not stick to the grill.) Brush the squab with olive oil and toasted sesame oil if using, and season both sides with salt, pepper, and freshly ground coriander seed. Salt lightly, since the soy in the marinade is also salty.

Grill on the skin side first for 6–7 minutes, then turn over and grill on the flesh side for 3–4 minutes. Return to the skin side for 2 minutes longer, then remove from the grill. Pour the reserved marinade over the birds and let them rest for 5 minutes before serving.

for the ginger-soy marinade

8 pieces star anise, lightly crushed

2 tablespoons grated fresh ginger

½ cup dark soy sauce

2 tablespoons honey

Juice of 1 lime

4 strips orange peel plus juice of the orange

for the squab

4 whole squab, about 1 pound each

Olive oil

1 tablespoon toasted sesame oil (optional)

Salt and pepper

Freshly ground coriander seed

‹ weighing your options ›

This is a good year-round recipe, so I pair it with seasonal side dishes.
Spring: Wild Leek Risotto, page 246
Summer: Sweet Corn and Fava Bean Succotash, page 230
Fall: Squash Roasted in Foil Packages, page 235
Winter: Macadamia Nut Couscous, page 243

Fried Rabbit
with Whole-Grain Mustard Sauce

for the marinaded rabbit

Two 3-pound rabbits*

1 clove garlic, thinly sliced

2 tablespoons soy sauce

2 tablespoons balsamic vinegar

1 pinch minced thyme

1 pinch minced rosemary

2 strips orange zest

¼ cup olive oil

for the whole-grain mustard sauce

2 shallots or 1 small white onion

2 tablespoons butter

½ cup white wine

3 cups fortified chicken stock (see Chef's Trick on the next page)

¼ cup crème fraîche (see box on page 29) or heavy cream

½ cup whole-grain mustard

*If possible, have your butcher bone the legs and the loins. The forelegs and the carcass can be used for stock.

My friend Steven Hall would always increase the frequency of his visits to Quilty's when I had this dish on the menu. Ordinarily already a fan of my cooking, he was especially taken with this dish. Like most of New York's single men, Steven doesn't do a whole lot of cooking at home (read: none), so I'm always pleased to feed him.

Why fry a rabbit? I've found that what is good for chicken is even better for rabbit. In fact, I think of rabbit as the überchicken—mild and tender like that bird, but with a more assertive flavor. Mustard has long been used with rabbit, and this piquant mustard sauce is just the right note against the crispy and savory fried meat. Since the rabbit's hind legs are its meatiest part, that is what I fry. There's really so little meat on the forelegs that I prefer to simmer them along with the carcass in the chicken stock that I use for the mustard sauce. They help fortify the flavor, and nothing is lost. I use the loins for a quick grill (suggestions follow this recipe).

SERVES 4

marinade the rabbit

Gently pound out the boned rabbit legs into a uniform, half-inch thickness.

Combine all marinade ingredients and pour over the rabbit legs. Turn over to evenly distribute the marinade, then refrigerate for 1–2 hours. (You can pour everything in a ziploc bag and toss it around to coat nicely.)

make the whole-grain mustard sauce

Sweat the shallots or onion in the butter in a saucepan over medium heat. When the shallots are soft, 3–4 minutes, pour in the wine and reduce it to a syrup. With such a small amount of wine, the sauce will become syrupy fairly quickly. Pour in the fortified stock along with the sachet that's in the stock. Simmer until the liquid has reduced by half. Temper in the crème fraîche (for details on tempering, see Chef's Trick on page 91), and reduce until the sauce very lightly coats a spoon. Discard the sachet.

Now you're ready to add the mustard, but here are just a few points to note before you do:

1. The mustard will act as a thickener, so the base can be a little lighter than you think it should be when you fold in the mustard.

2. Once you add the mustard, you cannot boil the sauce or you will break the mustard. I don't even simmer the sauce once I've added mustard, I just keep it warm.

3. Cooking the mustard, or even warming it, mellows its sharpness, so don't be surprised at how much you'll be adding.

Following the above steps, add the mustard and taste sauce for seasoning.

prepare the rabbit for frying

Preheat oven to 350°F. Have a rack ready over a baking sheet. Drain off the marinade and blot the rabbit dry on paper towels. Season the flour with salt and pepper, and set up your breading station (see Chef's Trick on page 197).

Dredge a piece of the rabbit in the seasoned flour and shake off any excess. Next dip it into the egg wash and again let any excess dip off. The idea is to get a thin but well-adhered crust. Finally, press the rabbit pieces into the bread crumbs, sprinkling them over with your fingers where you need extra coverage. Repeat the process with all the legs. Don't bread the rabbit more than a few minutes before you're ready to fry or the crust will become a little soggy.

for the breading
Flour for dredging
Salt and pepper
2 eggs, beaten with
    3 tablespoons cold
    water
2 cups fresh bread crumbs
    (see Chef's Trick on
    standard breading
    procedure on page 197)
2 cups pure vegetable oil for
    shallow frying (canola,
    safflower, light olive)

Chef's Trick: Fortified Chicken Stock While the rabbit legs are marinating, fortify your chicken stock with the rabbit forelegs and carcass. Simply simmer the rabbit gently in the stock with a sachet of 8 coriander seeds, a small handful of parsley stems, 1 bay leaf, and 8–12 black peppercorns. Cook for 40 minutes and strain. Your chicken stock is now fortified with the rabbit flavor. I use this method when I don't have enough trimmings to make a separate stock but want to take advantage of whatever flavor I can get from the meat (it could be any poultry).

Heat the oil—about an inch deep—in a wide skillet or 2 skillets over medium-high heat. When the oil shimmers, gently slide the rabbit in. The pieces will not be entirely submerged, but you'll cook 1 side until golden (3 minutes) and then turn and fry the other side. Moderate the heat if the rabbit seems to be browning too quickly. At this point, you have "set" the crust and cooked the rabbit most of the way through. The final cooking will happen in the oven. Transfer the fried rabbit to the rack atop a baking sheet and slide carefully into the oven. Bake 4–5 minutes. The rabbit can be served in 1 piece, known as a paillard, or cut into slices.

Serve the warm mustard sauce to the side—not on the hard-won crisp crust. In colder months, I like to serve this with Celery Root and Apple Remoulade (page 275), or Creamed Spinach with Sherried Currants (page 239). In summer, Sweet Corn and Fava Bean Succotash (page 230) makes a lighter seasonal accompaniment.

‹ weighing your options ›

The reserved rabbit loins are small, but well worth concocting a dish with. I like to wrap them with a thin piece of pancetta or blanched bacon, marinate them with something simple like good olive oil and a little citrus juice, and grill or pan-roast them for 2 minutes per side. They should have a little rosy center. Then I just slice them thin and serve as a first course with a salad, or as a garnish to a risotto, or between 2 slices of bread with a fruit mustard and a slice of Manchego or other well-aged cheese.

Chef's Trick: Standard Breading Procedure   It's very helpful to have the breading procedure hard-wired into your brain. From left to right: a shallow plate or container for the flour, seasoned with salt and pepper; next to that a container for the beaten eggs with water, known as an "egg wash"; and, last, your breading, which could be any number of things—ground nuts, cornmeal, cornflakes—but in this case fresh and fluffy bread crumbs.

I never buy the overtoasted dry variety of bread crumbs when fresh are so easy to make and lend an incredible texture to your fried food. Just trim off the crust of a day-old white or whole-grain peasant bread (avoid sourdough, which has too much character, or any overly seeded bread). Tear the bread into small pieces and pulse in a food processor until you have fine crumbs. This takes just a few pulses—if you overprocess, you'll wind up with a gluey paste.

Rabbit Sausage

This is the lazy cook's version of sausage. It involves a good amount of knife work, but no stuffing into sausage casings, which I admit is not one of my favorite chores. The forcemeat, as the sausage is called before being stuffed or cooked, is simply shaped into logs and wrapped in foil, then poached for twelve minutes. Once cool, you can slice and serve with an array of homemade condiments. I have listed a few options below. I also like to heat slices of the sausage in a sauté pan and make a warm salad with yellow potatoes and a spicy mushroom vinaigrette, the recipe for which is also included below.

SERVES 6

2 shallots, minced

2 tablespoons butter

4–6 dried prunes or dried apricots

1 tablespoon cognac or Armagnac (optional)

One 2½–3-pound rabbit

1 boneless, skinless chicken breast, cut into ¼-inch dice

3 ounces Serrano ham, prosciutto with a good layer of fat, or cooked ham cut into ¼-inch dice

1 rabbit liver (optional), ¼-inch diced (you can substitute 2 chicken livers)

Begin by sautéing the minced shallots in the butter until they are soft and just a little golden in color. Remove from pan and cool.

Rehydrate the prunes or apricots in 1 cup of simmering water mixed with the cognac or Armagnac, if you are using it. Turn off the heat and let the fruit plump up and soften, about 10 minutes. Drain and cut the fruit into ¼-inch dice.

Bone the rabbit, and discard any sinew you might find. The forcemeat is not going to be ground in a meat grinder, so you want only nice, sinew-free meat. Dice the meats into ¼-inch pieces. (You should have close to a pound.) Be faithful with your ¼-inch dice. If you find the cuts getting too large, go back over them once with a knife. The size matters because there is no grinding to even out the texture.

Keep the meats cold while working with them. Once they are diced, fold them all together in a chilled bowl. Add the diced fruit, rabbit or chicken liver, and cool shallots to the bowl. Beat the egg well and pour it over the contents of the bowl. Season with the orange zest, thyme, salt, pepper, and nutmeg. Fold gently to combine all ingredients. Let the flavors develop in the fridge for 2–12 hours.

Now you want to test the seasoning. You can't eat the meat raw, so take a pinch of the forcemeat and sauté it gently in a little olive oil until cooked through. Let the cooked sample sausage chill before tasting, since chilled food needs to be more highly seasoned. Add more salt and pepper and nutmeg if needed to lift the flavor. Roll the forcemeat in heavy foil into four 1-inch-diameter cylinders.

Bring water to a gentle simmer in a pan large enough to submerge the cylinders comfortably. Poach the sausages in their foil wrappers for 12 minutes, then remove the pan from the heat and let the sausage cool in the water.

When ready to serve, use a serrated knife to cut through the foil for even slices. Remove foil and serve for lunch, or as a first course for dinner, accompanied by whichever condiments you choose. I've selected a few ideas below. The cooked sausage will continue to develop its flavor in the fridge and will reach its peak in 3 days. After that, there's a slow decline in flavor, and I wouldn't recommend eating it past day 5. I would not freeze them.

1 large egg
½ teaspoon grated orange zest
Pinch minced thyme
Salt and pepper
Freshly grated nutmeg

‹ weighing your options ›

When serving the sausage cold, I like to pair it with at least one flavored mustard and a pickle of some kind.

- Fruited Mustards, page 274

- Celery Root and Apple Remoulade, page 275

- Pickled Wild Mushrooms, page 266

If you are serving the sausage warm, slice it and gently heat in a nonstick skillet with a little oil. Serve with yellow potatoes that have been cooked in their skins, peeled, and sliced into rounds, with a drizzle of Spicy Mushroom Dressing (page 260) on top. Serve, alternating slices of potato and sausage.

Pork Chops Smothered in Lentils

Pork chops figure prominently in my family's repertoire of everyday meals. A well-marbled chop can be hard to find in these days of leaner, meaner animal husbandry, but there are still some producers out there who appreciate the value of plump porkers (see Sources). In this recipe, cooked lentils are poured over seared pork chops to create an atmosphere of moist cooking that makes for both a tender chop and very flavorful lentils. No pan sauce is needed, since the lentils absorb all the delicious pan drippings. For even more fun, I top this one-pot wonder with an exotic and refreshing spiced mango yogurt.

SERVES 4

for the spiced mango yogurt
1 tablespoon butter
1 small mango, peeled and diced into ½-inch pieces
Pinch brown sugar
1 teaspoon ancho chile powder
Tiny pinch ground clove
1 teaspoon cinnamon
Tiny pinch cayenne
1 cup whole-milk yogurt
½ small red onion, minced
1 tablespoon lime juice

make the spiced mango yogurt
Heat the butter in a sauté pan until foamy, and add the mango with the pinch of sugar, the ancho powder, clove, cinnamon, and cayenne. Stir over medium heat until softened and browned, about 4 minutes. Cool and fold into the yogurt with the onion, lime juice, and herbs. Season with salt and freshly ground black pepper.

make the pork chops
Season the pork chops with salt and pepper.

Heat a large heavy-bottomed skillet over medium-high heat. Add the olive oil and butter to the pan. When the butter foams, slip in the pork chops, leaving at least ¼ inch of space between them. Sear each side 2–3 minutes, until chops are golden brown, then pour in the chicken stock and the lentils and shake the pan to evenly distribute. Bring the lentils to a simmer over the pork, reduce heat to low, and cover. Cook 10 minutes, then turn off the heat. Let the pork and lentils sit for another 5 minutes off the heat for all the flavors to settle into each other.

To serve the dish, divide the pork and lentils among 4 plates and spoon a large dollop of the mango yogurt on each, or pass yogurt around in a decorative bowl. Garnish with herbs. Serve this with Sugar Snap Peas with Browned Shallots, Pancetta, and Mint (page 236), or Baby Brussels Sprouts with Bacon, Chestnuts, and Pomegranate Seeds (page 242).

Pinch minced cilantro, mint, or basil, or all 3 combined, plus whole leaves for garnishing
Salt and pepper

for the pork chops
4 rib pork chops, at least 1 inch thick
Salt and pepper
1 tablespoon olive oil
2 tablespoons butter
$2/3$ cup chicken stock (see Appendix)
2 cups cooked French lentils (see recipe on page 144, but omit the mango and olives)

Medallions of Pork Breaded in Crushed Gingersnaps with Apples and Sage

I don't usually resort to boxed cookies as an ingredient for dinner, but I made an exception in this case. Gingersnaps, like Wheat Thins, are one of the staples that sustained us kids on long car trips to Nova Scotia on summer vacation. I can vividly recall sitting in the "way back" of the Ford Bronco (they were much smaller in the 1970s than they are today, and so was I), being cruelly bounced up and down while driving off-road to our campsite in Donald Roddy Rankin's cow pasture. My only companion was a box of gingersnaps. My brother and sister, by accident of birth order, were comfortably established on the back seat. Maybe my parents were clever and chose these cookies precisely because ginger calms the upset stomach. But ginger is also a wonderful complement to both pork and apples, and the cookies make a sweet and spicy crust for the thin medallions of meat.

SERVES 4

for the breading

2 cups crushed gingersnaps (pulsed in a food processor until they resemble fine cornmeal)

2 tablespoons ancho chile powder (optional)

1 teaspoon grated orange zest

1 tablespoon minced sage

1 teaspoon minced thyme

Flour, for dredging

2 eggs, beaten with 3 tablespoons cold water

prepare the gingersnap breading

Stir together the gingersnap crumbs, ancho, orange zest, sage, and thyme in a small bowl. Set up your breading station with the flour and egg wash (see page 197).

prepare the apples and sage

Peel and core the apples and cut into ½-inch-thick rings or wedges. (Do this right before cooking them so they don't turn brown.)

Heat a heavy skillet over medium heat. Dot the skillet with the butter. When it foams, slide the apple rings into the pan in a single layer. (Sauté two batches of apples if necessary or use more than one pan.) Sprinkle the curry powder (if using) and the brown sugar evenly all over the apples and cook until golden brown on each side, about 3 minutes per side.

Deglaze the pan with the cider vinegar. Turn off the heat and season the apples with a little salt, pepper, and nutmeg. Scatter the chopped sage over the top and give the apples one more flip or turn. (If you want a more saucelike accompaniment, add ½ cup of chicken stock to the apples just after adding the cider vinegar and swirl in a couple additional tablespoons of butter before seasoning.)

prepare the pork medallions

Cut the pork tenderloin into ½-inch-thick slices and lightly pound them out with a mallet or side of a knife, but don't make slices thinner than ¼ inch. Season the medallions lightly with salt and pepper and bread them following the standard breading technique—for details on this procedure, see page 197, replacing the fresh bread crumbs with the gingersnaps.

Preheat a slow oven (250°F) for keeping medallions warm.

Heat a nonstick skillet, or two if you are comfortable monitoring a couple of pans at the same time. If not, cook the pork in several batches. Heat half of the butter and oil in the pan over medium-high heat. When the butter foams, lay in as much pork as can fit without crowding. Cook medallions 2 minutes per side, until crust is set and browned. Lower the heat if the crust seems to be browning too quickly. Pork this thin will cook quickly. Wipe the skillet dry between batches and add fresh butter and oil as needed. Keep the pork warm while finishing the rest.

Serve 3 or 4 medallions per person with the apples and sage, and drizzle any juices or sauce around them.

for the apples and sage

2 crisp firm apples like Golden Delicious, Gala, Cortland, or Granny Smith
2 tablespoons butter
1 teaspoon curry powder (optional)
1 tablespoon brown sugar
2 tablespoons cider vinegar
Salt and pepper
Freshly grated nutmeg
Small handful roughly chopped sage leaves

for the medallions of pork

2–3 pork tenderloins, depending on size, about 2 pounds total
Salt and freshly ground pepper
3 tablespoons butter
1 tablespoon canola oil

‹ weighing your options ›

This dish evokes the fall harvest, when the apples, like the air, are crisp and refreshing. But the basic technique of quickly sautéing breaded medallions of pork can be used in other seasons with various crusts and accompaniments. Here are some of my favorites:

Spring: A crushed pine nut crust—lightly toast the nuts and pulse them in a food processor until they resemble coarse cornmeal. Serve with sautéed apricots or plums and rosemary.

Summer: A cornmeal crust—use regular cornmeal with Sweet Corn and Fava Bean Succotash, page 230.

Winter: An ancho chile and herbed bread crumb crust—use fresh bread crumbs seasoned with ancho chile powder and some minced fresh thyme, served with the Sautéed Wild Mushrooms on page 233.

Chipotle Barbecued Pork
with Peach-Radish Salsa

You can use either pork chops or pork tenderloin for this dish. Anytime you cook on the bone, you'll be rewarded with a more intense flavor, but I'm happy with the tenderloin too—it lives up to its billing and is indeed very tender. Chipotle is a fiercely hot, smoked jalapeño, usually sold in cans and packed in a vinegar and tomato base called adobo. I puree the chiles with their surrounding sauce, making sure to blend long enough to break up the chile seeds, which are where most of the heat is. Any leftover chipotle puree will keep almost indefinitely in the fridge if tightly covered. The peach radish salsa provides a sweet and cooling relief to this fiery barbecue sauce.

SERVES 6

**for the chipotle
barbecue sauce**
½ cup cider vinegar
½ cup brown sugar
2 tablespoons molasses
2 cloves garlic, minced
4 tablespoons soy sauce
¼ cup cold water
3 tablespoons chipotle
    puree*
2 tablespoons Dijon
    mustard

*To make the chipotle puree,
empty the contents of a small
can of chipotles in adobo into
a blender and puree until very
smooth, making sure all of the
seeds are broken down. For more
information on where to find
chipotles, see Sources.

prepare the chipotle barbecue sauce
Combine the cider vinegar, brown sugar, molasses, garlic, soy sauce, and cold water in a saucepan over low heat. Stir together and simmer 15–20 minutes to melt the sugar and develop the flavor.

Remove from the heat and stir in the chipotle puree and the mustard. Cool and brush about ⅔ of the barbecue sauce over all sides of the pork. You can marinate the chops in the barbecue sauce for about 30 minutes to an hour in the fridge if you have time; it is not necessary, but this will saturate the pork chops with flavor. Save the last ⅓ of sauce for basting the meat as it cooks.

prepare the peach-radish salsa
Fold all the salsa ingredients together in a bowl and let mellow at room temperature for an hour or so. Try not to refrigerate the salsa—this causes the fruit to "weep" or juice too much.

prepare the pork chops

Light your grill or heat a grill pan. Season the chops or tenderloin with salt and pepper and drizzle evenly with olive oil. For the chops, grill each side 5 minutes, placing chops in a medium-hot part of the grill. The tenderloin will cook a little faster, about 4 minutes per side, depending on thickness. Baste the pork every few minutes with the reserved barbecue sauce, and move the pork to a cooler spot on the grill if it seems to be blackening too quickly. The sugars in the marinade will cause some blackening, but this is all part of barbecuing (and it tastes really good). Rest the meat 3–5 minutes before serving.

Serve the chops with the salsa on the side. If you are using the tenderloin, slice the pork into ½-inch-thick slices and divide among plates or fan out on a platter with the salsa in the middle. Garnish with the cilantro or basil leaves. This dish goes well with Sweet Corn and Fava Bean Succotash (page 230) or, for a more substantial meal, Coconut-Simmered Fingerling Potatoes (page 251).

Six 1-inch-thick rib pork
  chops or 2½–3 pounds
  pork tenderloin

for the peach-radish salsa

3 ripe peaches, pitted and
  diced into ½-inch
  pieces
½ small red onion, diced
  fine
½ cup sliced red or pink
  radishes
½ mild green chile, like
  poblano, diced fine
2 tablespoons lime juice
A splash of orange juice
2 tablespoons extra virgin
  olive oil
A good pinch minced
  cilantro or basil leaves,
  plus whole leaves for
  garnish
Salt and pepper

Salt and freshly ground
  black pepper
4–6 tablespoons olive oil,
  for grilling

‹ leftover alert ›
You can also use this barbecue sauce on grilled chicken
or salmon or slathered on burgers.

Brined Pork Roast "Wild Boar" Style

Boar can be hard to find, so I approximate its unique wild flavor with traditional game seasonings like juniper, rosemary, and black pepper along with a few of my own flavors: toasted chile, orange zest, and allspice berries. By soaking the "boar" overnight in a brine, the herbs and spices are able to penetrate deeply into the pork and transform it from the ordinary to something *wild*. As it roasts, the "boar" perfumes the entire house, prompting the neighbors to ask, "What did you cook last night? It smelled wonderful!"

SERVES 6 (WITH LEFTOVERS)

for the brine

1 cup sugar

½ cup salt

⅓ cup lightly crushed juniper berries

3 tablespoons coriander seed, lightly crushed

3 tablespoons black peppercorns

6–8 whole allspice berries, crushed

2 bay leaves, torn into pieces

Zest of 1 orange, cut in long strips

4 cloves garlic, thinly sliced

prepare the brine

Choose a nonreactive vessel large enough to hold the pork loin and about a gallon of brine. Dissolve the sugar and salt in 2 cups of boiling water in your chosen pot. Stir in 3 quarts cold water, the spices, zest, garlic, and chile along with half the rosemary and half the thyme. Let the brine cool completely and then submerge the tied pork loin into the brine, weighing it down with a plate or two to keep it from surfacing. Cover the pot with plastic wrap and refrigerate the pork in its brine overnight.

make the pork roast

Preheat oven to 475°F. When ready to cook the pork, remove it from the brine (reserving 1 cup) and let the meat drain well on paper towels. Rub the loin with olive oil and a few grindings of black pepper—no salt will be needed, since the pork has absorbed it from the brine. Thread the remaining rosemary and thyme under the twine to cover the pork.

Roast the pork in a roasting pan and start it at this high temperature for 20 minutes to get a good sear on the roast. Then turn the oven down to 350°F, and baste from time to time with any pan drippings. If the pan seems dry, pour in the reserved cup of brine for basting. Cook approximately 20 minutes per pound, or to an internal temperature of 150°F when you remove it from the oven—it will continue to cook another 10 or so degrees while resting.

1 New Mexico or guajillo chile, toasted in a dry pan until it puffs up, seeded, and torn into small pieces, or 1 teaspoon dried red chile flakes
8 sprigs rosemary
6 sprigs thyme

for the pork
1 boneless pork roast (about 4 pounds), tied
Olive oil, for rubbing on the roast
Freshly ground black pepper

‹ weighing your options ›

At the point when I turn the oven down to 350°F, I like to toss red-skinned potatoes, cut in half, into the bottom of the roasting pan. They soak up all the pan drippings and get very well seasoned from the brine. A fruit chutney or relish with its sweet-and-sour tanginess is also a wonderful accompaniment. Try the Cranberry Relish with Green Chiles and Kumquat (page 272) or the Grated Apple and Horseradish Cream (page 275). As a side dish, I like to serve this with Roasted Cauliflower Gratin (page 240) or Black Pepper and Parsley Spaetzle (page 252).

Garlic-Studded Leg of Lamb
in Red Chile and Cumin Crust

Every cook should have a roast leg of lamb recipe in his or her repertoire. Lamb is one of the few animals still raised in the old-fashioned
way: lots of roaming around in grassy meadows—not tied up in
dreary feeding pens. Generally, the smaller the lamb, the sweeter and
milder the flavor. Most bone-in legs range between five and seven
pounds. By studding the leg with garlic and rosemary, you end up
with a roast that is perfumed throughout. A spicy rub of ancho chile
and cumin forms a wonderfully flavorful and crisp crust.

SERVES 6 (WITH LEFTOVERS)

**for the red chile and
cumin crust**

⅓ cup freshly ground
     cumin*

¼ cup freshly ground
     coriander seed*

¼ cup ancho chile powder*

Grated zest and juice of
     1 orange

½ cup olive oil

*There's no need to toast the
whole spices before grinding,
since they'll toast in the oven
while the lamb cooks.

prepare the crust
Mix together the spices, zest, juice, and olive oil to form a paste.

prepare the leg of lamb
Make up to 24 small slits all over the leg of lamb, concentrating on
the thicker, meatier part of the leg. Depending on the leg, sometimes
fewer slits are sufficient.

Press a quartered slice of garlic and a small sprig of rosemary into
each slit. The heat of the oven will cause these shallow slits to fuse
together quickly, so there's no real danger of losing precious juices.
Rub the studded leg all over with the spiced paste and let it marinate
in the fridge for 2–4 hours.

‹ leftover alert ›
Serve the lamb the next day, cold, with lemon-mint mayonnaise,
page 270, on a slice of crusty bread. Or have it as part of a
charcuterie plate for the next night's dinner, with an assortment
of olives, chilled vegetables, and sheep's-milk cheeses.

roast the lamb

Preheat oven to 450°F. Season the leg liberally with salt and pepper. Place the leg on a rack in a shallow roasting pan; you'll want to maximize the amount of heated air that can circulate around the leg to make a crisp crust. If you don't have a rack, you can improvise with 2–3 carrots and 2–3 stalks of celery laid side by side to lift the leg out of the pan.

Roast 20 minutes at the high temperature, then turn down the oven to 350°F and roast about an hour, basting with the collected juices every 20 minutes or so. Cook until a meat thermometer registers 138–142°F; the leg will continue to cook up to 10 degrees while it's resting.

Remove the leg to a carving platter to rest 20 minutes; like all roasts, the texture improves with a good interval of resting. See more on resting on page 190.

After resting, carve the lamb across the grain into very thin slices.

Because of the heavy spicing in the crust, the pan drippings are not auspicious for a pan sauce. Instead, I like to serve Fresh Mint and Coriander Sauce (page 271) with the lamb. You can add a side of Coconut-Simmered Fingerling Potatoes (page 251), Quinoa Salad with Pine Nuts, Dried Cherries, and Basil (page 248), or Orange and Radish Salad with Mint (page 229) for a lighter option.

for the leg of lamb

1 leg of lamb (6–7 pounds), bone in

6 cloves garlic, cut into quarters

1 large branch rosemary, leaves pulled off the main branch into small sprigs

Salt and pepper

Chef's Trick: In lieu of a meat thermometer, an old cook's trick is to insert a thin bladed knife or carving fork into the fattest part of the roast, let it sit there for 15 seconds, pull it out, and immediately press the middle of the probe to just under your bottom lip. If it is cool, the roast is rare, if it is warm to hot, it is medium rare to medium, and very hot means it's well done.

Spiced Lamb Meatballs in Eggplant "Leaves"

I have the good fortune to belong to a member-owned and -operated food coop here in Brooklyn. It's a unique place that dabbles in delicacies like smoked salmon and duck liver—all from creatures raised organically and sustainably. I occasionally run across a shipment of ground lamb from the Catskills region of New York State, and I snap some right up. I love Middle Eastern spices with ground lamb, so I season it heartily and shape it into small meatballs that I broil and wrap in thin slices of roasted eggplant. The wrapped meatballs are then topped with a piquant pomegranate and coriander yogurt sauce and popped into the waiting mouths of my family. I've found these meatballs good to serve as cocktail hors d'oeuvres—the eggplant leaves make them easy finger food.

SERVES 6

prepare the meatballs

Fold together the ground lamb, feta, garlic, scallions, ginger, coriander, cumin, chiles, cilantro, salt, pepper, and nutmeg in a bowl. Let flavors develop by resting the meat in the fridge while you roast the eggplant and make the yogurt sauce.

When ready to broil the meatballs, pinch off a small piece of the lamb mixture and sauté it in a drop or two of olive oil. This is the only way to taste for seasoning. Cook the pinch of lamb mixture until just pink inside and taste. Then add more salt and pepper if needed. Once you have seasoned the meat, shape it out into 24–36 small meatballs.

make the eggplant "leaves"

Preheat the broiler. I use a plastic Japanese mandoline to cut the eggplant into very thin, 1/8-inch slices, but a steady hand and a sharp knife will do the trick too. Once you have sliced the eggplant thin, cut the slices into roughly 1 1/2 inches wide by 5 inches long. This size will allow for shrinkage when the eggplant cooks, and the slice will wrap nicely around the small meatballs. Brush each eggplant strip lightly with olive oil and season with salt and pepper. Roast under the broiler on the second shelf from the top to avoid burning the thin slices. When the eggplant is browned and tender, it's ready. Let it cool before handling.

‹ weighing your options ›

When serving these as a main course, I pair them with the Macadamia Nut Couscous on page 243, and an exotic-tasting side salad like Orange and Radish Salad with Mint, page 229, or just some simply steamed rice.

for the lamb meatballs

1 1/2 pounds ground lamb (if you can't find ground lamb, you can buy lamb shoulder to grind at home)

3 ounces French feta*

1 clove garlic, minced

2 scallions, minced (white and a little of green part too)

2 teaspoons grated fresh ginger

1 teaspoon ground coriander seed

2 teaspoons ground cumin seed

2 jalapeños, minced, or 1 serrano chile, minced

Hearty pinch chopped cilantro

Blend of salt, pepper, and a little nutmeg to taste (1 teaspoon to start)

Olive oil, for sautéing test piece of meatball

for the eggplant "leaves"

2 Japanese or Asian eggplants, or 1 large purple eggplant

*French feta is milder than Greek, and I prefer it in this recipe.

Olive oil as needed for
    roasting
Salt and pepper

for the yogurt sauce
Seeds of 1 pomegranate,* or
    a fine dice of tomato if
    pomegranates are out of
    season
1 cup whole-milk yogurt,
    preferably Greek because
    it's so thick and rich
3 tablespoons minced
    cilantro, plus a few
    whole sprigs for
    garnishing
Salt and pepper

*Pick a pomegranate that feels
heavy for its size. This means the
seeds have ripened and have lots
of delicious juice in them. If
pomegranates are not in season,
you can use a scattering of finely
chopped fresh tomatoes.

make the yogurt sauce
Remove the seeds from the pomegranate: I do this by cutting the fruit
in half and plucking the seeds out from between the papery white
membranes. Don't wear anything that you mind having speckled
with pink dots of pomegranate juice! Stir together the yogurt, the
cilantro, and half the pomegranate seeds in a bowl. Reserve the rest
of the seeds to garnish the plates or platter with.

broil the meatballs
Place the meatballs on a baking sheet in the oven, on the second shelf
down from the top—if you put the meatballs too close to the broiler,
they will overbrown on the outside before cooking through (see note
below). Broil the meatballs until just a little pink inside. This will take
5–8 minutes depending on the size of your meatballs. Remove from
the broiler and rest 2–3 minutes before wrapping with the eggplant
"leaves."

NOTE: If you have an oven with a broiler "drawer," where the
flame is very close to the food, you'll want to bake your meatballs
in the oven at about 400°F instead, because they will burn if you
put them under the intense heat of such a close flame. Bake the
meatballs for 5–8 minutes, depending on size, and if you need to give
them a bit of browning, just pop them under the broiler for a few
seconds.

Wrap a strip of roasted eggplant around each meatball and top
with a half teaspoon or so of the yogurt sauce. Pass around as finger
food or serve 4–6 of them to each person as a main course.

NOTE: These meatballs taste best at room temperature—not too
hot or too chilled. If you have leftovers, bring them to room temperature before devouring.

Wrapping eggplant "leaves" around meatballs

Beef Tenderloin with Marrow Toasts and Spiced Tomato Chutney

Beef tenderloin is a luxurious cut of meat, but it has the reputation of being the triumph of texture over flavor. It's true—it doesn't have the full, beefy flavor of a strip steak or rib eye, but its very mildness makes it a wonderful vehicle for other tastes. I've paired it here with marrow toasts, which amplify the beefiness. Marrow is the fatty, unctuous center of the beef's leg and shoulder bones (femur is the best). Once the marrow is poached and salted, it is as deliciously satisfying as foie gras. The contrasting sweet and tart flavor of the tomato chutney makes this a memorable dish.

SERVES 6

for the marrow toasts

6 ounces marrow, removed from the bones (ask your butcher to do this or scoop it out with a spoon)

2 tablespoons minced shallots

2 tablespoons butter

Small handful chervil and a small handful chives, chopped

2 tablespoons lemon juice

Salt and pepper

6 slices brioche or rich bread like challah

⅔ cup Spiced Tomato Chutney (page 284)

poach the marrow

Cut the marrow into ¼-inch slices and soak in cold water in the fridge for 2 hours to draw off any blood.

Bring 1 quart of salted water (1 teaspoon salt per quart) to a simmer. Remove the marrow from the cold water and slip it into the simmering water. Poach the marrow gently for 2–3 minutes, just until it softens. Drain and chill in the fridge for about 15 minutes.

prepare the marrow butter

Sauté the minced shallots in the butter until softened. Put the cooled marrow and sautéed shallots into the bowl of a food processor with the chervil, chives, lemon juice, salt, and pepper. Process until smooth, scraping down the sides of the bowl once or twice. To serve, toast the brioche and spread with the room-temperature marrow mixture. If you've made the marrow ahead, just bring it to room temperature before serving. Garnish with a dollop of the Spiced Tomato Chutney and a sprinkle of coarse sea salt; I use sel gris.

roast the beef

Preheat oven to 450°F. Rub the beef all over with the olive oil, season liberally with salt and pepper, place it on a rack over a baking sheet to allow even airflow over and around the tenderloin, and roast without turning for 30 minutes.

Let the roast rest at least 10 minutes before slicing and you'll be rewarded with juicy, medium-rare beef. If you prefer your meat medium, cook for 5–8 more minutes. Serve with the marrow toasts.

for the beef

1 beef tenderloin, about 4 pounds, trimmed and tied
4 tablespoons olive oil
Salt and pepper

‹ weighing your options ›

I like to serve this with a variety of sides, such as Braised Belgian Endive with Citrus Cream and Walnuts (page 241) or Creamed Spinach with Sherried Currants (page 239). For a starch, try Celery Root Puree (page 232) or Porcini Potato Gratin (page 250). Another delicious garnish to this beef dish is to make a Roquefort or Stilton butter in place of the beef marrow: Process 3 ounces of Roquefort or Stilton and 3 ounces of softened butter in the food processor. Radishes are a natural complement to the blue cheese, so I pickle them lightly and serve in place of the tomato chutney. You'll find a recipe for Pickled Radishes recipe on page 265.

Beef Short Ribs Braised in Amarone with Dried Cherries and Black Olives

12 beef short ribs, on the
  bone
Salt and pepper
Scant pinch of ground cloves
3 tablespoons olive oil
1 Spanish onion, diced fine
1 small bulb fennel, diced
  fine, or celery, about
  ¾ cup
1 carrot, peeled and diced
  fine
2 tablespoons ancho chile
  powder, or 2 tablespoons
  tomato paste
1 bottle (750 ml) Amarone*
6 cups veal stock or water
Sachet of 8–12 coriander
  seeds, 1 strip orange
  peel, 3–4 whole cloves,
  8–12 black peppercorns,
  a small fistful of parsley
  stems, and 1 bay leaf

*If you have a hard time finding
Amarone, you can substitute
another full-bodied red wine and
add ½ cup of dried cherries to the
braising liquid to approximate the
fruitiness of this big wine.

John Bittici, the former owner of a delightfully dilapidated Greenwich Village speakeasy, introduced me to Amarone—an unusual Italian wine. After the first sip, I was a fan; I didn't know that a wine could have such depth and layers of flavor, with the richness and complexity of a good port. But Amarone is not a fortified wine (that is, a wine that has distilled alcohol added to it); it's all in the treatment of the grapes. The method is called "passito," whereby the grapes are dried in a cool area for up to four months to shrivel them. This concentrates the flavor and produces a very fruity wine. Amarone means "strongly bitter," but with a little guidance from your wine merchant you will find one that doesn't have this bitterness, and is instead full of lush fruit. Here are a few producers with very good reputations: Bertani, Tommaso Bussola, and Quintarelli. I enhance the fruity flavors by garnishing the sauce with dried cherries and oil-cured black olives, which are fruity in their own way.

A traditional gremolata is minced garlic, lemon zest, and minced parsley, scattered over an osso buco or other long-simmered dish to perk up the flavors and refresh the palate. This more baroque gremolata functions in the same way, but also echoes the deep fruity flavors of the Amarone.

SERVES 6

Preheat oven to 325°F. Season the ribs on all sides with the salt, pepper, and ground cloves. Heat the olive oil in a large casserole dish and brown the ribs until golden. If using water instead of veal stock, sprinkle the ribs with 2–3 tablespoons of flour—this will help thicken the sauce as it cooks. (Veal stock has enough natural gelatin to thicken the sauce on its own.)

Remove the beef from the casserole and let it rest on a platter. Pour out all but approximately 2 tablespoons of fat from the pan, then sauté the onion, fennel, and carrot over medium heat until lightly browned—about 4 minutes. Sprinkle the ancho powder over the vegetables, or dab on the tomato paste, if using. Cook the ancho or paste another 2–3 minutes. Pour in the Amarone, scraping up any fond (stuck-on bits) from the pan. Reduce the wine by half. Return the ribs and any juices that accumulated on the platter to the pan and add enough veal stock or water or a combination to come ⅔ of the way up the ribs. Add the herb sachet. Bring to a boil, immediately reduce to a simmer, cover tightly, and place the whole thing into your hot oven. Cook the ribs for a total of 2–2½ hours (until the ribs are very tender—your fork should easily pierce the braised ribs), turning the ribs in their cooking liquid halfway through. Let the ribs cool in their cooking liquid; they will stay moist and continue to exchange flavors with the broth as they cool.

make the dried cherry and olive gremolata while the ribs are braising

Fold together the cherries, olives, garlic, zest, and minced herbs.

When ready to serve, remove the ribs from the pan, keep warm, and reduce the broth until thick enough to coat a spoon. Pour sauce over and around the ribs and garnish with the gremolata.

‹ weighing your options ›

A dish as savory as this one is often best paired with a relatively plain starch or vegetable. I'm partial to either Celery Root Puree (page 232) or Porcini Potato Gratin (page 250). If you're feeling ambitious, a simple risotto garnished with plentiful shavings of Parmigiano-Reggiano is divine; you might want to try the Wild Leek Risotto on page 246. A green vegetable in season, lightly steamed, helps lighten up the meal.

for the dried cherry and olive gremolata

½ cup dried cherries, minced

½ cup oil-cured black olives, pitted and minced

1 teaspoon minced garlic

1 tablespoon grated lemon zest

2 tablespoons minced cilantro or parsley

Using a Microplane to grate lemon peel

Grilled Flank Steak
in Smoked Chile and Lime Marinade

A nicely charred flank steak and Mom's pasta with pesto made from basil plucked straight from the garden is my brother Michael's favorite birthday dinner. Although exposed through his travels to some pretty spectacular dishes, this remains his annual request. I think it has something to do with his love of camping. He's known to pack up a tent and a well-stocked cooler and head for the hills for a few days when civilization gets on his nerves. And flank steak is great camping food—it can be marinating while you drive, hike, or row to your campsite. When you arrive, build your fire and lay the steak on the grill for just three to four minutes per side (rare–medium rare), and you have a stress-free and delicious first-night dinner. (It is equally stress-free on the grill at home.) After it has rested a few minutes, it is absolutely critical to slice the steak very thin, across the grain at a slight downward angle or bias. Otherwise flank can be a very tough cut. The smoked chile and lime are my idea. But since my brother will teasingly accuse me of being a "food snob" whenever I get too fancy with my recipes, the fact that he loves this one means I'm right on target. Besides, as I feel compelled to remind him, I'm the chef.

SERVES 4–6

for the steak
1 flank steak (2–2½ pounds)
Salt and freshly ground black pepper

prepare the flank steak
Score the flank steak on one side by making shallow diagonal slices about an inch apart in both directions to create a diamond pattern on the surface. This scoring helps the marinade to penetrate the firm muscle and prevent it from curling up when placed on the grill.

prepare the smoked chile and lime marinade

Stir or whisk together all the marinade ingredients in a bowl and spread evenly over both sides of the steak. This is a strong marinade and will do its job in 2–3 hours. If you leave the marinade on much longer, the acid in the lime juice will begin to "cook" the meat, making it gray in color and too sour-tasting.

When ready to grill (or broil), pat the marinade off with paper towels, season well with salt and pepper, and lay the steak onto the hottest part of the grill (or under the broiler). You can rotate the steak by 45-degree intervals once or twice so the surface will char evenly. I'm not a stickler for perfect grill marks; I'm more interested in getting even cooking. After 3 minutes, turn the steak over and cook for another 3, making the same rotations on the second side. Rest the meat for 6–10 minutes before slicing. (For more on resting, see the box on page 190.) Carve the steak across the grain into very thin slices.

The flank is notoriously tough when cut too thick. Think of deli meat slices—almost that thin. Serve with German Butterball Potato Salad with Dill, page 249, or your own basil pesto on thin noodles like linguine or spaghettini.

for the smoked chile and lime marinade

2 tablespoons chipotle puree (see page 204)

Juice of 2 limes

2 tablespoons Dijon mustard

3 small or 2 large cloves garlic, mashed to a paste with 1 teaspoon salt

1 tablespoon freshly ground cumin

1 tablespoon minced rosemary

½ cup olive oil

Pan-Roasted New York Strip Steak
with Balsamic Vinegar

One of the fringe benefits of being a professional cook is that you're around a lot of talented people who are prone to sharing their brilliant discoveries with you. This dish is the result of such generosity and a little bit of serendipity—a priceless combination. The late Jan Sendel and I were working together one night at Mesa Grill. After cooking for our standard four hundred people that night, Jan noticed that the pan he had perched on the edge of the grill to rest his steaks on all night had developed a really lovely fond (stuck-on meat juices). He decided to loosen the fond with a hearty splash of balsamic vinegar. Then he swirled in a knob of butter and poured the sauce over an end cut of steak (a traditional cook's snack). He crowed over his discovery, and we all tasted a slice. It was indeed the best steak sauce ever. I use this basic technique whenever I want a straightforward steak with a simple but perfect sauce.

SERVES 4

2 tablespoons olive oil
Four 1-inch-thick New York strip steaks (8–10 ounces each)
Salt and freshly ground black pepper
2/3 cup real balsamic vinegar (the label should read "Aceto Balsamico Tradizionale" or "made in the traditional style")
4 tablespoons butter, chilled and cut in small pieces

Heat a heavy skillet, large enough to comfortably fit all four steaks, or use two pans. Add olive oil to just coat the pan in a thin film. Season the steaks liberally with salt and pepper. When the pan is hot, add the steaks and sear over high heat for 1–2 minutes on the first side before turning down the heat to medium. Continue to cook on the first side for a total of 4 minutes. Turn the steaks over and cook the second side—3 minutes for a medium-rare temperature, 4 minutes for medium. These times are based on a 1-inch-thick steak, so adjust times downward if steaks are thinner.

Remove the steaks from the pan and let them rest 5–8 minutes on a carving platter. Meanwhile, with the pan over medium-low heat, pour in the vinegar. Use a wooden spoon or a whisk to loosen the fond. When the vinegar has reduced to a syrup, whisk in the pieces of cold butter. Add a drop or two of water if the sauce becomes too thick. Taste for seasoning, and add salt and pepper if needed. Pour the sauce into a sauce boat or directly onto the steaks. I prefer to leave this steak unsliced—it stays warmer. Serve 1 steak per person.

‹ weighing your options ›

This dish pairs up nicely with Sesame-Roasted Green Beans (page 237) or Sautéed Wild Mushrooms (page 233). For more of a substantial meal, add Risotto with Oven-Cured Tomatoes (page 244) or Macadamia Nut Couscous (page 243).

With Michael

Chef's Trick: Whenever you want the fond, or stuck-on juices, to be part of the sauce, you need to match the size of the pan carefully to the size of the food that will be browning in it. Too much extra room will cause the fond to burn and turn bitter, making it unusable for the sauce. Too little room, and the food will steam and not brown. Ideally you want to have ¼–½ inch of space between the pieces of food and around them at the edge of the pan. Use high heat at the beginning of the browning process to prevent the food sticking to the pan, but once this is accomplished, moderate the heat to medium—for the same reason, to again avoid burning the fond.

Meat and Poultry   221

Venison with Fox Grape Poivrade

You don't have to wait until the fall hunting season to enjoy venison; it's raised year-round and is a deliciously lean and flavorful meat. This particular recipe is inspired by the fall harvest of wild fox grapes (a close cousin to Concord grapes), but I've included some seasonal variations at the end of the recipe. As children, my brother and sister and I used to swing Tarzan-style (forget Jane) through the thick ropey vines of a patch of fox grapes near our house. Both fox grapes and Concord grapes are super grapey—perfect for grape jelly, but disastrous if you try to make wine from them. The grapes make a lively poivrade—a traditional game sauce that is usually made with vinegar, white wine, and heavily seasoned with poivre (crushed peppercorns).

Our good friends Peter and Joann Langrock manage to get their hands on some wild venison from time to time. Sometimes it's a buck offered as barter for Peter's expert legal advice, sometimes it's just happenstance, like on the frigid and dark November evening when my parents' housekeeper, Melanie Pratt, was heading home and her headlights picked out a deer lying in our driveway. Knowing that my parents were just then en route to the airport to fly to Europe, she called Peter Langrock. Someone had shot a doe during muzzle-loading season (after the rifle and bow seasons are over), and she had staggered onto our property before collapsing. Apparently the hunter had lost her trail. Peter called the game warden and described the circumstances, and the warden very reasonably told him to go ahead and dress it out—no sense letting the poor animal go to waste. So in the bitter cold, Peter field-dressed the deer and hung it from the rafters of our barn. Hanging is necessary to tenderize the meat of such an active animal—it also develops the flavor, as the meat concentrates a bit by drying.

Later that month, Michael, Luke, and I were up for a long weekend. We were treated to a well-chosen cut from this very venison at the Langrocks' farmhouse in Salisbury. When Peter and Joann cook for friends, there's always something on the menu that they shot, caught, raised, or plucked right out of their fields. What could be better than to be a guest at a well-set table with properly cellared wines, local delicacies, and accomplished storytellers? I'm always consulted over how long to sauté the deep red medallions of venison while Joann heats her well-seasoned cast-iron skillets and Peter fixes the second round of martinis.

SERVES 6

prepare the fox grape poivrade

Toss the cinnamon, coriander, juniper, and pepper into a warmed skillet over medium heat, shaking now and then, and toast until fragrant, about 3–4 minutes. Place the toasted spices along with the grapes, orange peel, ginger, and 1–2 tablespoons cold water in a saucepan over medium-low heat. Simmer, stirring occasionally, until the grapes deflate and cook down to a thick puree. This will take about 20 minutes. Taste for seasoning and add a pinch of sugar, if needed, to round out the grape flavor. Pass the puree through a sieve to remove the pits, skins, and spices.

In a medium-heavy saucepan, sauté the shallots in the butter until they are golden brown. Pour in the wine or port and cook down to reduce by half. Add the veal stock (or demi-glace and water) and the grape puree. Simmer while skimming from time to time, until the sauce coats the back of a spoon. Season to taste with salt and freshly grated nutmeg. Hold the sauce until ready to serve. (See Chef's Trick on next page.)

cook the venison

Cut the venison across the grain into ½-inch-thick medallions. Pound the medallions lightly to achieve the uniform thickness—this is so important for even cooking. Heat two cast-iron or other heavy skillets over medium-high heat. Season the medallions with salt and pepper and add 2 tablespoons of butter to each skillet. When the butter has melted, quickly slip the medallions into the pans before

for the fox grape poivrade

1 stick cinnamon

10–12 coriander seeds, lightly crushed

8–10 juniper berries, lightly crushed

8–10 black peppercorns, lightly crushed

1 pint fox or Concord grapes, stems removed

2 strips orange peel

1 teaspoon grated fresh ginger

A pinch of sugar, if needed, to correct for excessive tartness

2 shallots, thinly sliced

1 tablespoon butter

½ cup full-bodied red wine (like a Côte-du-Rhône) or a ruby port

2 cups veal stock (see Appendix), or 1 cup commercial demi-glace plus 1 cup water

Salt and freshly grated
    nutmeg

for the venison
2½–3 pounds trimmed
    venison from the hind
    leg or the loin (the leg is
    less expensive but is
    somewhat less tender)
Salt and freshly ground
    black pepper
4–6 tablespoons butter,
    as needed

the butter browns too much. (When the meat hits the pan, the temperature will drop and you'll have no problem with burning the butter. Just act quickly, but safely.) You won't want to cook these medallions much longer than 1 minute per side. Venison is very lean, and will be tough and dry if cooked beyond medium-rare.

Rest the cooked medallions on a warm platter for 2–3 minutes. Collect any juices from the platter and add them to the poivrade to fortify its flavor, then reduce the sauce lightly again to coat a spoon. Serve the medallions on heated plates—they are so thin that they won't stay hot for long without some help. Dress each plate with an ounce or two of the warm sauce.

Chef's Trick: Rich, reduced sauces like this one can easily form a gelatinous skin, which mars the silky texture you're aiming for. When holding a sauce, keep it warm in a shallow water bath and cover the container with a piece of plastic wrap to prevent a "skin" from forming on the surface.

In cooler months, I like to serve the venison with my Celery Root Puree
(page 232) and a garnish of Glazed Chestnuts (page 234).
Here are some warmer weather ideas for venison:

Spring: Medallions of Venison with Morel and Asparagus Fricassee

Cook the venison medallions as above. For the fricassee, parcook about
$\frac{1}{2}$ pound of asparagus—cut into 1-inch lengths in boiling, salted water for
2 minutes, shock them in an ice bath, and drain. Cut about $\frac{1}{4}$ pound of morels
in half and sauté in a little butter with a minced shallot until lightly browned
and tender. Deglaze the pan with a dash of cognac and pour in some heavy
cream and a tablespoon or so of veal stock or demi-glace if you have some.
Simmer the sauce to thicken lightly, add the cooked asparagus to warm
through, and season with salt and pepper. Serve the fricassee under the
sautéed medallions.

**Summer: Grilled Venison Chops Wrapped in Applewood-Smoked Bacon
with Lemon-Herb Butter**

For a change of pace, I like to grill venison chops in summertime. Marinate the
chops for an hour or so with a dash of red wine vinegar, minced thyme,
rosemary, and olive oil. Lightly blanch the bacon in water to remove some of
the smokiness. Wrap a slice around the circumference of each chop and
secure it with a toothpick. Season the meat with salt and pepper and grill
3 minutes per side, until medium rare. Top each chop with a tablespoon or so
of room-temperature lemon-herb compound butter (see page 175). Hopefully,
this comes from your stash of frozen compound butters ready for just this kind
of thing. Serve with Sweet Corn and Fava Bean Succotash (page 230) or
Summer Tomato and Sweet Onion Salad (page 114).

Orange and Radish Salad with Mint

Sweet Corn and Fava Bean Succotash

Fennel Kraut

Celery Root Puree

Sautéed Wild Mushrooms

Glazed Chestnuts

Squash Roasted in Foil Packages

Sugar Snap Peas with Browned Shallots, Pancetta, and Mint

Sesame-Roasted Green Beans

Sweet and Hot Peppers with Almonds

Creamed Spinach with Sherried Currants

Roasted Cauliflower Gratin

Braised Belgian Endive with Citrus Cream and Walnuts

Baby Brussels Sprouts with Bacon, Chestnuts, and Pomegranate Seeds

Macadamia Nut Couscous

Risotto with Oven-Cured Tomatoes

Wild Leek Risotto

Quinoa Salad with Pine Nuts, Dried Cherries, and Basil

German Butterball Potato Salad with Dill

Porcini Potato Gratin

Coconut-Simmered Fingerling Potatoes

Black Pepper and Parsley Spaetzle

Spaetzle Gratin with Browned Onions, Gruyère, and Ham

VEGETABLES AND SIDE DISHES

Side dishes are like the accessories to a great outfit—you can do without them, but why should you, when they can add so much pizzazz to an otherwise ordinary ensemble? To take the fashion analogy one step further, you can mix and match with the seasons. In cooler weather, a simple roast chicken is transformed into an elegant dinner with the addition of Squash Roasted in Foil Packages or Sautéed Wild Mushrooms. In the summer, you might choose to pair the same bird with Sweet Corn and Fava Bean Succotash or Sesame-Roasted Green Beans. Whatever you're serving, a thoughtful pairing with a side dish or two makes the meal special. I've culled through my long list of recipes and offer my favorites here. All the seasons are represented, and I've included suggestions for seasonal variations to many of the recipes. These dishes are based on ingredients that are easy to find and simple to prepare in a reasonable amount of time.

I hope that a few of the techniques become part of the way you cook and that you'll want to experiment once you're comfortable with the methods. For example, roasting firm vegetables like winter squash in foil packages is easily adapted to root vegetables like beets, celery root, turnips, sweet potatoes, and the like. The idea is to infuse the vegetables with a highly seasoned vapor created from flavored butter or oil, herbs, and spices that are trapped together in the tightly wrapped foil package. The possible combinations are endless.

Another useful technique is one I learned at the first restaurant I worked in, Al Forno, in Providence, Rhode Island. One of the two pieces of kitchen equipment we had in the tiny space was a pizza oven, which we soon realized had far more ambitious uses than just pizza. In fact, the pizza went on the wood-fired grill; it was the vegetables that went into the pizza oven! I became addicted to those crispy, sweet vegetables sizzling on the metal trays that I shuffled around the oven. I needed the concentration and quickness of a Manhattan parking garage attendant to keep all the various trays of vegetables and pastas in the "first in, first out" order. I learned to use all my senses to tell when the food was ready, judging by the color and aroma of the vegetables and the slow, redolent boil of the cream sauce around the browning pastas. It is this high-heat method that I use to roast the Sesame-Roasted Green Beans in this section. The beans are roasted at 450°F to quickly caramelize the natural sugars of the vegetable, and then they are dressed in a vinaigrette to balance out their sweetness. The idea is to quickly cook the vegetables so they don't dry out, while at the same time accentuating their flavor by deeply roasting them. This method works equally well with asparagus, sweet peppers, brussels sprouts, carrots, and even potatoes for quick oven fries.

At work in the restaurant

Orange and Radish Salad with Mint

I serve this side salad in the winter months, when its lovely color and sweetness brighten up the long, dark days. It's a wonderful accompaniment to simply grilled or roasted fish or a lamb dish. Play with a variety of oranges and their cousins: blood oranges, Seville oranges, clementines, tangerines, tangelos—they all work well in this recipe.

SERVES 6

Use a small knife to remove the peel and all the pith from the oranges. Slice them crosswise into ¼-inch-thick rounds, reserving any juices. Arrange the slices on a platter in slightly overlapping layers. Scatter the onions and radishes evenly over the oranges. Whisk together the vinegar, reserved orange juices, and oil in a small bowl. Spoon this dressing over the salad and garnish with grains of the coarse sea salt, the pepper, and the freshly cut mint.

6 oranges

½ red onion, thinly sliced

1 dozen red or pink radishes, thinly sliced or quartered for extra crunch

1 tablespoon red wine vinegar

2 tablespoons extra virgin olive oil

Coarse sea salt to taste

Freshly ground black pepper to taste

Small handful mint leaves, chiffonade

‹ weighing your options ›
In warmer months, I like to substitute avocado or thinly sliced raw zucchini for the oranges.

Sweet Corn and Fava Bean Succotash

Succotash is a Native American dish from the Narragansett Indians of southern New England. It usually consists of corn with lima beans, but I find limas too starchy with the corn and prefer favas, which are creamier. But you can substitute green beans or even snap peas in this dish.

SERVES 6

3 tablespoons butter

1 leek, white part only, cleaned and thinly sliced

6–8 shiitake mushroom or white mushroom caps, cleaned and thinly sliced

4–6 ears sweet corn, kernels cut off the cobs

1 cup shelled fava beans, blanched and removed from the inner shell

3 slices bacon, cut into ¼-inch dice and rendered until crisp (or use leftover Smithfield ham or any other smoked country ham)

Small handful basil leaves, cut into thin ribbons or torn by hand

Salt and pepper

Freshly grated nutmeg to taste

Melt 2 tablespoons of the butter in a skillet. Add the leeks and cook slowly over low heat until the leeks soften. Increase the heat to medium, add the mushrooms, and cook until they have wilted, about 4 minutes. Stir in the corn and immediately add about 2 tablespoons cold water—this will prevent the corn from browning, and the resulting steam will quickly cook the corn. Fold in the fava beans and the crisped bacon, and cook to heat through. Swirl in the last tablespoon of butter with the basil and season to taste with salt, pepper, and nutmeg.

Fennel Kraut

Kraut means "cabbage" in German, and typically the cabbage is pickled into sauerkraut. This dish borrows the cabbage technique for fennel instead of cabbage. With its natural anise flavor, it makes a wonderful accent to simply grilled salmon, chicken, or lamb.

SERVES 6

Shave the fennel as thinly as possible. (I use a Japanese mandoline, but a very sharp knife will also work.) Place the fennel in a nonreactive bowl and stir in the salt, sugar, vinegar, orange juice and orange zest, and ground anise or fennel seed. Cover and let the fennel marinate at room temperature for 2 hours. Drain off the liquid that has accumulated at the bottom of the bowl but don't squeeze the fennel. Garnish with the minced herbs just before serving. The fennel will keep in the fridge for 10 days. If you plan to store some of the fennel, sprinkle the fresh herbs only over the part that you're serving. If the herbs are added to the kraut all at once, it will turn an unlovely shade of khaki within an hour or so.

2 bulbs fennel, washed and trimmed of any brown spots

2 tablespoons salt

1 tablespoon sugar

½ cup rice vinegar or white wine vinegar

Zest and juice of 1 orange

½ teaspoon ground anise or fennel seed

2 tablespoons minced fresh tarragon or cilantro (optional)

Front: tomatillos, endive, and kumquats. Back: fennel, endive, and fingerling potatoes. Stalks of lemongrass in between.

Celery Root Puree

I just love this gnarled and ugly root! It's the underdog of the vegetable world. It has its very own texture and flavor; it is not as starchy as most roots, and has a distinctly piquant taste. To pump up the body of the puree, I cook the celery root and apple in water first, then transfer the root and the apple to a hot oven to dry out before being pureed. This step really adds a nice creaminess to the final dish. I used to serve this at Quilty's with my Venison with Fox Grape Poivrade (page 222) and Glazed Chestnuts (page 234). Very few of my guests could name the snowy white puree on their plates, but they sure loved it.

SERVES 6

½ lemon
1 large celery root (about 1 pound)
1 firm, sweet apple—Fuji, Gala, or Empire—peeled and quartered
⅓ cup heavy cream
2 tablespoons butter, softened
Salt and pepper
Freshly grated nutmeg

Preheat oven to 350°F. Prepare a bowl of acidulated water by squeezing the ½ lemon into 2 quarts of cold water. This will prevent the celery root from browning while you prepare it for cooking. Peel the celery root with a sharp paring knife. Remove any dark blemishes. Cut the root into 1-inch cubes and drop immediately into the acidulated water.

Bring 3 quarts of salted water to a boil. Add the celery root and the apple and cook until both are tender—about 15–20 minutes. Drain and lay out the celery root and apple in a single layer on a baking sheet. Bake the root and apple until no more steam rises from them, about 5 minutes.

Heat the cream and butter in a saucepan. Transfer the root and apple to a food processor, and puree until reasonably smooth. Pour in the cream and the butter and process until very smooth, about 4 minutes. Season with salt, pepper, and nutmeg. Serve hot. If you need to hold the puree for a while, cover it in plastic wrap and place in a hot-water bath over low heat.

Sautéed Wild Mushrooms

Many varieties of wild mushrooms are now cultivated, and hence are available year-round, but certain stubborn species defy the hand of man, and these are the kind I like best. Morels and porcini in the spring, puffballs in the summer, chanterelles and hen-of-the-woods in the late summer and fall, and of course truffles in the winter. What are sold as premium or exotic mushrooms are very good too: shiitakes, oyster mushrooms, cultivated hen-of-the-woods, and portobellos. I'm offering a recipe here that can be dressed up with the addition of Madeira and veal stock for a more elegant side dish, but it is also perfectly delicious without these refinements.

SERVES 6

Use a large skillet or two smaller ones—you want to brown the mushrooms and not steam them, so you don't want to overcrowd your pan. Heat the olive oil and butter over medium-high heat until the butter sizzles. Quickly add the sliced mushrooms and toss or stir the pan once to coat them in the fat. Leave the mushrooms undisturbed for 2–3 minutes, allowing them to brown. Scatter the shallots over the mushrooms and stir or flip the mushrooms by shaking the pan firmly to brown the second side for 3–4 minutes more. Season with salt, pepper, and thyme. If using, pour in the Madeira and let it reduce for 1 minute, then pour in the veal stock. Let the sauce reduce until it coats a spoon, and serve.

1 tablespoon olive oil
2 tablespoons butter
1 pound mixed wild or cultivated mushrooms, trimmed and sliced into 1/4-inch-thick pieces
2 shallots, peeled and thinly sliced
Salt and pepper
2 teaspoons minced fresh thyme
2 tablespoons Madeira (optional)
1/4 cup veal stock (optional; see Appendix, or use good-quality commercial stock)

My mother with a big bag of morels

Glazed Chestnuts

I find freshly roasted chestnuts irresistible—especially when offered in a little paper cone on the streets of Paris or Vienna. But, truth be told, I've always found the chestnuts a little dry and crumbly. So I cook them first in water to remove the skins, then glaze them in a sweet syrup to ensure that they're creamy and delicious. Serve these with venison, pork, pork sausages, goose, duck, or turkey.

SERVES 6

1½ pounds fresh chestnuts
1 cup chicken stock (see Appendix, or use organic, low-sodium boxed)
½ cup dark brown sugar
½ cup Madeira or sherry (optional)
2 strips orange peel
2 tablespoons butter

Bring 3 quarts of lightly salted water to a boil. Drop in the whole chestnuts and cook them until a fork can pierce the shells—about 20 minutes. Strain and allow to cool in a bowl. When they are cool enough to handle, but still warm, carefully pierce the hard outer shell with the tip of a paring knife. Peel off the shell and the inner brown skin. If the chestnuts cool too much, reheat them in the water to make this chore easier. When all the chestnuts have been peeled, place them in a shallow skillet with the chicken stock, brown sugar, Madeira or sherry (if using), and orange peel. Bring to a simmer and cook until a syrupy glaze forms over the chestnuts, shaking the pan occasionally, for a total of about 15 minutes. Remove the orange peel, swirl in the butter, and serve.

Squash Roasted in Foil Packages

The foil packages create a flavorful steam bath for the squash. You can use any compound butters you have in the freezer, herbs on hand, and whole spices like star anise and cinnamon. I love to design each package like a small still life—they look so beautiful both before and after they've been in the oven. I prefer kabocha squash for its creamy texture and wonderful flavor, but other varieties are fine substitutes: acorn, butternut, and Hubbard squashes, or even sweet potatoes. The maple syrup, which is wood-fired, adds a rich smoky flavor to the squash that is a sweet complement to the spiced smokiness of the chipotles—smoked jalapeño peppers.

SERVES 6

Preheat oven to 400°F. Lay the sheets of foil out on a work surface. In the center of each piece, place 2 cups of diced squash, 1 tablespoon butter, 1 tablespoon maple syrup, ½ teaspoon chipotle puree (if using), 1 stick cinnamon, 2 strips orange peel, 3 pieces star anise or cloves, and 1 sprig of thyme or sage. Season the contents of the packages with salt and pepper. Squeeze the juice from the peeled orange evenly over each package. Carefully fold the foil to enclose the contents, making sure that no opening exists for the steam to escape. If your foil is thin, use a double layer. Place the packages on a baking sheet and into the hot oven. Roast the squash for 25–30 minutes. Serve along with the juices that have accumulated in the package, discarding the whole spices, herbs, and orange peel.

‹ weighing your options ›
For the fall: Fennel with Orange Peel, Saffron, and Pernod,
or Carrots with Brown Sugar and Cardamom
For the spring: Peaches or Nectarines with Whole Vanilla Beans
For the summer: Fresh Figs with Port and Star Anise

3 sheets of heavy-duty foil wrap, each sheet approximately 12 inches by 15 inches

6 cups 1-inch-cubed squash (approximately 2 pounds)

3 tablespoons butter

3 tablespoons maple syrup

1½ teaspoons chipotle puree (optional; see page 204)

3 sticks cinnamon

6 strips orange peel and juice of the orange

6 pieces whole star anise, or 6 whole cloves

3 sprigs thyme or sage

Salt and freshly ground black pepper

Vegetables and Side Dishes 235

Sugar Snap Peas
with Browned Shallots, Pancetta, and Mint

I find that sugar snaps are the most reliably sweet and tender peas available in the markets. Shell peas are often sold overly mature and thus are too starchy, and snow peas have too much pod and not enough pea. Look for plump shells with no yellowing or browning—be sure to enjoy snacking on a few of them raw before giving the rest up to the recipes.

SERVES 6

1 pound sugar snap peas, strings removed
1 teaspoon olive oil
¼ pound pancetta or bacon, diced small
3 shallots, thinly sliced
1 teaspoon grated lemon zest
2 tablespoons mint or tarragon leaves, freshly minced
1 tablespoon butter
Salt and pepper

Bring 2 quarts of salted water to a boil. Dump the peas into the pot and blanch them for 15 seconds, then refresh them by straining them and running cold water over them. Heat a heavy skillet with the olive oil, add the pancetta, and cook over medium heat until it is half crisp, about 4 minutes. Add the shallots and brown them well. Tip out any excess fat. Stir the blanched peas into the browned shallots and pancetta and cook until warm. Sprinkle in the zest and the herbs, swirl in the butter, and season lightly with salt and pepper.

Sesame-Roasted Green Beans

This dish is loosely based on the Chinese technique of dry-roasting vegetables. There is always some oil used, but it is kept at a minimum. When beans are roasted at a high heat, their natural sugars caramelize and they become wonderfully crisp. You can certainly use a wok if you prefer that to the oven. I dress them while still warm with a sesame vinaigrette and a sprinkle of good sea salt. Be careful—they're addictive! Look for young, thin beans, as they will be sweeter and less starchy than the big ones.

SERVES 6

Preheat oven to 450°F. Toss the beans in a bowl with the olive oil to coat. Lay the beans out in a single layer on a baking sheet, place them in the hot oven, and roast until browned and crispy, about 10 minutes. Transfer the beans to a serving bowl and toss them with the dressing and the sesame seeds, then sprinkle sea salt to taste all over them. Serve warm or at room temperature.

1½ pounds young, thin green beans, stemmed
2 tablespoons olive oil
¼ cup Sesame Vinaigrette (page 262)
2 tablespoons lightly toasted sesame seeds
Sea salt to taste

‹ weighing your options ›
Asparagus is great this way as well, simply dressed with extra virgin olive oil and lemon juice. Quartered baby artichokes can also be roasted at high heat and served with lemon-mint mayonnaise (see page 270). Sliced sweet potatoes can be roasted and sprinkled with cider vinegar and a bit of salt, pepper, and cumin.

Sweet and Hot Peppers with Almonds

This is a side dish that can easily double as a cocktail snack or part of an hors d'oeuvre buffet. Choose various colors of peppers—red, yellow, orange. The lovely visuals and textures of this dish make it a dramatic addition to simply grilled chicken, heartier fish like salmon or tuna, or a frittata for a lunch or light dinner. You can keep these stewed peppers for up to two weeks in the refrigerator.

ABOUT 2 CUPS

½ cup olive oil

4 cloves garlic, thinly sliced

4 sweet peppers of any color—red, orange, or yellow—seeded and sliced into ½-inch-wide strips

2 red serrano chiles or red jalapeños, seeded and thinly sliced (green are fine as well—the red color is more for presentation)

1 tablespoon grated lemon zest

2 tablespoons lemon juice

½ cup sliced almonds, toasted

Salt to taste

Heat the olive oil over low heat in a heavy skillet. Add the garlic, sweet peppers, and chiles. Stir well to coat all the vegetables in oil. Cook very slowly, stirring occasionally, until peppers are very soft—about 45 minutes. Stir in the lemon zest and juice and the toasted almonds. Season lightly with salt. Serve at room temperature.

Creamed Spinach with Sherried Currants

Steakhouses of the world—eat your hearts out! This is the best creamed spinach ever (if I do say so myself). The whole spinach leaves and sherried currants update the old classic, and you don't feel like you're eating baby food.

SERVES 6

Simmer the heavy cream over medium-low heat until it has reduced by half. Meanwhile, bring 3 quarts of salted water to a boil. Plunge the spinach into the boiling water and quench for 10 seconds. Immediately remove the spinach with a slotted spoon or spider and shock it in an ice bath to stop the cooking. Drain spinach well on paper towels.

Heat the vinegar with ½ cup of water in a small saucepan. Add the currants to the vinegar and water solution and steep over low heat until the currants plump, about 10 minutes. Drain. Melt the butter in a large skillet. Add the drained spinach leaves to the skillet and pour in the reduced heavy cream and the plumped currants. Stir constantly over medium heat until the spinach is hot. Season to taste with salt, pepper, and nutmeg.

1½ cups heavy cream, or coconut milk for a more exotic flavor
2 pounds flat-leaf spinach, washed and stemmed
3 tablespoons aged sherry vinegar
¼ cup dried currants
2 tablespoons butter
Salt and pepper
Freshly grated nutmeg to taste

Roasted Cauliflower Gratin

The humble cauliflower is a surprisingly versatile vegetable. I coax more flavor out of it by roasting it before turning it into an ultra-smooth puree, which is then gratinéed with a mixture of Gruyère and Parmesan. This is a great side dish for roasts, steaks, and chops.

SERVES 6

1 large head cauliflower,
    sliced into ¼-inch-thick
    pieces with some stem
    attached
3 tablespoons melted butter,
    plus 2 tablespoons
    softened butter for the
    puree
½ cup heavy cream
1 cup chicken stock
Salt and pepper
½ cup finely grated Gruyère
¼ cup finely grated
    Parmigiano-Reggiano

Preheat oven to 400°F. Toss the sliced cauliflower with the melted butter to coat. Spread the cauliflower out on a baking sheet and roast for about 20 minutes, or until the cauliflower is a deep golden brown.

Warm the cream and the stock together in a small saucepan. Transfer the roasted cauliflower to a food processor and puree until it is smooth, while slowly pouring in the stock and cream mixture. Season the puree with salt and pepper. Spread the puree out into a 9-by-11, 2-inch-deep casserole dish. Dot the top with the remaining 2 tablespoons of butter and sprinkle evenly with both cheeses. Bake the casserole until the cheese browns, about 10 minutes.

‹ weighing your options ›
Roasted cauliflower can stand up to some assertive flavors. Another variation
I like is to toss the roasted cauliflower (the florets, not the puree) with
2 tablespoons minced capers, ¼ cup golden raisins, 1 teaspoon lemon zest,
1 tablespoon extra virgin olive oil, and 2 tablespoons chopped fresh dill.
Season with salt and pepper and serve warm with chicken or a roast, or serve it at
room temperature as part of an antipasto buffet.

Braised Belgian Endive with Citrus Cream and Walnuts

In this country, we're more likely to eat endive raw in salads than cooked. But it has a lovely, subtly bitter flavor when braised, and the citrus cream and walnuts make it a sophisticated side dish for duck, quail, or squab.

SERVES 6

Preheat oven to 400°F. Cut the endives in half lengthwise. Melt the butter in a skillet and place the endives cut side down in the butter. Sprinkle endives with the sugar and cook over medium heat until they are browned, about 6 minutes, and then season with salt and pepper. Pour the citrus juices and zests over the endives and cook to reduce to a syrup. Transfer the endives and the citrus syrup to a casserole dish. Pour the heavy cream evenly over the endives, nestle the thyme among them, and dot the top with the goat cheese. Bake until cream has reduced and is producing fat, slow-bursting bubbles around the edge of the casserole dish and the goat cheese has browned a bit. Take the endives out of the oven and garnish with the chopped walnuts and the kumquats, if using.

6 whole Belgian endives
2 tablespoons butter
1 tablespoon sugar
Salt and pepper
Zest and juice of 1 orange
Zest and juice of 1 lemon
1 cup heavy cream
1 sprig thyme
4 ounces fresh goat cheese
½ cup walnuts, lightly toasted and chopped
6 kumquats, thinly sliced, for garnish (optional)

Baby Brussels Sprouts
with Bacon, Chestnuts, and Pomegranate Seeds

I find brussels sprouts kind of amusing. They are like miniature heads of cabbage. And while they do indeed have a cabbage-like flavor, they are distinctly their own vegetable. I like to pair them with strong partners like bacon and chestnuts (you can substitute walnuts) and introduce some acidity and crunch via the pomegranate seeds. This is a very satisfying side dish; it makes a great side to turkey on Thanksgiving and is also good with roasted chicken, duck, pork, or venison.

SERVES 6

1 pound baby brussels
    sprouts, preferably the
    size of a nickel, but no
    larger than a quarter
4 slices bacon, cut into
    ½-inch dice
1 small onion, diced fine
⅔ cup chicken stock or water
¾ cup cooked and peeled
    chestnuts, or ½ cup
    walnut pieces*
½ cup pomegranate seeds
    and 3 tablespoons of
    pomegranate juice,
    or 3 tablespoons red
    wine vinegar
2 tablespoons butter
Salt and pepper

*For more on cooking chestnuts,
see recipe for Glazed Chestnuts on
page 234.

Peel off the outermost leaves of the brussels sprouts and score the stem end with an X. Cook the sprouts in 3 quarts of boiling, salted water for 6–8 minutes, until tender. Drain and rinse under cold water to stop the cooking. Drain on paper towels. Render the bacon until halfway crisp in a large skillet. Add the onions to the bacon fat and sauté them until they are slightly browned. Add the parcooked brussels sprouts to the pan and cook over medium-low heat until the sprouts begin to brown, about 8–10 minutes. Pour in the chicken stock or water and reduce it by two-thirds. Add the chestnuts or walnuts and the pomegranate seeds and juice or red wine vinegar. Shake or stir the ingredients together until everything has warmed through. Swirl in the butter at the end and season to taste with salt and pepper.

Macadamia Nut Couscous

Couscous is a form of pasta that cooks very quickly and easily because it has been parcooked and shaped into fine grains. It is traditionally steamed over a simmering stew in a couscousier in its native North Africa. But making good couscous is really as simple as rehydrating it in boiling stock or water and just adding flavorful garnishes. I make this version in the winter months, when a little influence from sunnier climates is welcome.

SERVES 6

Melt the butter in a saucepan. Add the onions and cook over medium heat until they are golden brown, about 8 minutes. Sprinkle the saffron, cumin, coriander, cinnamon, and lemon zest over the onions. Add the couscous and stir well to coat with the spices. Pour in the boiling stock or water, all at once, with the 1 teaspoon of salt. Cover and remove from the heat. After 5 minutes, remove the cover and fluff the couscous with a fork. Fold in the macadamia nuts and the herbs. Season to taste with salt and freshly ground black pepper and the oil, if using.

1 tablespoon butter

1 small onion, thinly sliced

Small pinch saffron threads, or $1/4$ teaspoon ground turmeric

2 teaspoons ground cumin

1 teaspoon ground coriander seed

$1/4$ teaspoon ground cinnamon

2 teaspoons grated lemon zest

1 cup couscous

$1\frac{1}{2}$ cups boiling chicken stock (see Appendix, or use organic, low-sodium boxed) or water

1 teaspoon salt

$2/3$ cup chopped, toasted macadamia nuts

2 tablespoons minced tarragon or cilantro

Salt and pepper

2 teaspoons nut oil, like hazelnut or walnut (optional)

Risotto with Oven-Cured Tomatoes

SERVES 6

for the oven-cured tomatoes

2 pounds ripe plum
    tomatoes
Sea salt, as needed
4 cloves garlic, thinly sliced
2 tablespoons minced thyme
2 tablespoons grated lemon
    zest
4 tablespoons extra virgin
    olive oil

prepare the oven-cured tomatoes

Preheat oven to 200°F. Cut tomatoes in half lengthwise and arrange them cut side up on a foil-lined baking sheet. Sprinkle each tomato with sea salt, a couple of slices of garlic, and a pinch each of the thyme and lemon zest. Drizzle the olive oil over all the tomatoes. Place the tomatoes in the oven and cook 4–6 hours, until they have shriveled and lightly browned. You don't want them dry like fruit leather, but you do want them to shrink up so that the flavors are greatly reduced and concentrated. If storing, package them up with their cooking juices; they will keep for up to 10 days in the fridge.

make the risotto

NOTE: Review the method of risotto making in greater detail in Wild Leek Risotto on page 246.

Sauté the onion in 1 tablespoon butter until translucent. Add the rice and toast for 3 minutes. Pour in the wine and cook until the wine is completely absorbed. Season rice with ½ teaspoon of salt. Pour in the first addition of hot stock to cover the rice. Stir frequently. Add stock in batches until rice is al dente, about 20 minutes. Remove from heat. Fold in the tomatoes, remaining butter, and the cheese. Stir vigorously. Garnish with the minced herbs and season to taste with salt and freshly ground black pepper.

‹ **weighing your options** ›
Once you have mastered the basic risotto-making technique, you should have fun adding as many seasonal variations as you'd like. Here are a few ideas:

Spring: Risotto with Pan-Roasted Morels (page 54)

Fall: Risotto with Roasted Squash and Wild Mushrooms (see Squash Roasted in Foil Packages, page 235, and Sautéed Wild Mushrooms, page 233)

Winter: Quail or Squab with Black Truffle and Savoy Cabbage (see quail recipe on page 184 or squab recipe on page 192; finely shred the savoy cabbage and thinly shave the black truffle and fold them into the risotto at the end)

for the risotto

1 small onion, minced

3 tablespoons butter, divided

1½ cups carnaroli or arborio rice

¼ cup dry white wine

½ teaspoon salt

3½ cups (approximately) hot chicken stock (see Appendix or use organic, low-sodium boxed)

1 cup Oven-Cured Tomatoes, roughly chopped

⅓ cup Pecorino Romano cheese (you can use Parmigiano-Reggiano, but it may be too sweet with the concentrated tomatoes)

¼ cup minced fresh herbs (parsley, sorrel, tarragon)

Salt and pepper to taste

Wild Leek Risotto

Finding wild leeks (or ramps, as they are also called) is not an every-day event (see page 92). But if you visit a farmers market in the early spring, up until May, you are likely to come across them. Their territory ranges from Canada through New England down as far as Georgia and west as far as Minnesota. Ramps have a more pungent flavor than cultivated leeks, but this risotto is also delicious using store-bought leeks with the simple addition of garlic to approximate the wild flavor. The default rice for risotto is short-grained arborio rice. It is fine, but not the best choice for a creamy and firmly al dente risotto. Instead, I use carnaroli when I can find it; it holds its shape and doesn't require constant stirring to develop a wonderful creaminess. My favorite tool for risotto making is a sturdy wooden spoon that doesn't do damage to the pan with all the stirring and that feels good in my hand.

SERVES 6

½ pound wild leeks, or 1 pound cultivated leeks plus 3 cloves garlic
1 tablespoon butter
1½ cups carnaroli or arborio rice
¼ cup dry white wine
½ teaspoon salt
3 cups (approximately) hot chicken stock (see Appendix, or use organic, low-sodium boxed)

Clean the wild leeks by trimming the root, slipping off the outermost layer of skin on the bulb end, and cutting off the green leaves to be used as a garnish. Wash the leeks well and cut the stems and bulbs into ¼-inch-thick slices. Cut the green tops into thin ribbons and reserve ¼ cup of them. If you are working with cultivated leeks, trim the green off and discard, split the white part in half, and wash well in cold water. Cut the white part into ¼-inch-thick slices. Peel and thinly slice the garlic, if using.

Heat the butter in a wide saucepan over medium-low heat. Stir in the wild leeks, or the cultivated leeks and garlic. Cook until the vegetables are soft, stirring occasionally, for about 4 minutes. Avoid coloring the leeks—use a lid to trap the steam if necessary. Once the leeks are tender, pour in the rice. Turn up the heat to medium and let the rice toast for 3 minutes, stirring occasionally. Pour in the wine and let it boil until it evaporates. Season with ½ teaspoon of salt. Salting now helps the grains absorb the full flavor from the leeks and the broth.

Begin ladling in the hot stock. The first addition of stock should just cover the rice. Bring the rice to a simmer and stir every couple of minutes until the stock has been absorbed. From now on, you will be adding the stock in ever-smaller additions to make sure that you don't add too much and overcook the rice. Stir as often as you like, but certainly every few minutes to prevent scorching. After 15 minutes, taste a few grains of rice—if they are still quite firm, ladle in another addition of stock. The risotto will continue to cook even when it is removed from the heat, so you always want to stop when the rice is still firm in the center (al dente). When you are ready to finish the risotto, give it a few very vigorous strokes. Remove the rice from the heat and add the parsley, lemon zest, and the reserved wild leek tops, if using. Stir in the butter and the cheese, taste for seasoning, and add salt and pepper as needed.

Serve immediately on its own as a first course, or as a side dish for salmon, lamb, squab, or duck.

¼ cup freshly chopped parsley
1 teaspoon freshly grated lemon zest
2 tablespoons butter
⅓ cup finely grated Parmigiano-Reggiano
Salt and pepper to taste

Quinoa Salad
with Pine Nuts, Dried Cherries, and Basil

Quinoa, pronounced "keen-wah," looks like a grain, but is actually the seed of a plant that is distantly related to spinach. Once I was introduced to quinoa, I made it part of my diet—it is nutty and delicious as well as healthful. Quinoa is very high in protein and has an almost perfect balance of amino acids, a trait shared only with amaranth and buckwheat. I generally serve it cold as a salad, where I think its unique flavor is at its best. Cracked wheat or bulgur wheat are reasonable substitutions.

SERVES 6

for the quinoa

1½ cups quinoa, well rinsed
in cold water and
drained
3 cups water
1 teaspoon salt

for the salad

4 cups cooked quinoa
(above)
½ bulb fennel, finely diced
½ cup toasted pine nuts,
lightly chopped
⅓ cup minced dried cherries
or currants
¼ cup Aged Sherry–Walnut
Vinaigrette (page 261)
Small handful basil leaves,
torn or cut into ribbons
Salt and pepper to taste

cook the quinoa

Add the quinoa to a heavy skillet and dry-toast it over medium heat until quinoa is light brown and fragrant, about 4 minutes. Bring 3 cups water to a boil in a saucepan with 1 teaspoon salt. Transfer the quinoa to the boiling water, bring back to a simmer, and cover. Cook over low heat for 15 minutes. Spoon the quinoa out onto a plate or baking sheet to cool.

make the salad

Toss all the ingredients together in a large bowl, seasoning to taste with the salt and freshly ground black pepper. Serve chilled or at room temperature with grilled pork chops, lamb, duck, or chicken.

German Butterball Potato Salad with Dill

German Butterball potatoes are an heirloom variety worth seeking out. They are yellow fleshed with a pronounced potato flavor. Fine substitutes are Yellow Finns or small Yukon Gold potatoes—but smaller is better when making potato salad, because the high skin-to-flesh ratio means better flavor. In fact, even though it's a bit of a pain, cooking the potatoes in their skins and peeling them while still warm is really the way to go. This kind of chore is why my mother has a television in her kitchen!

SERVES 6

Bring the potatoes to a boil in 3 quarts of water with the bay leaf and 2 teaspoons of salt. Cook at a slow boil for 20–25 minutes, until they are tender throughout.

While the potatoes are cooking, render the bacon in a skillet until crisp, then drain on paper towels. Sauté the diced onion in the bacon fat until soft and lightly browned. Peel the potatoes when they're cool enough to handle. Slice into $\frac{1}{4}$-inch-thick or half-moon slices. Place the cut potatoes in a large bowl. Whisk together the mustard, vinegar, and oil in a small bowl, and drizzle this dressing over the potatoes. Scrape the cooked onions and the bacon fat into the bowl with the potatoes and add the crisped bacon and the dill. Season to taste with salt and pepper. Let the salad age 2–3 hours before serving. Serve cold, at room temperature, or warm.

$1\frac{1}{2}$ pounds German Butterball or other yellow-fleshed potatoes, scrubbed clean but not peeled

1 bay leaf

2 teaspoons salt

$\frac{1}{4}$ pound bacon, cut into $\frac{1}{4}$-inch pieces

1 large onion, diced

2 teaspoons Dijon mustard

$\frac{1}{4}$ cup cider vinegar

$\frac{1}{2}$ cup vegetable oil (canola, peanut, or light olive)

$\frac{1}{3}$ cup freshly chopped dill

Salt and freshly ground black pepper

Porcini Potato Gratin

I'm a completely devoted fan of potatoes cooked with cream and cheese, and I haven't yet met anyone who isn't. The deep flavor of each bite means you don't need to eat a lot of it to be satisfied. I've added dried porcinis for an unexpected twist to this classic gratin dauphinois.

SERVES 6

1 clove garlic, smashed

1½ pounds Yukon Gold or russet potatoes, peeled and sliced into very thin rounds (⅛ inch thick)

1½ cups heavy cream

1 cup milk

Salt and pepper

Freshly grated nutmeg to taste

1 ounce dried porcinis, rehydrated in 1 cup of simmering chicken stock (see Appendix, or use organic, low-sodium boxed) or water, then minced

1 cup grated Gruyère

Preheat oven to 400°F. Rub the inside of a 2-quart gratin dish with the smashed garlic. Place the sliced potatoes, cream, and milk in a heavy saucepan. Season with salt, pepper, and nutmeg. Taste the milk and cream mixture—it should be highly seasoned, since it serves as the seasoning for the potatoes. Bring the potato and cream mixture to a boil, fold in the minced porcinis, and transfer to the gratin dish. Scatter the grated cheese evenly over the surface of the potatoes and set the dish in the oven. Bake for 40–50 minutes, until potatoes are tender when pierced with a small knife. Let the gratin settle for 10–15 minutes before cutting and serving.

Coconut-Simmered Fingerling Potatoes

The addition of coconut and ginger makes these somewhat exotic potatoes a wonderful match for tuna, salmon, or duck. The initial cooking over rock salt and herbs deepens the potato flavor. If you choose, you can stop there for fabulous miniature baked potatoes—just split them and add a bit of butter or crème fraîche and a pinch of minced chives or pickled horseradish. But you should try them simmered in this aromatic coconut broth at least once—they're really special.

SERVES 6

Preheat oven to 400°F. Spread rock salt out on a baking sheet. Strew the herbs over the salt and nestle the potatoes into the salt bed. Roast the potatoes for 30 minutes or until the potatoes are tender when pierced with a sharp knife. Carefully brush all the salt crystals off the potatoes. You can store the rock salt in a covered container in a dry place and use it again.

Meanwhile, bring the coconut milk, ginger, lemon zest, and cilantro stems (if using) to a boil. Reduce the heat to a simmer and cook the coconut milk slowly, until it has reduced by about half and coats a spoon. Swirl in the butter and strain the sauce through a sieve to remove ginger, zest, and cilantro stems. Slice the roasted potatoes in half lengthwise and place them in a skillet with the strained coconut milk. Simmer until potatoes are warm through and have absorbed some of the broth, about 5 minutes. Season lightly with salt and pepper. Garnish with the minced cilantro or thyme, if using. Serve the potatoes with a generous spoonful of the sauce.

for the potatoes

1 pound rock salt

2 sprigs thyme

2 sprigs rosemary

1½ pounds fingerling potatoes

for the coconut cream

One 12-ounce can unsweetened coconut milk

2 tablespoons grated fresh ginger

Zest of 1 lemon

Handful cilantro stems (optional)

2 tablespoons butter

Salt and pepper

2 tablespoons minced cilantro or thyme, for garnish (optional)

‹ weighing your options ›

If you add a nice squeeze of lime juice to some of the remaining coconut broth in the pan, this makes an excellent sauce for simply cooked tuna, salmon, or duck.

Black Pepper and Parsley Spaetzle

Literally translated, *spaetzle* means "little sparrows" in German. I suppose if you sort of squint your eyes and concentrate on little sparrows, you might just see them. I see irregular little squiggles of the easiest homemade egg noodles in the world. Unlike Italian fresh pasta, which usually requires rolling and cutting into shapes, spaetzle are pressed through a fine colander or spaetzle maker directly into the boiling water. There is a second technique that is fun to master—rolling out the dough on a cutting board and cutting very thin, long dumplings right into the water with a sharp knife. I think this is for the advanced spaetzle students, though. I just recently got to that level myself! Depending on how dense the dough is, you can have tiny little squiggles (loose dough) or large, dense, more regular shapes (firmer dough). It's really up to what you're looking for.

This recipe is for the looser kind—I find them more tender and a joy to eat. Once spaetzle are cooked, they can be held for a day in the refrigerator before warming or browning in butter or baking with golden onions, cheese, and ham into a delicious gratin. When you've had just about enough potatoes, these little noodles are an ideal side dish for any stews or saucy meat dishes.

SERVES 6

3 cups flour, sifted
1 teaspoon salt
1 teaspoon medium-ground
    black pepper
1 tablespoon grated lemon
    zest
1/3 cup chopped parsley
4 eggs
1 cup milk

Combine the flour, salt, pepper, lemon zest, and parsley in a bowl and make a well in the center. Separately, whisk together the eggs and the milk. Pour the wet ingredients into the well and mix everything together with your hands until the dough is smooth and elastic, about 2 minutes. Let the dough rest in the fridge for an hour before cooking.

Bring a large pot of salted water to a boil. Set up an ice bath with a strainer next to the pot; the ice bath will quickly shock the cooked noodles. They should immediately be removed from the ice bath to drain.

Push the dough through a colander with small holes or a spaetzle maker over the pot of boiling water. You will do this in 3 or 4 batches, since the time it takes to push all the dough through would create unequal cooking time for the noodles. Cook the noodles for 5–6 minutes; they will tend to float to the top when they're done. Scoop out the cooked noodles with a strainer and plunge immediately into the ice bath; repeat with each batch. When cold (about 2 minutes), drain the spaetzle on a clean dish towel. You can keep the spaetzle in a container; they won't stick together.

At this point you have a few options:

- warm the spaetzle in melted butter and serve with buttered bread crumbs
- brown the spaetzle in butter until they're golden and crisp
- layer the spaetzle with browned onions, cheese, and ham and pop in the oven for a delicious gratin (recipe on page 254).

Spaetzle Gratin
with Browned Onions, Gruyère, and Ham

SERVES 6

2 tablespoons butter

2 onions, thinly sliced

1 recipe Black Pepper and Parsley Spaetzle (see page 252)

¼ pound thinly sliced Westphalian or Smithfield ham, or other cold smoked ham

1 firm, tart apple, peeled

½ cup heavy cream

4 ounces Gruyère, grated

Salt and pepper

Freshly grated nutmeg

Preheat oven to 400°F. Heat a large skillet and add the butter and the sliced onions. Cook onions until well browned, about 10 minutes. In a 2-quart casserole, layer half the spaetzle with half the amount of onions and ham, and grate half the apple right into the dish. Drizzle the layer with half of the cream and the cheese. Repeat this process for the next layer. Season with salt, pepper, and nutmeg. Bake the casserole for 25–30 minutes, until cheese has melted and is golden brown. Let gratin settle for 10 minutes before serving.

This gratin is great with pork or veal roasts, or served as a lunch or light dinner with a green salad.

Food & Wine *Best New Chef Award, 1998*

BUTTER

We've all probably made butter at least once by accident by overwhipping our heavy cream for dessert after an already exhausting dinner party. But if you ever tasted this sort of butter, you know how bland and un-butterlike it is. That is because you'd have to knead a lot of the buttermilk out of it to get a buttery taste and texture. Salt is usually added to commercial butter for flavor and to extend the shelf life, but a good butter needs no salt. In fact, the best butters are unsalted and are made from cultured cream. Cultured cream has had a starter culture added to it, much like in cheese making. This culture makes for a more complex, ripened, nutty flavor and a lovely, waxy, modeling-clay-like texture that is a joy to work with. But all this love and attention comes at a price, so I save the cultured butter for butter-centric uses like compound butters and for a smear on a good, crusty slice of bread. For cooking I use Cabot's unsalted butter and keep only one stick out at a time. The rest I store in the freezer, since unsalted butter is highly perishable. Vermont Butter & Cheese Company makes a cultured butter that is as good if not better than the European imports (see Sources). A great butter shouldn't be taken for granted—it's a labor of love by the producers and a real treat for the rest of us.

When you melt butter, you'll notice that it is made up of three components: water, which causes steam and sizzling and quickly evaporates; butter fat, which is what you get when you clarify butter—it is the oily, pure fat part of butter; and the solids, which contain salts and natural sugars—this is the part that browns and becomes nutty in a beurre noisette or browned butter sauce.

When gently cooking vegetables in butter, you want to keep all three of these components together for a creamy sauce that clings to the vegetables. The easiest way to do this is to whisk a tablespoon or two of cold water into the melting butter before it separates. The water will create an emulsion that keeps all the components suspended together. This emulsion will coat the vegetables and not feel oily on the palate. If you get the emulsion too hot, it can break, so this must be done over medium-low heat. Once you have created the emulsion, it is ideal for rewarming previously blanched vegetables, but it is not ideal for cooking vegetables from the raw state.

BUYING VEGETABLES
IN THEIR PEAK SEASON

We are both blessed and cursed by the incredible bounty on our supermarket produce shelves, where you can find berries, tomatoes, asparagus, and apples year-round. But how do they taste? To be fair to the produce, it really does have a peak season when it tastes best. You can do very well at farmers markets and roadside stands if you know what to look for. But even these close-to-the-land sources will often try to provide everything under the sun for their customers—tomatoes in January and asparagus in October. Eating well can be a challenge, but if you follow the seasons you'll pay less and enjoy more.

Here are some very general tips for buying produce from the supermarket:

- Fruits and vegetables should feel "heavy for their size." This means they haven't lost moisture through aging on the shelves or in the warehouse.
- Skins and peels should have a healthy sheen and not look wrinkled, dented, or bruised.
- Many fruits have such thick skins that taking a sniff doesn't tell you anything at all, but berries tend to taste as good as they smell, especially strawberries, so go ahead and get your nose in there. Pears and apples are also particularly fragrant when in peak form.

Pass up any sad, wilted-looking produce—their best days are long gone. Once you train your eye to the virtues of fresh fruits and vegetables, you can spot them a mile away. My father can pick out wild asparagus growing along the roads of Vermont while driving along at fifty miles per hour. Train yourself to be a modern-day forager-gatherer. Acquiring this skill is important in allowing yourself to get the best deals and to enjoy all the glorious food that's around.

Here is a rough guide to seasonal produce. It is not by any means comprehensive, but it encompasses most of the usual suspects. Within each season there are products that don't arrive exactly when expected (depending on weather, mainly), so keep looking for them as the season wears on—they'll show up eventually! Some fruits and vegetables like to straddle two seasons, and some show up all year long, as in the case of mangoes and bananas, which are grown in the tropics. And standbys like onions, carrots, potatoes, and garlic are available year-round.

SPRING
(late March through mid-June)
Ramps (wild leeks), asparagus, morels, artichokes, fennel, leeks, peas, shallots, fava beans, new potatoes, beets (and their greens), scallions, radishes, spinach, carrots, rhubarb, apricots, strawberries, and cherries.

SUMMER
(late June through mid-September)
Raspberries, blackberries, mangoes, blueberries, summer squashes, eggplant, corn, tomatoes, okra, chile peppers, sweet peppers, sweet onions, potatoes, figs, nectarines, peaches, melons, cucumbers, hen-of-the-woods mushrooms, chanterelles, lettuces, herbs, bok choy, green beans, papayas, and grapes.

FALL
(late September through mid-December)
Apples, artichokes, beets, pears, quince, persimmon, cardoons, cauliflower, chestnuts, fall squashes, pomegranates, plums, salsify, cippolini, chards, cranberries, Concord grapes, table grapes, chanterelles, porcini, white truffles, potatoes, sweet potatoes, yams, and garlic.

WINTER
(late December through mid-March)
Grapefruit, oranges, clementines, blood oranges, Seville oranges, pineapples, kumquats, fresh dates, turnips, brussels sprouts, broccoli, lemons, mustard greens, collards, kale, celery root, cabbages, radicchio, endives, avocados, and cauliflower.

Spicy Mushroom Dressing

Aged Sherry–Walnut Vinaigrette

Sesame Vinaigrette

Juniper Vinaigrette

Coconut-Curry Dressing

Red Chile Oil

Pickled Radishes

Pickled Wild Mushrooms

Tomato Salsas

Mayonnaise and Variations

Smoked Chile and Caper Remoulade

Fresh Mint and Coriander Sauce

Cranberry Relish with Green Chiles and Kumquat

Dried Fig and Almond Chutney

Fruited Mustards

Celery Root and Apple Remoulade

Grated Apple and Horseradish Cream

Cumin-Cured Cherry Tomatoes

My Green Sauce

Salsa Verde Picante

Papaya-Ginger Salsa

Port-Plumped Prunes

Beurre Noisette and Variations

Homemade Flavored Vinegars

Spiced Tomato Chutney

Onion-Sage Confit

DRESSINGS, PICKLES, AND RELISHES

A sauce doesn't have to be a classical reduction of a slow-simmered meat stock, though that kind of sauce is wonderful too. Today, a sauce can be a salsa, chutney, vinaigrette, relish, or even a dab of fruited mustard or a drizzle of flavored oil. And I find that a jar of homemade Pickled Radishes or Cumin-Cured Cherry Tomatoes in the fridge provides a source of explosive flavor that acts like an exclamation point to your meal. These recipes are simple by design. I want to encourage you to create your own stash of unique sauces that will give you flexibility when you're looking for just the right flavor note to pair with your food.

The beauty of these items is that a great many of them will keep in the fridge for weeks, if not longer, with little loss of flavor and texture. (All but the tomato salsas, that is, which should be used the day they're made.) Having an inventory of several homemade condiments allows you to be spontaneous and innovative when putting a meal together. For example, a drizzle of the Juniper Vinaigrette over a roasted pork chop with apples and fall vegetables makes a meal that is completely in tune with the crisp autumn weather. Alternately, brushing that same pork chop with some of the mildly spicy Red Chile Oil and serving the Papaya-Ginger Salsa on the side expresses a simple and playful Asian idiom. Surprise yourself with the kind of pairings you can create. Simply grilled, roasted, or fried foods often just need a quick, flavorful sauce and a seasonal side dish to make a great meal.

Spicy Mushroom Dressing

The first step in this recipe is to make a concentrated mushroom syrup. At this point you can continue on and finish the dressing, or divert some or all of the syrup into small portions to be frozen (see Weighing Your Options, next page). As a dressing, it is fabulous on warm potatoes, with hearty greens like frisée and endive, or as a quick sauce for pan-seared scallops or salmon.

MAKES APPROXIMATELY 1 CUP MUSHROOM SYRUP AND 1½ CUPS VINAIGRETTE

1½ pounds white mushrooms, cleaned and trimmed, plus any wild mushroom stems you might have left over from another dish
1 onion, diced
2 cloves garlic
3 tablespoons olive oil
1 teaspoon salt
1 bay leaf
5 cups cold water
3 tablespoons sherry vinegar
½ cup extra virgin olive oil
½ teaspoon dried chile flakes
2 teaspoons minced thyme
Salt and freshly ground black pepper

Put the cleaned mushrooms, onion, and whole garlic in the bowl of a food processor and pulse briefly until vegetables become a coarse puree. Do this in batches if necessary. Heat a heavy skillet over medium heat with the olive oil. Transfer the mushroom mixture to the skillet, add the salt and bay leaf, and stir once or twice. Reduce heat to low and let the mushrooms cook down to a deeply browned paste, about 20 minutes.

Pour in the cold water, bring to a simmer, and cook about 30 minutes, until the water has reduced down by about ⅔. Strain out the solids, pressing on them firmly to extract as much flavor as possible. Transfer the strained mushroom stock to a small, clean saucepan and reduce over low heat until a syrupy consistency develops—thick enough to coat a spoon. Cool. This is your mushroom syrup or glace. You should have about 1 cup.

Whisk together the mushroom syrup, the sherry vinegar, olive oil, chile flakes, and thyme in a bowl. Season to taste with salt and pepper.

Aged Sherry–Walnut Vinaigrette

This is one of my everyday vinaigrettes. The wood aging of the sherry vinegar creates a wonderfully complex flavor that is enhanced by the walnut oil. Sherry vinegar is a little more expensive than red wine vinegar, but it has a higher acidity so you use less. Pair this dressing with strongly flavored salad greens, cheeses, nuts, and seasonal fruits, like in my Seasonal Country Salad on page 116.

MAKES APPROXIMATELY 1 CUP

Toss the minced shallots with the salt in a bowl and let the shallots "weep" for a few minutes. This helps them flavor the vinaigrette more quickly. Whisk in the mustard and sherry vinegar. Slowly drizzle in the walnut oil and the olive oil. It's not important to keep this vinaigrette emulsified. If the oil and vinegar separate, just stir vigorously to recombine them before using. Season with the pepper and more salt if needed. This vinaigrette will keep several weeks in the fridge.

1 shallot, peeled and
    minced
1 teaspoon salt
1 teaspoon Dijon mustard
¼ cup aged sherry vinegar
3 tablespoons walnut or
    hazelnut oil*
¾ cup extra virgin olive oil
Freshly ground black pepper

*Once oil has been opened, store it in the fridge to slow down the oxidation that leads to rancidity—especially a problem for nut oils.

‹ weighing your options ›

After cooling the mushroom syrup from the preceding page, you can pour it into an ice cube tray, freeze it, then wrap each block tightly in wax paper and put in a freezer bag for an instant vegetable-based bouillon. See the introduction to the Spicy Mushroom Dressing recipe for ideas on how to use these mushroom cubes. You can also make double the amount so you will have enough for that dressing recipe and an equal amount to store. It will last ten days in the fridge.

Sesame Vinaigrette

1 shallot, peeled and minced
1 teaspoon salt
1 clove garlic, minced
1 tablespoon minced ginger
2 tablespoons lemon juice
¼ cup rice vinegar or white
    wine vinegar
3 tablespoons toasted
    sesame oil
¼ cup Red Chile Oil (page
    264)
¼ cup canola oil

You can replace the red chile oil in this recipe with a more neutral oil like canola or safflower if you don't want the heat. I use this on the Sesame-Roasted Green Beans on page 237 and as a marinade for shrimp or scallops. If you double the quantity of vinegar and lemon juice, you can even turn the shellfish into an Asian-inspired ceviche.

MAKES APPROXIMATELY 1 CUP

Toss the shallots in a bowl with the salt and let them "weep" for a few minutes to help them quickly flavor the vinaigrette. Combine with the remaining ingredients and let them age 1–2 hours in the fridge for maximum flavor. This vinaigrette will keep up to 2 weeks in the fridge.

Juniper Vinaigrette

2 tablespoons coarsely
    chopped juniper berries
1 shallot, peeled and minced
¼ cup red wine or aged
    sherry vinegar
2 tablespoons walnut or
    hazelnut oil
½ cup extra virgin olive oil
1 tablespoon freshly grated
    orange zest
1 tablespoon minced
    rosemary
Salt and pepper

This vinaigrette is too assertive for most greens or lettuces, but is great for drizzling on roasted root vegetables like parsnips, carrots, and beets. It also makes a fine finish for simply prepared quail, pork, or duck. Just spoon some over the warm meats. I think juniper really evokes the fall harvest and hunting season, so think about including fall fruits in your menu too: apples, pears, quince, and chestnuts.

MAKES APPROXIMATELY 1 CUP

Stir all ingredients in a bowl. Let this vinaigrette age 1–2 hours in the fridge before using. It will keep for 2 weeks in the fridge.

Coconut-Curry Dressing

This is a very versatile, light sauce for fish or shellfish. It's also great for pulling together a salad composed of cold leftover chicken, lamb, duck, or pork, garnished with crunchy fruits like apples and pears and whatever toasted nuts you have on hand. This will keep about one week in the fridge.

MAKES 1½ CUPS

Heat the olive oil in a saucepan and sauté the apple, onion, ginger, garlic, and chile until softened, about 4 minutes. Stir in the curry powder and cook 2 minutes, then pour in the coconut milk. Simmer the sauce for 5 minutes, turn off the heat, and let the flavors steep together and cool. Transfer the contents of the saucepan to a blender. Add the lemon juice and vinegar and puree until smooth. With the machine running, slowly incorporate the oil and season to taste with salt and pepper.

1 tablespoon olive oil
1 tart apple, peeled and diced fine
1 onion, diced fine
1 tablespoon grated fresh ginger
1 clove garlic, minced
1 green chile, poblano or Jalapeño, seeded and minced
2 teaspoons medium-hot curry powder (like a Madras curry)
½ cup coconut milk
2 tablespoons lemon juice
2 tablespoons rice vinegar (champagne or white wine vinegar can be substituted)
¼ cup canola oil
Salt and freshly ground black pepper

Red Chile Oil

My favorite red chile of all is the ancho. It is a ripened and dried poblano chile that is sold both as a whole pod and as a roasted and ground powder. (The pods should be soaked in hot water until soft, and then the flesh can be scraped from the skins. The flesh is a gorgeous deep-red color and is used to thicken and flavor chiles, stews, and sauces.) More often, though, I use it in its powdered form. Ancho is more sweet than hot since the ripening and drying create a raisin-like flavor. The powder will easily bleed its lovely color into whatever you're cooking and has mild thickening properties as well when whisked into a vinaigrette or sauce. Once made into this flavored oil, you can drizzle it over any dish that could use a little splash of color and mild heat.

MAKES APPROXIMATELY 1 CUP

2 cloves garlic
1 tablespoon olive oil
¼ cup ancho chile powder
   (see Sources)
1 cup canola oil
1 teaspoon salt

In a small pan, sauté the whole cloves of garlic in the olive oil until they are golden brown and tender. Cover the pan while sautéing the garlic to trap the steam and keep it from burning. Transfer the garlic and any oil from the pan to a blender. Add the ancho powder, canola oil, and salt and run on low speed for 5 full minutes. This amount of time is necessary to really suspend the chile in the oil so it can develop its full flavor. Pour the contents of the blender into a coffee filter or a double layer of cheesecloth suspended over a cup. The oil should drip out slowly over the course of several hours. Don't press on the solids or the oil will be cloudy. You can keep the oil in the fridge for up to 2 weeks.

Pickled Radishes

There's nothing like a pinch of these peppery, tart, and salty radishes to perk up a slice of cold roast, sandwich, or a grilled piece of tuna. There are several varieties of radish available, known mostly by color—pink, white, red, breakfast radish, icicle radish. I use any of these or in combination, but I avoid black radish and daikon, which are too strongly flavored for this recipe.

MAKES APPROXIMATELY 2 CUPS

Combine the shallot, ginger, lemon juice, vinegar, and sesame oil in a nonreactive bowl. Toss in the radishes and stir well to coat. Sprinkle in the salt and sugar and stir again. Let the radishes pickle at room temperature for several hours before using. They will keep 2–3 weeks in the fridge.

1 shallot, minced

1 tablespoon grated fresh ginger

2 tablespoons lemon juice

½ cup rice vinegar, or substitute champagne or white wine vinegar

2 tablespoons toasted sesame oil

2 bunches of radishes (about 24–30 radishes), thinly sliced, or just quartered for extra crunch

2 tablespoons salt

1 teaspoon sugar

‹ weighing your options ›
I like to fold in a small handful of minced cilantro just before serving. If you are lucky enough to run across shiso, which is a Japanese mint, it is also a great last-minute addition.

Pickled Wild Mushrooms

Wild mushrooms are very perishable, and this light pickling is a great way to preserve them while creating a zesty condiment for a wide range of foods—grilled sausages or a meaty tuna or salmon steak, or grilled country bread with a dab of aged goat cheese for a quick and satisfying snack or hors d'oeuvre. They will last about two weeks in the fridge.

MAKES 1 QUART

¼ cup extra virgin olive oil, plus 2 tablespoons for sautéing mushrooms

1½ pounds of a combination of chanterelles, oyster mushrooms, and shiitakes, stems removed and meat cut into ¼-inch-thick slices

Salt and pepper

2 shallots, peeled and minced

2 cloves garlic, minced

½ bulb fennel, diced fine

⅓ cup dried apricots, diced fine

2 tablespoons dried currants

⅓ cup apple cider vinegar

2 tablespoons sherry vinegar

Zest of 1 lemon

3 tablespoons minced tarragon

Heat 2 heavy medium-size skillets and pour 1 tablespoon of olive oil into each pan. When the oil shimmers, toss half the mushrooms into each pan. Cook over medium-high heat until the mushrooms begin to brown a bit and soften, about 4 minutes. Season lightly with salt and pepper, then transfer them to a plate to cool.

Meanwhile, mix the shallots, garlic, fennel, apricots, currants, cider and sherry vinegars, lemon zest, tarragon, and the remaining ¼ cup of olive oil together in a large bowl. Fold the cooled mushrooms into the ingredients in the bowl and season liberally with salt and pepper. Let "pickle" at room temperature for 2 hours before storing covered in the refrigerator for up to 2 weeks.

Chef's Trick: When serving these fabulous fungi, be sure to stir the contents up from the bottom, as things will tend to settle with time. (Don't I know it!)

Tomato Salsas

Tomato is a fruit, and when ripe, quite a sweet one at that. I find that some acidity from citrus fruits or vinegar with background notes from red onions or shallots make a tomato salsa a very welcome addition to the summer dinner table. Tomatoes are fragile and don't refrigerate well, so use these salsas soon after they're made. Here are three distinctly different expressions of tomato salsa that can be paired up with grilled fish, tacos, steaks, on burgers, or just with a bag of crispy tortilla chips!

tomato, basil, and caper salsa

MAKES 2 CUPS

Heat the olive oil in a small skillet. When it shimmers add the onions and sauté until lightly golden. Pour the balsamic vinegar into the pan and simmer with the onions for about 2 minutes. Put the tomatoes in a nonreactive bowl, and pour in the onions with the balsamic vinegar. Season with the capers, basil, and salt and pepper to taste. Let stand at room temperature to develop the flavors for 30 minutes or so before serving.

2 tablespoons olive oil
1 onion, thinly sliced
¼ cup balsamic vinegar
2 ripe beefsteak tomatoes,
    seeded and cut into
    ½-inch dice
2 tablespoons capers,
    roughly chopped
Small handful basil leaves,
    torn or cut into ribbons
Salt and freshly ground
    black pepper

tomato and citrus salsa

MAKES 2 CUPS

2 ripe red beefsteak
    tomatoes, seeded and cut
    into ½-inch dice
2 shallots, peeled and thinly
    sliced
Seedless sections of 1 lemon
    (see Chef's Trick)
Juice and sections of 1 lime
Seedless sections of 1 orange
    (see Chef's Trick)
2 tablespoons extra virgin
    olive oil
Salt and freshly ground black
    pepper
2 tablespoons freshly minced
    herbs like cilantro,
    tarragon, and basil

Simply combine all ingredients in a nonreactive bowl and serve after the flavors have mellowed for 30 minutes or so.

Chef's Trick: For seedless sections, cut both ends off the citrus fruit and stand it upright on a cutting board. With a sharp knife take off all of the peel and pith until just the fruit remains. Then slide the blade of the knife in between the membranes, making a V-shape cut for each section. Do this over a bowl to collect any juices, and remove the seeds by hand.

yellow tomato, blistered chile, and mango salsa

MAKES 2 CUPS

2 tablespoons olive oil
1 poblano chile or
    2 jalapeño chiles
2 ripe yellow beefsteak
    tomatoes, seeded and
    cut into ½-inch dice
1 mango, peeled, pitted, and
    cut into ½-inch dice
½ red onion, diced fine
Juice of 1 lime
Handful cilantro leaves,
    minced
2 tablespoons olive oil
Salt and pepper

Heat the olive oil in a skillet until it shimmers, add the chile(s), and blister the skin on medium heat until entirely blackened. Transfer the chile(s) to a small bowl, and cover immediately with plastic wrap to loosen the skins via the trapped steam. When cool enough to handle, peel and seed the chile(s) and dice fine. (Wash your hands after dicing the jalapeños because the heat will stay on your fingertips.) Combine the diced chiles with the tomatoes, mango, red onion, lime juice, cilantro, and olive oil. Stir well but gently. Season to taste with salt and pepper.

Mayonnaise and Variations

Homemade mayonnaise is easy to make and can be the basis for so many flavorful spinoffs. However, it does have a shorter shelf life than store-bought—it will only hold up to five days in your fridge. I use mainly canola oil with just a touch of extra olive oil for flavor. This allows the essential "egginess" to come through. Aioli, or garlic mayonnaise, would be a case where you'd want the olive oil flavor to shine.

basic mayonnaise

MAKES APPROXIMATELY 2 CUPS

Room temperature ingredients will hold the emulsion better; temperature variations are the enemy of emulsions like mayonnaise, so be sure to take your eggs out of the refrigerator and let them come to room temperature. Using a standing mixer or a handheld electric mixer (unless you have a particularly strong arm), beat together the egg yolks and whole egg with the mustard, lemon juice, and vinegar until a pale yellow color develops. In a slow, steady stream, beat in the canola oil. Add a few drops of cold water if the mayonnaise appears too firm or in danger of breaking. Beat in the olive oil and season to taste with salt and pepper. Mayonnaise should be highly seasoned, so don't be too shy with the salt.

2 egg yolks, at room
    temperature
1 whole egg, at room
    temperature
1 tablespoon Dijon mustard
1 tablespoon lemon juice
1 teaspoon red wine vinegar
1½ cups canola oil
¼ cup extra virgin olive oil
Salt and pepper

lemon-dill mayonnaise

1 cup mayonnaise,
   homemade or high-
   quality store-bought
1 shallot, peeled and minced
3 tablespoons minced fresh
   dill
1 tablespoon grated lemon
   zest
1 tablespoon lemon juice
Salt and small pinch of
   cayenne pepper

This is a great sauce for leftover leg of lamb or folded into cold diced chicken or turkey for a quick salad or sandwich. It makes a great foil for grilled salmon as well.

MAKES APPROXIMATELY 1 CUP

Mix together all ingredients in a nonreactive bowl, seasoning to taste with the salt and cayenne pepper.

‹ weighing your options ›
For lemon-mint mayonnaise, substitute 3 tablespoons
minced fresh mint for the dill.

garlic-anchovy mayonnaise

1 cup mayonnaise,
   homemade or high-
   quality store-bought
1 teaspoon mashed
   anchovies or anchovy
   paste
2 teaspoons lemon juice
1 clove garlic, mashed into a
   paste with a pinch of salt
1 teaspoon cold water
Pinch basil leaves, freshly
   torn or cut into ribbons
   (optional)
Salt and freshly ground
   black pepper

I use this most frequently as a quick sauce for dipping the leaves of a freshly steamed artichoke as a predinner snack.

MAKES APPROXIMATELY 1 CUP

Simply stir together all the ingredients in a nonreactive bowl, seasoning to taste with salt and a generous amount of pepper.

Smoked Chile and Caper Remoulade

MAKES APPROXIMATELY 1¼ CUPS

Stir together all ingredients in a nonreactive bowl, seasoning to taste with salt and pepper.

1 cup mayonnaise, homemade or high-quality store-bought
2 teaspoons chipotle puree (see page 204)
2 tablespoons capers, minced
1 tablespoon lemon juice
1 tablespoon Dijon mustard
2 tablespoons minced cilantro leaves or parsley
Salt and freshly ground black pepper

Fresh Mint and Coriander Sauce

This recipe is an updated version of an old-fashioned mint sauce. It is a fresh herb-based sauce that makes a fragrant addition to so many dishes: fish, lamb, poultry, and simply grilled or roasted vegetables all spring to mind.

MAKES APPROXIMATELY 2 CUPS

Combine the sugar, vinegar, and water and stir until the sugar dissolves. Add the shallots, coriander seed, chopped herbs, and salt and mix well. This sauce will keep well in the fridge for up to 2 weeks. It will turn an unlovely shade of green, but the flavor will remain vibrant.

¼ cup sugar
½ cup white wine or champagne vinegar
¼ cup cold water
6 shallots, peeled and minced
1 tablespoon freshly ground coriander seed
⅔ cup minced fresh mint leaves
⅓ cup minced fresh cilantro leaves
2 teaspoons salt

Cranberry Relish with Green Chiles and Kumquat

This is a chunky, piquant cranberry relish with attitude! Your turkey had better be up to the challenge. Actually, it is a great accompaniment to most birds—squab, duck, quail, pheasant, and goose. The leftover relish will keep for up to two weeks in the fridge.

MAKES APPROXIMATELY 1 QUART

2 tablespoons butter

1 red onion, diced fine

2 tablespoons grated fresh ginger

2 teaspoons curry powder

Two 1-pound bags fresh cranberries, picked over for stems and rinsed*

1½ cups orange juice

1 cup dark brown sugar

2 poblano chiles, roasted, peeled, seeded, and diced fine

12–15 kumquats, thinly sliced, or substitute orange or tangerine sections

Salt and freshly ground black pepper

2 tablespoons minced fresh cilantro or sage as garnish (optional)

Heat a saucepan over medium heat, melt the butter, and sauté the onion and ginger until soft, about 3 minutes. Stir in the curry powder and cook for 2 minutes more. Add the cranberries, orange juice, and brown sugar to the pan and stir once or twice to combine. Turn heat down to a simmer and let cook slowly until the cranberries have popped open, about 15 minutes. Fold in the poblanos and kumquats and let the relish cool before seasoning to taste with salt and pepper. Garnish with cilantro or sage, if using, just before serving. These flavors are at their best at room temperature, so if you've made this in advance, take it out of the fridge at least 2 hours before serving.

‹ weighing your options ›
Don't just think poultry with this vibrant sauce. It's a great match for pork and venison too.

*Note: If fresh cranberries are not in season, you can use dried.

Dried Fig and Almond Chutney

This is strictly my own definition of chutney—a chunky fruit-based sauce that is sweet, tart, and spicy all at once and makes simple food taste fabulously complex. You can use any dried fruit or fresh fruit in season. Good variations can be made with prunes or dried apricots. I use this chutney on grilled pork or veal chops or as part of a cured meats and cheese platter.

MAKES APPROXIMATELY 1 QUART

Use a paring knife to remove the stem end of the figs and cut them into quarters. Pour the cold water into a saucepan and add the figs, ginger, shallots, port, orange juice and zest, and vinegar to the pan. Simmer until the figs have plumped up and absorbed most of the liquid, about 20 minutes. Cool the figs and fold in the toasted almonds. Season to taste with a little salt, pepper, and freshly grated nutmeg.

¼ pound dried figs
2 cups cold water
1 tablespoon minced ginger
2 shallots, peeled and
    minced
1 cup port
Zest and juice of 1 orange
3 tablespoons red wine
    vinegar
½ cup toasted almond slices
    or slivers
Salt and freshly ground
    black pepper
Freshly grated nutmeg

‹ weighing your options ›
If it is fresh fig season, I make a similar relish by lightly grilling the figs and folding them together with roasted and peeled poblano chiles, grilled red onion, a splash of balsamic vinegar, and a drizzle of extra virgin olive oil. Then you can garnish with some minced cilantro or basil if you like.

Fruited Mustards

This is really not a recipe at all, just an invitation to tinker a bit. When I'm uninspired by the jar of Dijon mustard in my fridge, but I want that lovely mustardy bite to go with a sausage or on a sandwich, I just melt a little of my favorite fruit jelly or jam in a small pan and fold it in with the mustard. Why pay premium prices for the gourmet store varieties when you can do it so easily yourself? The proportion changes depending on how sharp or sweet I want the final sauce to be. As a general rule, I usually use two parts mustard to one part fruit. You can add even more flavor nuance by reducing wine or port or cider with some fresh fruit like currants, apricots, cherries, plums, whatever. You can leave them in large chunks for texture, or puree them for a smoother sauce. Also experiment with whole-grain mustard as a base.

Celery Root and Apple Remoulade

This is my twist on a classic French condiment. I've replaced the traditional mayonnaise base with crème fraîche and added the sweetness and crunch of apple. While I usually serve this as a garnish with pâté, I can eat it in huge spoonfuls as is!

MAKES APPROXIMATELY 3 CUPS

Stir together the crème fraîche, mustard, and lemon juice in a bowl. Cut both the celery root and the apple into thin matchstick slices (you should have about 3 cups total between both the celery root and apple), and toss immediately in the crème fraîche mixture to prevent their turning brown. Stir well and season with salt, pepper, and herbs, if using. Let the sauce sit for an hour in the fridge to let the flavors marry together. This remoulade will keep up to 5 days in the fridge.

1 cup crème fraîche (see box on page 29)
3 tablespoons Dijon mustard
2 tablespoons lemon juice
1 celery root, trimmed and peeled
1 crisp apple—Gala, Fuji, Granny Smith—peeled
Salt and freshly ground black pepper
2 tablespoons minced herb of your choice—thyme, tarragon, or cilantro (optional)

Grated Apple and Horseradish Cream

This is in some ways similar to the preceding remoulade, but the horseradish provides a lovely tangy bite that makes it perfect with hot or cold roasts of any kind—particularly roast beef. Fresh horseradish is becoming easier to find, but prepared will do nicely too.

MAKES APPROXIMATELY 1 CUP

Fold all ingredients together in a nonreactive bowl, seasoning to taste with salt and pepper. You can store this for up to 10 days in the fridge.

$\frac{1}{2}$ cup finely grated fresh horseradish tossed with 2 tablespoons white wine vinegar, or 4 tablespoons prepared horseradish, drained
$\frac{2}{3}$ cup crème fraîche
1 crisp apple—Fuji, Gala or Granny Smith—peeled and grated directly into the crème fraîche
Salt and freshly ground black pepper

Cumin-Cured Cherry Tomatoes

Oven-curing tomatoes is like preserving a little bit of the sun. Drying the tomatoes out in an oven at low heat with the help of salt intensifies their flavor and allows the tomatoes to keep for up to a month in the fridge. They also freeze very well when protected with a healthy coating of olive oil before packaging them into freezer bags. I use them for a splash of color and vibrant flavor for so many things: salads, soups, sandwiches, and quick sautés of fish or meat. They're particularly good as a garnish to beans and lentils—like wonderfully savory candy.

MAKES APPROXIMATELY 2 CUPS

3 pints cherry tomatoes of any color—a combination is nice

Coarse sea salt

4 cloves garlic, sliced paper thin

¼ cup coarsely ground cumin seed

⅔ cup olive oil

Preheat oven to 225°F. Wash and stem the tomatoes and cut in half. Line two baking sheets with foil. Place the tomatoes in a single layer, cut side up, on the sheets. Season each face with several grains of the sea salt, a slice or two of garlic, and a tiny pinch of cumin. Then drizzle the tomatoes as evenly as you can with the olive oil. Seasoning each tomato as precisely as you can yields the best results. Place the tomatoes in the oven and let them cook/cure for 3–4 hours. The tomatoes should shrivel a bit but not be too leathery.

My Green Sauce

This is the sauce to make when you find yourself with several miscellaneous bundles of herbs in your fridge. It's a real brine lover's paradise. The capers, olives, and herbs combine to make a playful sauce for oily fish like salmon and tuna and a great condiment for cold roasts.

MAKES APPROXIMATELY 1½ CUPS

Use herbs in any combination you like—lots of parsley will yield a very bright green sauce. Put all the ingredients except the olive oil and salt and pepper in a nonreactive bowl. Stir well to combine and then slowly incorporate the olive oil while stirring. Season to taste with salt and pepper. This sauce is best if it is used the day it's made, but it will hold a few days in the fridge.

½ cup pitted and finely chopped green olives

2 tablespoons capers, drained and chopped

4–6 gherkins, chopped

1 tablespoon Dijon mustard

1 teaspoon mashed anchovies or anchovy paste

2 tablespoons red wine vinegar

1 teaspoon lemon zest

2 cloves garlic, peeled and mashed to a paste

1 cup minced fresh herbs in any combination— parsley, tarragon, chervil, cilantro, basil, mint, thyme, chives

½ cup extra virgin olive oil

Coarse sea salt and freshly ground black pepper

Salsa Verde Picante

This is another version of a green sauce, made from lightly cooked tomatillos and green chiles for a crisp, light salsa that is great with fish or just a bag of corn chips! Stir some of this sauce into a ripe, mashed avocado and you have a great guacamole. If you cannot find tomatillos, you can substitute green cherry tomatoes. Just don't cook them—place them in the blender raw.

MAKES APPROXIMATELY 2 CUPS

½ pound tomatillos, husks removed and rinsed

2 jalapeño or serrano chiles, cut in half

1 small white onion, sliced

1 cup lightly packed cilantro leaves

Honey to taste

Salt

Bring 3 quarts of salted water to a boil, drop in the tomatillos, and cook for 8 minutes. Drain and refresh under cold water. Put the tomatillos, chiles, onion, and cilantro into a blender. Puree until smooth. Season to taste with a little honey and salt. This salsa is best if used the day it's made.

Papaya-Ginger Salsa

Ripe papaya has a sweet and funky flavor all its own. The ginger harmonizes with its tropical roots and makes it a natural pairing with fish that swim in or migrate to the southern oceans, like tuna, mahimahi, pompano, and grouper. This salsa also tastes great with grilled duck breasts, particularly if they've been marinated with a combination of sesame oil and soy.

MAKES APPROXIMATELY 2 CUPS

Simply stir together all the ingredients in a nonreactive bowl, seasoning to taste with salt and pepper. This salsa will keep up to 3 days in the fridge, but the natural pectin in the papaya will cause it to "seize up" after a day, so just loosen the salsa by stirring in a couple of tablespoons of cold water. Taste again to see if it needs more salt and pepper.

1 small or ½ large papaya, peeled, seeded, and cut into ½-inch dice

1 small red onion, diced fine

2 tablespoons minced fresh ginger

1 poblano or jalapeño chile, thinly sliced

1 teaspoon ancho chile powder (optional)

Juice of 1 lime

2 tablespoons rice vinegar or white wine vinegar

3 tablespoons extra virgin olive oil

2 tablespoons minced cilantro

Salt and freshly ground black pepper

Port-Plumped Prunes

As much fun to say as they are to eat, these prunes are particularly enjoyable during the holiday months, when just about everything seems to be spiked with some kind of alcohol! Actually, the alcohol burns off in the cooking process, just leaving the flavor of the port behind. These spiked prunes are a wonderful garnish for pork, venison, or squab. They also make a delicious and elegant cocktail snack when used to top goat cheese crostini.

MAKES APPROXIMATELY 1 QUART

1 cup port
1 cup cold water
3 pieces whole star anise
1 stick cinnamon
6 cardamom pods
1 cup prunes
Zest and juice of 1 orange
¼ cup sugar
Julienne of orange peel, for garnish (optional)

Bring the port and water to a simmer in a saucepan. Meanwhile, dry-toast the spices in a skillet for 2 minutes to release their fragrance. Add the toasted spices, prunes, orange juice and zest, and sugar to the pan. Simmer gently until the prunes have softened and "plumped" and the liquid has reduced to a light syrup—about 20 minutes. Remove the prunes and strain the sauce over them. Serve either warm or at room temperature. If you like, top the prunes with a julienne of orange peel to add a bit of color. These prunes will keep for up to 2 weeks in the fridge.

❮ weighing your options ❯

These prunes can be the inspiration for a more elegant sauce for pork, duck, or venison. Just sauté a couple of sliced shallots in butter, add the prunes and their syrup, stir in some veal stock or good-quality commercial demi-glace (see Sources), and reduce until the sauce coats a spoon. Adjust the balance with a splash of red wine vinegar and a swirl of chilled butter at the end. Season to taste with salt, pepper, and freshly grated nutmeg.

Beurre Noisette and Variations

This is by far the simplest of the classic French sauces. Butter is heated until the solids toast and turn a nutty hazelnut (noisette) color. At this point, you can liven up the flavor profile by adding herbs, spices, vinegar, or lemon juice and capers. In fact, the most well-known browned butter sauce is beurre meuniere, which is finished with minced parsley and lemon juice and then poured over a delicate white fish like flounder, sole, or skate. I always add capers to these preparations for a briny boost.

MAKES ABOUT ½ CUP

Melt the butter in a small saucepan over medium heat, swirling the pan occasionally to let the butter brown evenly. When the butter stops foaming, keep a close eye on the color—it will darken quickly at this point. You want the solids to turn a rich, golden brown like the color of unpeeled hazelnuts. Once you get the butter to this shade, immediately remove it from the heat and pour in the lemon juice to stop the cooking and balance the flavor. At this point, add your garnishes and season to taste with salt and pepper.

for basic browned butter
1 stick unsalted butter
1 tablespoon lemon juice
Salt and pepper

VARIATIONS:

Pistachio-Cardamom: ¼ cup chopped, toasted pistachios and ⅛ teaspoon ground cardamom

Saffron-Orange: ¼ teaspoon saffron threads and juice and zest of 1 orange (orange juice replaces lemon juice)

Truffle-Sherry: 1 tablespoon minced fresh or preserved black truffles and 1 tablespoon aged sherry vinegar (vinegar replaces lemon juice)

Homemade Flavored Vinegars

I'm very attracted to bottles of flavored vinegars whenever I see them decorating the shelves of gourmet food shops. But I never buy them, because making your own is so much fun and so easy—not to mention more affordable. The basic idea is to fill a glass bottle or jar with dried herbs (the herbs must be dried or you will get a murky vinegar), spices, chiles, fresh and reasonably fleshy fruit like peaches, apricots, or cherries, and garlic or shallots in any combination that strikes your fancy. You want to match the strength of the vinegar to the flavoring ingredients. For example, use white wine or champagne vinegar for delicate herbs like lemon thyme, dill, and cilantro. Cider, rice, or red wine vinegar is suitable for more robust flavors like garlic, dried chiles, and heartier herbs like sage and rosemary. Flavored vinegars can be used in vinaigrettes, as part of a marinade, or as a splash of acid added just at the end of a long-simmering soup or stew to perk up the flavor.

step 1

Choose your flavoring ingredients and match them with the right vinegar. For each wine-sized bottle of vinegar, the flavorings should compose about a quarter of the volume. This is not an exact science, but a general rule that you can play with once you are more comfortable with your homemade vinegars. Here are some suggested pairings:

- hot chile peppers with basil and garlic in red or white wine or rice vinegar
- cinnamon sticks, orange peel, whole star anise, and whole cloves in cider vinegar
- fresh peaches, sage, and rosemary in white wine vinegar

- fennel seed, oregano, marjoram, and cumin seed in white wine vinegar
- cilantro, lemongrass, ginger, and dried chiles in rice vinegar
- dill flowers, thinly sliced lemon wheels, and black peppercorns in champagne vinegar

All herbs should be completely dry. You can use commercial dried herbs, or what I like to do is buy fresh herbs in bunches and hang them upside down in my kitchen for a week to dry them. The nice branches look quite dramatic in the jar.

If you are using fresh fruit or citrus, blanch the fruit in boiling water for 15 seconds, then shock in an ice bath. Peel fresh fruit, if desired.

step 2

Gently warm the vinegar in a pot but don't let it boil, which will reduce its acidity. Tuck your flavoring ingredients into the jar or bottle, then pour in the warm vinegar. Be sure that the aromatics are completely submerged. If anything has a tendency to float (like dried chiles), thread them on a wooden skewer to keep them in line. Cover the jar or bottle and let the flavors develop in a cool spot for 1–2 months.

Spiced Tomato Chutney

This is a very assertive chutney that pairs nicely with rich meats like the marrow toasts on page 214. The dates in the recipe help round out the intensity of the spices and the vinegar and make it very bold and satisfying. But you don't need a big beefy dinner for this chutney. It's also great spread on a crouton under a slice of marinated goat cheese as a quick cocktail snack or quick bite while making dinner. Just pop the whole thing under the broiler for a few seconds to let the cheese get warm and melting. These are addictive!

MAKES APPROXIMATELY 2 CUPS

1 tablespoons vegetable oil

2 cloves garlic, minced

1 tablespoon minced ginger

1 stick cinnamon

6 cardamom pods

2 whole cloves

1 New Mexico chile,*
    or 1 teaspoon crushed
    red chile flakes

1 pound ripe plum
    tomatoes, roughly
    chopped

½ cup pitted dates, diced

¾ cup cider vinegar

2 tablespoons light brown
    sugar

Salt and freshly ground
    black pepper

Heat the oil in a skillet over medium heat. Add the garlic, ginger, cinnamon, cardamom, cloves, and chile and stir together for 2 minutes to release their oils. Add the tomatoes, dates, and vinegar to the skillet and sprinkle with the sugar. Cook over medium-low heat, stirring occasionally, until the tomatoes are very soft and glossy from the reduced vinegar and sugar syrup. This takes about 20 minutes. Remove from heat, cool, and pick out the whole spices—cinnamon sticks, cloves, and cardamom pods—with a fork or spoon. Season to taste with salt and pepper. The chutney will keep for 2 weeks in the fridge.

*To prepare the New Mexico chile, dry-toast it in a skillet over medium heat until the chile puffs up with steam and becomes fragrant, about 2 minutes. Open the pod, remove the seeds, and chop the chile with a knife or in a spice mill into ¼-inch pieces.

Onion-Sage Confit

Onions are naturally sweet, and slow cooking only accentuates this trait. I love to add the sage early in their cooking so it really permeates the whole dish. Thyme is also nice, and in that case I would omit the cider vinegar and replace it with about a quarter cup of diced, briny black olives or oil-cured olives.

MAKES APPROXIMATELY 1½ CUPS

Heat the olive oil and butter together in a heavy skillet over medium heat. Stir in the onions and coat them well with the oil and butter, add the sage, and cook over medium-low heat while stirring occasionally for 25–30 minutes, or until the onions are deeply browned and very soft. Sprinkle the vinegar over the onions and add the dried currants, if desired. Season lightly with salt and pepper. You don't want this too salty—it gets in the way of the lovely sweet flavor—but lots of pepper is divine!

2 tablespoons olive oil
1 tablespoon butter
2 large onions, sliced thin
8–10 sage leaves, cut into
   ¼-inch ribbons
1 tablespoon cider vinegar
   or sherry vinegar
2 tablespoons dried
   currants (optional)
Salt and freshly ground
   black pepper

‹ weighing your options ›
I love this marmalade as a garnish for poultry dishes.
It serves as a great condiment for leftover chicken or turkey
sandwiches. It is also goes well with pork chops or ham.

POTS DE CRÈME

Bittersweet Chocolate
Butterscotch
Marsala with Orange Zest

OPEN-FACED FRUIT TARTS

Dough for Individual Tarts
Apple Tarts with Almond-Ginger Streusel
Raspberry Tarts with Cardamom Sugar

Mohr im Hemd

Quark Cheesecake with a Spiced Nut Crust
Gweürztraminer Syrup
Frosted Green Grapes

Simple Chocolate Cake

Warm Berry and Mango Gratin in Mascarpone Chantilly

Strawberry-Rhubarb Shortcake

Caramelized Pineapple with Vanilla Bean and Star Anise Sauce

Chocolate Bread Pudding

Riesling Poached Pears with Pistachio Custard Sauce

Maple Lace Cookies

Cinnamon-Cayenne Sugar Cookies

Oatmeal, Chocolate Chip, and Pecan Cookies

DESSERTS

Most chefs will tell you that the pastry arts are a completely different discipline from savory cooking, and that for the most part we prefer to leave it to the professionals. I'm just as smitten with complex pastries and ornate desserts as the next person, provided I am eating—not making—them. However, since Quilty's was such a small restaurant, I wore both chef and pastry chef hats. The desserts I made at Quilty's had to be simple but still dramatic on the plate. I accomplished this by using great ingredients with interesting flavor combinations, and simple techniques that are easily mastered, like open-faced fruit tarts and simple custards. I cook the same desserts at home without having to simplify them at all. These desserts provide maximum impact with minimal fuss.

As a student in Vienna in the early 1980s, I still remember my first slice of Sacher torte in the Hotel Sacher itself. I was eighteen and had just begun my winter semester studying classical music and German at an American international school. Juergen Hammer had called to say that he and his *Stammtisch* from Mainz were in town and wanted me to join them at the hotel for lunch. A *Stammtisch* is a noisy table of regulars at a restaurant. This particular group was a cross-section of the prominent burghers of Mainz. Juergen and his wife, Gisela, are good friends of my parents, and Juergen couldn't resist an opportunity to tease his friends' daughter a little. What business did I have sitting at the head of the table of eight raucous German men in an elegant private room of the Hotel Sacher? However I ended up there, I'll never forget it—and I have a purloined monogrammed ashtray from the hotel to remember it by.

While in Vienna, I stayed with other family friends, the Esterhazys. Esterhazy is a well-known name in Austria and Hungary—it's a little like an American saying that she spent her vacation with her family friends the Cabots or the Lodges. This branch of the Esterhazys is old aristocracy but also a thoroughly modern family engaged in pursuing careers in the arts and in charitable work. My parents fell in love with the Esterhazys and vice versa when my father was a Fulbright scholar in the 1950s and the Esterhazys had a spare room to let to interesting young people. The two families have been trading visits between Vienna and Vermont ever since.

During my stay I had plenty of time to wander the streets during the day—the fringe benefit of not taking one's studies seriously. I spent long hours in the afternoons in the cafés, which were often situated on prime people-watching corners. The *Frauen* behind the pastry counters looked like they had not only sampled every dessert but like they were made of butter, sugar, and flour themselves—a perfect integration of work and worker. I'm not commenting on their size, just the fact of their serenity and obvious surrender to their position.

Another family favorite dessert is Mohr im Hemd, "Moor in a shirt." My mother got this recipe from Mathis Esterhazy's wife, Eva; it is a lightly souffled chocolate and nut cake drenched in a dark chocolate sauce (the moor, presumably) then topped with a fluffy cloud of *Schlag* (the German word for whipped cream—and we can guess it is the moor's shirt).

While many of my favorite desserts happen to involve chocolate, I also have a fondness for freshly picked fruit. As kids, we were sent out into the wild raspberry and blackberry bushes in the late afternoon. We picked the warm-from-the-sun and fully fragrant berries for a dessert that involved no more than pouring cold heavy cream over them. The raspberries were my favorite. I loved the contrast between the tender fruit and the crunchy seeds and how they turned the cream a delightful shade of pink. Wild strawberries and blueberries were also much prized, but they were harder to come by despite their relatively puny defenses—no sharp brambles, but instead low-lying groundcover that made them hard to spot. Intriguing when you think how nature has designed defenses for just about all things that are good to eat—either camouflage, thorns, toxins, or swift retreats. There is something satisfying about learning what wild things you can safely eat. It is like a little glimpse into our more primitive past (and by this I don't mean the time before microwaves).

In between the red maple, birch, and weeping willows, my parents planted dwarf fruit trees on the lawn. By building their own house and employing us kids as pint-size gardeners, they had an opportunity to shape the landscape in any way the Vermont climate could support. So we had sweet cherries and sour cherries, prune plums and pears. I loved the strategy my father employed to outwit the birds (more of a challenge than you would think, given my father's distinct advantage in brainpower) that were eating all the sour cherries before we could pick them ourselves: he bought a two-dollar rubber snake from the discount store and draped it over a high branch. The birds were completely fooled—well, at least for that first season.

The sour cherries were the best, until it came time to pit them. But my mother had an ingenious tool for this—a bent hairpin. It does the least damage to the fruit of any pitter I've ever seen. I treasure these memories of working with my mother at the kitchen table. These were the times to ask questions about family history. Who was the better cook, Grandma Spayde or Grandma Sparks? Why didn't Uncle Bill have any kids? Remind me which bridges Grandpa Spayde bid the steel for? I didn't have to ask how to cook, I just watched my mother's deft movements and helped out where I could until it became second nature to taste and retaste. The sour cherry pie we made from our own tree was certainly something to look forward to every year, and as a bonus, the cherries froze pretty well too, so we could get a taste of summer when there was a couple feet of snow on the ground.

But in between these memorable dessert events, there were the more prosaic, daily sweet-tooth fixes. I loved the fact that my father couldn't resist a midafternoon Fudgesicle from the freezer during haying season or a handful of Hershey's Miniatures in the pocket of his denim farm coat when he went down to feed the chickens. It brought our big papa down to the level of us kids for a little while. When my sister, Liza, and I were preschoolers in Mainz, Germany, my father would escort us down to the banks of the Rhine River for an ice cream most summer evenings. When I think back on those nights, I realize it was never really clear who was taking whom. And that in fact is one of life's secrets—enjoy your food like a child, and you'll always have an immense source of pleasure.

Pots de Crème

I learned this recipe from my high school French teacher, Madame Bourcier, and it remains one of my favorite desserts. It is a very simple recipe for chocolate pots de crème, which is basically chocolate pudding for grown-ups. This one is dense and rich and requires no cooking at all—just setting up time in the fridge. My mother has adopted this recipe as one of her classic dinner-party desserts, after which my father offers the coup de grâce—a selection of very fiery eaux-de-vie that my parents bring back from the Alsace and Vienna.

There are so many devoted fans of these small but intensely flavored custards that there is even a Web site catering to the collector of pots de crème pots (www.potsdecreme.com)! Restaurants will often serve a duo or trio of custards, but I content myself with one flavor at a time.

bittersweet chocolate pots de crème

This is a no-bake custard—the heat of the scalded milk and cream essentially cook the egg yolks, and the chocolate itself firms up nicely when chilled.

SERVES 6–8

8 ounces bittersweet
    chocolate, chopped fine
2 egg yolks
¼ cup sugar
2 tablespoons cognac or
    1 tablespoon vanilla
    extract
⅛ teaspoon salt
1 cup milk
½ cup heavy cream

Put the chocolate, egg yolks, sugar, cognac or vanilla extract, and salt in a blender. Pour the milk and cream into a saucepan and set over high heat. As soon as the milk and cream have come to a scald,* pour the hot liquid into the blender and puree on high speed for 2 minutes. Pour the custard into 6–8 pots de crème cups or small ramekins and chill for at least 4 hours before serving.

*To scald means to bring the milk just up to under a boil so you get a skin on top.

butterscotch pots de crème

I've loved butterscotch since childhood, but these days I appreciate a somewhat less sweet butterscotch flavor. So I add a little Scotch to the custard. I felt since it was already in the name, it must be a good idea. The alcohol burns off and leaves behind a complex, wood-aged flavor that cuts through the intense sweetness of traditional butterscotch. While the first recipe is not baked, this one is, and the key for achieving a smooth custard is to cook the eggs slowly and evenly—this is achieved through a relatively low oven temperature and with the protection of a water bath, or bain marie, surrounding the custard cups.

SERVES 6

Preheat oven to 325°F. Melt the butter in a saucepan and whisk in the sugar and the Scotch. Cook for 3 minutes, until the sugar liquefies and the alcohol burns off. Meanwhile, in a separate saucepan scald (see footnote on preceding page) the heavy cream and milk together and pour into the sugar, butter, and Scotch mixture, whisking until the hot liquid is thoroughly combined.

Whisk together the eggs, egg yolks, and salt in a large bowl. Slowly drizzle in the hot cream mixture, whisking to combine. Strain this custard base through a fine sieve to remove any small lumps. At this point you are ready to fill your pots de crème cups or ramekins and prepare the bain marie. Your bain marie pan should be at least 2 inches deep and should easily accommodate all the cups, with about 2 inches of space between them.

3 tablespoons unsalted butter
1 cup dark brown sugar
¼ cup Scotch whiskey
1½ cups heavy cream
1½ cups milk
2 eggs
4 egg yolks
⅛ teaspoon salt

to prepare the bain marie
Heat approximately 3 quarts of water on the stove to just under a boil. Place the custard cups in the pan that will become your bain

marie, and fill the cups ⅔ of the way with the custard base. It is much easier to move a dry pan into the oven than one filled with hot water, so pull out the middle rack and place the pan on top of it, and then bring over the hot water. Slowly pour the water in at one of the corners, being very careful to not let water splash into the ramekins. If you're using proper pots de crème cups, they have individual lids that you'll use, which makes this a moot point. Pour the water in to rise halfway up the sides of the custard cups. Cover the whole pan with foil and gently push the oven rack into position.

Bake 25–30 minutes or until there is a nickel-size jiggle in the center of each custard. Remove the custards immediately from the hot water and let them cool on a rack.

‹ weighing your options ›

This custard is delicious both warm and chilled, but straight from the oven is a bit too hot and the texture won't be quite right. I serve with either a dollop of crème fraîche or lightly sweetened whipped cream.

marsala pots de crème with orange zest

This recipe has the flavors of the classic warm egg custard zabaglione, but because it is baked instead of being whisked over a water bath on the stove, it is more stable and can be served chilled as well as warm. Marsala is a fortified wine from Italy and the dry variety is used here, but experiment with the sweet one if you like.

SERVES 6

2½ cups heavy cream

¾ cup sugar

3 large strips orange peel, pith carefully removed

6 egg yolks

3 tablespoons dry marsala

Preheat oven to 325°F. Heat the cream, sugar, and orange peel in a pan and stir until the sugar dissolves and the cream has reached a scald (see footnote on page 290). Whisk the egg yolks until smooth in a medium bowl. Remove the orange peel from the cream mixture and slowly pour the cream into the eggs while whisking constantly. Strain this custard base through a fine sieve. Stir in the marsala and divide among 6 pots de crème cups or ramekins. Place the cups in a bain marie (for more on this, see procedure in Butterscotch Pots de Créme recipe, page 291), cover the whole pan tightly with foil, and bake for 25–30 minutes. The custards should still have a nickel-size jiggle in the center. Remove immediately from the hot water and cool on a rack.

‹ weighing your options ›
These marsala custards have the most fragrance when served warm with just a dollop of whipped cream, but I also love them chilled with a glass of marsala to reinforce the flavor. You can boost the orange flavor by sectioning an orange or two, lightly sautéing the sections in a little butter and sugar, and spooning them on top of each dessert. But the easiest accompaniment of all is to buy some very fresh hazelnut biscotti to dunk into the custard.

CHOCOLATE

I'm an admitted chocoholic, and I have no intention of reforming. I keep a bar of good bittersweet chocolate within arm's reach at all times, but am very moderate in my consumption—one or two squares of high-quality, well-balanced chocolate is enough to keep me on an even keel. I'm not sure if this is due to the caffeine content, the theobromine (another feel-good brain chemical found in chocolate), or the sheer pleasure of the chocolate releasing its complex flavor as it melts on my tongue. Whatever it is, I seem to be hard-wired to appreciate it. I've recently had to cut way back on coffee—it was speeding up my system in an unpleasant way—so now, without my liquid caffeine fix, chocolate is even more important to me.

In the past few years, the variety and quality of chocolate available has increased tremendously, with artisan producers popping up in the United States, like Scharffen Berger (San Francisco) and Jacques Torres (New York), adding to Old World artisan chocolatiers like Michel Cluizel (France), El Rey (Venezuela), and Valrhona (France)—see Sources. All of these producers have a variety of chocolates in their lines, from milk to bittersweet, semisweet and dark, which you should explore according to the intensity of your sweet tooth. For baking, my general rule is the better the chocolate, the better your final dessert will be. While all of the brands I have mentioned are wonderful for baking (and any old type of consumption), I tend to stick to Valrhona.

You may notice many chocolate bars now list a percentage on their labels. For instance, Scharffen Berger makes four different chocolate bars—a 41 percent milk, a 62 percent semisweet, a 70 percent bittersweet, and an 82 percent extra dark. The percentage refers to the fraction (by weight) of the bar that comes from the cacao bean. This means that for a one-ounce chocolate bar marked 75 percent cacao, three-quarters is unsweetened chocolate, which leaves little room for other ingredients like milk and sweeteners. A quick rule of thumb is that the higher the cacao percentage, the less sweet the chocolate will be.

If you aren't used to semisweet or dark chocolate—chocolates with a high cacao percentage—it may be hard to swallow at first, because of its slightly bitter taste. But the flavors of these off-sweet chocolates are much more complex, and as you eat more of the darker stuff, it becomes more palatable and quite enjoyable. Dark chocolate is really more of an adult chocolate. It's

like growing up and learning to eat stinky cheese. When you first try it, you can't believe people actually eat it (and rave about it!). But then all of a sudden you can't get enough of it.

Another benefit of eating dark chocolate is that it is higher in healthy antioxidants than milk chocolate. Research has shown that all chocolate is packed with high-quality polyphenol antioxidants—beneficial compounds similar to those found in fruits, vegetables, and red wines that scientists say may reduce the risk for developing cancer and heart disease. Their research also shows that dark chocolate contains twice the number of antioxidants as milk chocolate. So you have a built-in reason for eating it, right there!

Chocolate is susceptible to moisture and absorbs external odors, so you should store it tightly wrapped in a cool, dry place away from light and air. The ideal temperature for storing chocolate is between 54°F and 68°F (12°–20°C). At higher temperatures, the chocolate will soften and lose its gloss. Lower storage temperatures are less risky.

Open-Faced Fruit Tarts

I never thought it would be possible to assemble and bake a fresh fruit tart to order in a busy restaurant, but that is exactly what we did at Al Forno in Providence, Rhode Island. This was my first restaurant job fresh out of cooking school, and my hands would shake as I tried to line up the fruit in perfect symmetry while orders kept pouring into my tiny salad and dessert station. George Germon, an owner of Al Forno, would take pity on me and slice the apples and silently hand them to me as I just as silently tried not to weep. I learned a lot of valuable lessons there, and this tart reminds me of how much pleasure there is in pushing yourself to your limits to please your guests or friends or family—and yourself.

There are many options in choosing a type of pastry crust, and I prefer a sweet, short-crust pastry for fruit tarts. This style is crumbly and buttery rather than flaky and stands up well under the juices of fresh fruit. I also like the technique of incorporating the butter into the flour, though it is kind of counterintuitive. We're always told to touch the butter as little as possible, to work with only your fingertips to avoid melting the butter and creating a tough dough. But in this case, you will actually be smearing the dough with your palms on a work surface in a technique called "fraisage." You will smear the dough away, then gather it up again in a ball and rest it in the fridge to firm up and let the gluten relax. I find it very easy to work with and incomparable in flavor.

sweet tart dough for six individual tarts

Sift the flour into a large bowl and stir in the sugar, lemon zest, and salt. Cut the butter into ¼-inch cubes, toss them into the bowl, and coat well with the flour mixture. Crumble the butter into the flour using the tips of your fingers or a pastry cutter until the mixture resembles coarse cornmeal. You can also cut the butter into the flour in your food processor using quick short pulses.

Whisk together the egg yolks and heavy cream in a small bowl. Pour this over the flour and butter mixture and stir together with a fork. Gather the dough into a ball, patting any stray dry areas into the mass. Turn the dough out onto a lightly floured work surface and with the heel of your hand begin smearing the dough away from the mass in small sections. When all the dough has been smeared, scrape it up and gather it back into a ball. Divide into 6 smaller balls and pat each down into a disk. Wrap each disk tightly with plastic wrap and let relax in the fridge at least 2 hours before rolling out.

When ready to assemble your tarts, roll each disk into a 6-inch-diameter circle. Dough should be ⅛ to ¼ inch thick. Chill until firm.

2¾ cups flour
½ cup sugar
1 teaspoon freshly grated lemon zest
¼ teaspoon salt
2 sticks chilled unsalted butter
2 egg yolks
¼ cup heavy cream

apple tarts with almond-ginger streusel

MAKES 6 INDIVIDUAL TARTS

Preheat oven to 400°F.

prepare the streusel
Combine the sugar, ginger, flour, and almonds in a medium-size bowl. Stir the dry ingredients together, then cut the butter into the dry ingredients with two forks, your fingers, or a pastry cutter.

prepare the filling
Cut each apple in half lengthwise and remove the stem and core. Lay each half on a cutting board and make 10–12 slices per half. Each tart will use approximately ⅔ of an apple.

for the almond-ginger streusel
2 tablespoons light brown sugar
1 teaspoon ground ginger
2 tablespoons flour
3 tablespoons lightly toasted sliced almonds
4 tablespoons butter, softened

for the apple tart

4 Golden Delicious apples,
washed and dried

1 recipe Sweet Tart Dough
(see page 297)

assemble the tarts

Roll out the dough into 6 disks, $\frac{1}{8}$–$\frac{1}{4}$ inch thick and approximately 6 inches in diameter. Lay out on a foil- or parchment-lined baking sheet and chill until firm.

Start at the outer edge of the dough and lay the apples on in slightly overlapping and concentric circles until you reach the center. Divide the streusel topping among the 6 tarts, dotting it on over the entire surface. Bake the tarts on baking sheet lined with foil, parchment, or a Silpat (a synthetic rubberized nonstick pan liner) for 25 minutes, until the fruit is cooked and the crust is a golden brown color. Let the tarts rest 2–3 minutes before trying to remove them from the tray.

Serve with vanilla ice cream, whipped cream, or just a dusting of powdered sugar.

❮ weighing your options ❯

Pears, plums, and nectarines are equally good in this tart.
If using pears, look for slightly underripe, starchy ones like Bosc
or Comice that will hold up during cooking.

raspberry tarts with cardamom sugar

MAKES 6 INDIVIDUAL TARTS

Preheat oven to 400°F. Roll out the dough into 6 disks, ⅛–¼ inch thick and approximately 6 inches in diameter. Lay out on a foil- or parchment-lined baking sheet and chill until firm.

assemble the tarts

Starting at the outer edge of each tart, line up the berries like little soldiers in concentric circles until you reach the middle. Dot each tart with the butter. Stir together the sugar, cardamom, and zest in a small bowl, and divide among the tarts, sprinkling evenly over the surface. Bake for 20–25 minutes, until the berries are glazed with the butter and sugar and the crust is golden brown. Serve warm with a dusting of powdered sugar and vanilla ice cream or crème fraîche.

1 recipe Sweet Tart Dough (see page 297)

4 pints raspberries

3 tablespoons unsalted butter, cut into ¼-inch cubes

6 tablespoons sugar

½ teaspoon ground cardamom

1 teaspoon grated orange zest

Powdered sugar, for dusting

Putting the finishing touches
on the cake

Chef's Trick: For this recipe, bring your eggs to room temperature, which will give you better volume in your soufflé.

Mohr im Hemd

As I mentioned in the chapter introduction, Mohr im Hemd translates to "Moor in a shirt." Precisely why it is called this, I can't tell you. What I do know is that it is a very easy dessert to prepare and will probably make its way into your dessert file too. It is basically a souffléd chocolate and nut cake drenched in a warm chocolate sauce and topped with whipped cream. What's not to love?

SERVES 6

Preheat oven to 375°F.

Butter 6 small ramekins and dust the insides lightly with sugar.

prepare the soufflé cakes

Whip the butter and ⅛ cup of the sugar in a bowl with an electric mixer until creamy. Melt the chocolate over a double boiler and pour it into the butter mixture. Stir in the nuts, egg yolks, and vanilla, making sure to scrape down the sides of the bowl to incorporate all the ingredients. Beat the egg whites and the remaining ⅛ cup sugar in a clean bowl of an electric mixer until stiff peaks form. Fold the whites into the chocolate mixture. Fill the prepared ramekins ¾ full and bake uncovered in a water bath, or bain marie (see pages 291–292) for 30 minutes.

meanwhile, make the sauce and whip the cream

Melt the chocolate and cream, and crème de cacao, if using, in a double boiler and stir until smooth. With an electric mixer, beat the cream with the sugar until soft peaks form. Remove the cakes from the oven and run a knife around the edge of each ramekin. Unmold each cake onto a plate. Spoon the warm chocolate sauce over the top of each cake until it drips down the sides and onto the plate. Top with a dollop of whipped cream and serve immediately.

for the soufflé cakes

4 tablespoons butter, at room temperature

¼ cup sugar

2 ounces semisweet chocolate

¼ cup finely ground walnuts, or half walnuts and half almonds

4 eggs, separated

1 teaspoon vanilla extract

for the chocolate sauce

4 ounces semisweet chocolate, such as Baker's

½ cup heavy cream

2 tablespoons crème de cacao (optional)

for the whipped cream

½ cup heavy cream

1 teaspoon sugar

Quark Cheesecake with a Spiced Nut Crust

I live in New York, so I have easy access to arguably the best cheese-cake in the world. The only trouble is that I prefer a lighter, less sweet style than the famous New York cheesecake. I modeled this recipe on the Italian ricotta cheesecakes, and found that the combination of quark—a German- and Austrian-style fresh farmer cheese—and yogurt makes a refreshing and tender dessert. The cheese and yogurt mixture needs to be pureed and hung in a cheesecloth to drain it of some of its moisture, so start with this step and proceed to the nut crust from there.

MAKES 1 CHEESECAKE,
USING A 9-INCH SPRINGFORM PAN

for the cheese

3 cups quark or fresh ricotta

1 cup whole-milk yogurt,
    preferably Greek style*

*If you cannot find Greek-style yogurt, you can use any whole-milk yogurt (I prefer organic), but drain it in a cheesecloth of its excess liquid so it is nice and thick.

prepare the cheese

Place the quark or ricotta and yogurt into a food processor and puree until smooth. Transfer this mixture to a sieve lined with cheesecloth and set over a bowl. Let the cheese and yogurt hang in the fridge until no more liquid drips out. This can be done overnight or 4–6 hours before you bake the cheesecake.

prepare the spiced nut crust

Pulse the nuts and 1 tablespoon of the sugar in a food processor until fine. Place the crushed nuts in a bowl and stir in the remaining sugar, the flour, cinnamon, clove, cardamom, and salt. Cut the butter into the dry ingredients with a pastry cutter or with the tips of your fingers until it resembles coarse cornmeal. Pour the beaten egg over the mixture and combine thoroughly with a fork. Turn the dough out onto a lightly floured work surface and knead a few times. Gather it into a ball, flatten out to a disk, and cover tightly with plastic wrap. Chill the dough for at least 1 hour before rolling out.

Preheat oven to 350°F. Butter the bottom of a 9-inch springform pan and cut out a round of parchment or wax paper to snuggly fit into the bottom. Butter the sides of the pan. Roll out the nut dough to ⅛-inch thickness and cut it to an 11-inch circle. Transfer the dough to your pan and press it halfway up the sides of the pan, trying not to stretch it as you go or it will inevitably shrink back. Top the nut dough with foil, pressing it into the corners of the pan. Fill with pie weights or dried beans, making sure to get the weights all the way into the edges. Bake the dough for 20 minutes, remove the weights and foil, and bake it for another 10 minutes. Remove and let cool. Reduce oven temperature to 300°F.

prepare the filling

Transfer the drained cheese mixture to a bowl and stir in the lemon and orange zests and sugar. Whisk in the eggs 1 at a time. Pour this filling into the springform pan on top of the prebaked crust. Bake at 300°F for 35–40 minutes, until the sides are set and there is a quarter-size jiggle in the center of the cake if you gently shake the pan. The cake will continue to set as it cools.

for the spiced nut crust

½ cup lightly toasted
   almonds
¼ cup lightly toasted
   walnuts
¼ cup sugar
1 cup flour
½ teaspoon cinnamon
Pinch of ground clove
Pinch of ground cardamom
¼ teaspoon salt
1 stick unsalted butter,
   chilled and cut into
   ¼-inch pieces
1 egg, beaten
Foil and dried beans for
   weighing down the
   crust

for the filling

Finely grated zest of 1
   lemon
Finely grated zest of 1
   orange
1 cup sugar
4 eggs

❮ weighing your options ❯

I like to serve this cheesecake with a drizzle of Gewürztraminer Syrup (see recipe on following page). Gewürztraminer is a spicy Alsatian wine with lovely floral notes that when reduced with additional spices is a sensational dessert sauce. Also, a fun and easy garnish is to frost green grapes with a little sugar (see next page, also) and serve small clusters of these frosted grapes on each plate—it makes a real vintner's harvest dessert.

gewürztraminer syrup

MAKES APPROXIMATELY ⅔ CUP WINE SYRUP

1 bottle good-quality
    gewürztraminer wine
    (750 ml, standard size)
Peel of 1 orange, pith
    carefully removed
6 cardamom pods
1 teaspoon minced fresh
    ginger

Pour the wine into a nonreactive saucepan with the orange peel and cardamom pods. Reduce by simmering slowly over low heat until the wine becomes syrupy. Add the ginger and let it steep in the wine syrup for 10 minutes off the heat. Strain the syrup and let cool to room temperature.

frosted green grapes

1 pound green grapes,
    washed and separated
    into small clusters
1 egg white, whisked until
    just foamy
1 cup sugar, poured out onto
    a plate

Dip the grapes first into the egg white, then roll them in the sugar and let them air-dry on a rack. Store them in an airtight container at room temperature.

Simple Chocolate Cake

Having a reliable chocolate cake in your repertoire is like having a little black dress in your closet—it's always appropriate. But because the recipe is so simple, every ingredient must be top-notch. I'm devoted to Valrhona Caraque (67 percent cocoa solids) for my bittersweet chocolate, but Lindt, Ghirardelli, and Scharffen Berger all produce very fine chocolate as well.

MAKES ONE 9-INCH CAKE
IN A SPRINGFORM PAN

Preheat oven to 350°F. Butter a 9-inch springform pan. Melt the chocolate, butter, and sugar together over a double boiler and stir until smooth. Cool. Whisk the egg yolks into the cooled chocolate mixture, then stir in the cognac or vanilla extract, flour, and salt. Beat the egg whites in a clean bowl to just firm peaks—be careful not to overbeat, or they will become dry and difficult to incorporate into the batter. Fold 1/3 of the egg whites into the batter to lighten it. Then gently fold in the remaining whites until no streaks of white remain. Pour the batter into the pan and bake for approximately 30 minutes, until the cake springs back when pressed in the center with your fingertips. Cool on a rack for 2 hours before unmolding.

Serve with a dusting of powdered sugar and some ripe berries as garnish.

12 ounces bittersweet chocolate, chopped into small pieces
2/3 cup unsalted butter
3/4 cup sugar
5 large eggs, separated
1 tablespoon cognac or vanilla extract
1/4 cup flour
1/4 teaspoon salt
Powdered sugar and ripe berries, for dusting and garnish

Warm Berry and Mango Gratin in Mascarpone Chantilly

This bubbly dessert gratin is a variation of the one I learned to make at Al Forno in Providence, Rhode Island. We baked it to order in the infernally hot pizza oven (700-plus degrees) until the berries popped open in the cream and the top glazed to a golden brown crust. But you don't need a pizza oven yourself. Your home oven set to 450°F is just fine. It just takes a few minutes longer.

SERVES 6

for the pastry cream
1 cup milk
1 egg
1 egg yolk
2 tablespoons flour
2 tablespoons sugar
Half a fresh vanilla bean,
    scraped, or ¼ teaspoon
    vanilla extract

**for the mascarpone
chantilly**
1 recipe Pastry Cream
    (see above)
1 cup mascarpone cheese,
    at room temperature
½ cup heavy cream, whipped
    to soft peaks

First you'll make a pastry cream and then fold in both mascarpone and whipped cream.

prepare the pastry cream
Scald the milk (see footnote on page 290). Whisk together the egg, egg yolk, flour, and sugar in a small bowl. Slowly pour the scalded milk into the egg mixture while whisking constantly. When all the milk has been incorporated, pour it back into the pan and return to the heat. Bring to a boil while stirring constantly. Cook for 2 minutes to cook out the raw flavor of the flour. Stir in the vanilla beans or vanilla extract. Pass through a sieve to remove any lumps and cover with plastic wrap pressed right down onto the surface of the pastry cream to prevent a skin from forming. Cool.

make the mascarpone chantilly
In a large bowl, fold together the cooled pastry cream, mascarpone, and whipped cream.

assemble the gratin
Preheat oven to 450°F. Scatter the berries and diced mango over the bottom of a 9-by-11-inch baking dish with low sides. (Low sides in the pan allow for better browning, because the air current moves

easily over the surface of the food.) Spoon the mascarpone chantilly evenly over the berries and mango. Place dish in the hot oven for about 10 minutes, and cook until the berries have popped open a bit and the surface of the gratin has browned. Serve warm from the oven.

for the fruit filling

1 pint each: raspberries, blackberries, and blueberries

1 ripe mango, peeled and cut into ½-inch dice

Michael, always an appreciative eater

‹ weighing your options ›

I like to serve this dessert with crisp homemade cookies. My mother's recipe for Maple Lace Cookies (see page 314) is perfect here. And when you fold them into tuile shapes by draping them over a rolling pin or a dowel, they can function like dessert "tortilla chips" for scooping up the berries and cream.

Strawberry-Rhubarb Shortcake

We have an abundance of wild strawberries in Vermont, and these local gems are my favorites for any strawberry dessert, but any ripe cultivated strawberries macerated with just a little sugar are terrific too. I find that combining strawberries and rhubarb brings out the best of both fruits. This dessert is really about assembling the components: the biscuits, fruit, and whipped cream form a whole much greater than the sum of its parts.

SERVES 6–8

for the biscuits

2¾ cups flour

3 tablespoons sugar,
    plus 1 tablespoon for
    sprinkling on tops of
    biscuits

1 tablespoon plus 1
    teaspoon baking powder

1 teaspoon salt

½ teaspoon freshly grated
    lemon zest

⅛ teaspoon ground
    cardamom

8 tablespoons unsalted
    butter

1 cup heavy cream, plus
    2 tablespoons for
    brushing the tops of
    the biscuits

Preheat oven to 375°F. Sift together the flour, the 3 tablespoons of sugar, all the baking powder, and the salt in a large bowl. Stir in the lemon zest and the cardamom. Cut the butter into small pieces and incorporate it into the flour with your fingers or a pastry cutter until the mixture resembles fine cornmeal. Pour in the 1 cup of heavy cream and combine with a fork until the dough just comes together; it's all right to have dry patches here and there, they will be kneaded into the mass.

Turn the dough out onto a lightly floured work surface and knead just a few times, then form the dough into a ball. Roll the ball out to ¾ inch thick and cut into 6–8 rounds or rectangles. Place the biscuits on a parchment-lined or greased baking sheet and chill in the fridge for 30 minutes before baking.

NOTE: If your baking sheet is of the thin variety, you may want to nestle a second pan under it; biscuits tend to brown quickly on the bottom.

**while the biscuits are chilling in the fridge,
make the rhubarb compote**

Simply place all the compote ingredients in a nonreactive saucepan over medium heat. Cover for the first 5 minutes, then uncover and let the rhubarb wilt down to a puree for another 5 minutes. Remove the cinnamon stick and cloves and cool.

Brush the tops of the biscuits with the 2 tablespoons of cream, sprinkle with the remaining 1 tablespoon of sugar, and bake 25–30 minutes, until golden brown.

while the biscuits are baking,
prepare the strawberries and cream
Toss the sliced berries with the sugar and let them juice a little. Whip the cream with the sugar and vanilla until soft peaks are formed—keep this in the fridge until ready to use.

assemble the shortcakes
Let the biscuits cool and then cut them in half horizontally. Spread each bottom with a generous spoonful of the rhubarb puree and a mound of the strawberries. Add a dollop of the whipped cream and perch the top of the biscuit on top. Garnish with another dollop of whipped cream and a few of the strawberries. Add a sprig of mint if desired or a dusting of powdered sugar, or both.

for the rhubarb compote
1 pound rhubarb stalks, trimmed, peeled, and cut into 1-inch lengths (about 3 cups)
½ cup sugar
1 stick cinnamon
6 cloves
½ teaspoon grated fresh ginger
1 teaspoon grated fresh orange zest
¼ cup port or full-bodied red wine

for the strawberries
2 pints strawberries, hulled and sliced
1 tablespoon sugar

for the whipped cream
1 cup very cold heavy cream
1 tablespoon sugar
½ teaspoon vanilla extract

Sprigs of mint for garnish (optional)
Powdered sugar for dusting (optional)

Caramelized Pineapple
with Vanilla Bean and Star Anise Sauce

I always enjoy putting on a little show from my kitchen for friends and family, and this dessert does the trick nicely. You will be flaming the rum in the pan on the stovetop, and will dazzle everyone with your ability to create great leaping flames while keeping your eyebrows intact! Actually, the flames are pretty tame, and I'll describe how best to keep them under strict control.

SERVES 6

4 tablespoons butter—
   2 tablespoons for
   sautéing the pineapple,
   and 2 tablespoons for
   finishing the sauce
1 ripe golden pineapple,
   peeled, cored, and cut
   into ½-inch-thick slices
½ cup dark rum
½ cup pineapple juice
1 vanilla bean, seeds scraped
   out and reserved
1 teaspoon ground star anise
¼ cup dark brown sugar
1 tablespoon cider vinegar
1 pint good-quality vanilla
   ice cream
Fresh mint, for garnish

Heat a large heavy-bottomed skillet with 2 tablespoons of the butter over medium heat. When the butter foams, slip the pineapple slices into the pan in 2 or 3 batches; you only want a single layer of pineapple in the pan at a time. Increase the heat to medium-high and brown each side of the pineapple slices (this should take about 2–3 minutes). Transfer the slices to a plate while finishing the sauce.

Pull the pan off the burner and pour the rum in, keeping your face well away from the pan until the alcohol burns off. This may happen immediately if the alcohol ignites, or may happen as you return the pan to the burner and the fumes ignite there. The small amount of rum used in this recipe will burn off quickly, either by flaming or simply reducing in the pan. In any case, just keep the pan at arm's length until this happens. Once the rum has reduced by half its volume, pour in the pineapple juice with the scraped vanilla beans, star anise, and sugar. Turn the heat down to medium and simmer sauce until it is thick and syrupy. Pour in the cider vinegar and whisk in the final 2 tablespoons of butter. Pour the sauce directly over the browned pineapple slices and serve with a scoop of vanilla ice cream in the middle of each slice and garnish with a sprig of mint.

Chocolate Bread Pudding

I usually have at least half a loaf of some kind of bread in my basket that is just a little too stale for sandwiches, but perfect for French toast or bread pudding. And the rest of the ingredients for this dish are garden-variety pantry items, making this a very rich and satisfying chocolate dessert that couldn't be easier to make.

SERVES 6–8

Preheat oven to 325°F. Lightly butter a 9-by-11-inch, 2-inch-deep casserole dish. Over low heat, melt together the chocolate, sugar, heavy cream, and butter in a saucepan and stir until smooth. Cool this mixture to room temperature.

Whisk together the eggs and the vanilla in a large bowl until eggs are well broken up. Pour the chocolate mixture into the eggs and stir until well combined. Add the bread cubes and coat well with the custard. Pour everything into the casserole dish and bake 30–35 minutes, until the pudding is firm to the touch. Serve warm or cold with a little whipped cream.

6 ounces bittersweet chocolate (I prefer Valrhona or Sharffen Berger), chopped into small bits

½ cup sugar

2 cups heavy cream

4 tablespoons unsalted butter, plus butter for greasing the casserole dish

3 large eggs

1 teaspoon vanilla extract

3½ cups firm white bread cut into ½-inch cubes

Whipped cream for garnish (optional)

Riesling Poached Pears with Pistachio Custard Sauce

This is the dessert to make when you find that none of the fruit at your market is quite ripe enough to serve. Firm pears are ideal for this recipe, since the poaching softens and sweetens them. In fact, ripe pears would fall apart while cooking. Riesling has the right sweetness and flavor notes, but you can use Muscat Beaumes de Venise or another fruity white wine. The custard sauce is optional; you could easily just serve the pears with some of the syrup.

SERVES 6

for the poached pears

1 bottle of Riesling

1 vanilla bean, scraped, seeds reserved for the sauce

1 teaspoon grated fresh ginger

Peel of 1 lemon, pith completely removed

4 whole cloves

3 tablespoons pear brandy

2 cups cold water

6 firm pears, like Bosc or Comice

poach the pears

Combine all the ingredients for the poached pears (except the pears themselves) in a nonreactive saucepan. Cut each pear in half, skin on, and remove the cores with a melon baller or paring knife. Drop each half into the poaching liquid as it is ready. When all the pears have been placed in the liquid, fold a piece of parchment and press it down onto the surface of the liquid to keep the pears submerged. If the pears are not quite submerged, add a little more cold water. Bring the liquid to a boil over high heat, turn it down to low, and cook just at a simmer for 40–45 minutes, until pears are tender. Remove pears and reduce the cooking liquid down to ¼ cup of syrup.

while the pears are poaching, prepare the pistachio custard sauce

Combine the cream, milk, pistachio paste, and orange zest in a small saucepan. Bring to a scald (see footnote on page 290), remove from heat, and cover. Let the flavors steep together for 30 minutes. Strain through a fine sieve. Return the flavored milk and cream to the saucepan.

Whisk together the egg yolks and sugar in a bowl for a few minutes, until the sugar has dissolved and the eggs are thick and pale yellow. Reheat the cream to a scald and slowly pour into the eggs while whisking constantly. When all the cream has been poured into the eggs, return this mixture to the saucepan, add the reserved vanilla seeds, and cook over low heat (being careful not to let the custard boil), stirring with a wooden spoon (not a whisk, which would incorporate air bubbles), until the custard coats the spoon. Strain again through a fine sieve and cool.

To serve, spoon out a generous puddle of the pistachio custard sauce onto each plate (if using), and arrange 2 halves of poached pear over the top. Drizzle the pears with the reduced poaching liquid. Lightly chop the reserved toasted pistachios and garnish the pears with them.

for the pistachio custard sauce (optional)

¾ cup heavy cream

¾ cup milk

¾ cup lightly toasted pistachios pureed to a paste in a food processor, plus ¼ cup toasted whole pistachios for garnish

1 teaspoon freshly grated orange zest

Reserved seeds from 1 vanilla bean

4 egg yolks

¼ cup sugar

Luke loves it!

Maple Lace Cookies

½ cup real maple syrup
4 tablespoons butter
⅛ teaspoon baking soda
½ cup flour
¼ teaspoon baking powder
⅛ teaspoon salt
¼ cup sliced almonds or
    peeled hazelnuts,
    roughly chopped

Preheat oven to 350°F. Combine the maple syrup and butter in a saucepan over medium-high heat and bring to a boil. Let the mixture boil rapidly, while stirring, for 30 seconds. Sift together the baking soda, flour, baking powder, and salt in a bowl, and pour the mixture (all at once) into the syrup and butter, stirring well to combine. Once the mixture is combined, remove the saucepan from the heat and fold in the nuts. The batter will look lumpy at this point, but it will smooth out in the oven. Drop the batter by ½ teaspoons onto a greased baking sheet, leaving space between each cookie. Bake 6–8 minutes, until lightly browned.

Remove from the oven and scrape up each cookie with a spatula while still hot. Drape it over a rolling pin or dowel, or even some thin waterglasses laid on their sides, to achieve the curved tile shape known as a "tuile." Let all the cookies cool on the pin or dowel.

NOTE: Keep your oven on while you are shaping the cookies, because if they start to harden you can pop them back in for a few seconds to soften up the sugars, which will buy you some time to get them all shaped.

Cinnamon-Cayenne Sugar Cookies

These are sugar cookies with attitude. They may look sweet, buttery, and demure, but they pack a sneaky heat. You can make the dough several weeks ahead and keep it rolled in cylinders in the freezer, then just thaw, slice, and bake. A cold glass of milk is important to have on hand.

MAKES 4 DOZEN COOKIES

Preheat oven to 325°F. Using an electric mixer, cream together the butter, sugar, vanilla, and salt. With the mixer on low speed, add the egg yolk. Pour in the flour, cinnamon, and cayenne and mix until well combined. Roll the dough into 2 cylinders, each about 1 inch in diameter. Chill at least 1 hour in fridge before slicing and baking.

Remove from the fridge and slice each cylinder into ¼-inch-thick slices. Sprinkle each cookie with some large-crystal or regular granulated sugar. Bake on a parchment-lined baking sheet or on a Silpat (rubber nonstick baking surface) for approximately 12 minutes or until cookies are lightly browned. Cool on a baking rack. Store at room temperature in a cookie jar or other airtight container.

8 tablespoons unsalted butter, at room temperature
½ cup sugar
1 teaspoon vanilla extract
¼ teaspoon salt
1 egg yolk
2 cups flour
1 tablespoon ground cinnamon
1 teaspoon cayenne
3 tablespoons large-crystal sugar for sprinkling, or regular granulated sugar

Oatmeal, Chocolate Chip, and Pecan Cookies

Somehow, the addition of oatmeal to these chewy, gooey cookies makes me feel like they must be good for me! They certainly taste good, and that's usually my yardstick for making cookies—or anything else, for that matter.

MAKES ABOUT 3 DOZEN COOKIES

8 tablespoons unsalted butter, at room temperature

¾ cup sugar

1 cup light brown sugar, firmly packed

1 teaspoon salt

1 teaspoon vanilla extract

2 large eggs

1½ cups flour

1 teaspoon baking soda

½ teaspoon ground cinnamon

¼ teaspoon ground nutmeg

⅛ teaspoon ground clove

1 cup quick-cooking oats

2 cups chopped pecans

2 teaspoons freshly grated orange zest

12 ounces semisweet chocolate chips

Preheat oven to 350°F. Line a large cookie sheet with parchment or a Silpat (rubber nonstick baking mat). Using an electric mixer, beat the butter in a bowl until light and fluffy. Add both sugars, salt, and vanilla, and beat until well mixed, about 3 minutes. Stir in eggs, one at a time. Sift together the flour, baking soda, cinnamon, nutmeg, and clove in a separate bowl. Add half of the flour mixture to the butter with the mixer on low speed. Once the flour has been incorporated, add the second half. Stir in the oats, pecans, orange zest, and chocolate chips. Drop the dough, by the tablespoon, onto the cookie sheet and bake for 10–12 minutes or until golden. Remove from the oven and cool the cookies a rack. Store at room temperature in a cookie jar or other airtight container.

chicken stock

This is my basic version of chicken stock, appropriate for sauces, braises, soups, or any grain dishes. I don't salt my chicken stock, because it makes it cloudy and inhibits your versatility, if you want to make risotto or a reduced sauce. See Weighing Your Options on page 320 for variations.

MAKES 2 QUARTS

Rinse the chicken parts under cold water. Put them in a stockpot with 10 cups of cold water, bring to a boil, and skim off the foam that rises to the surface. Reduce the heat to a simmer and add the onions, celery, carrots, bay leaves, thyme, parsley, and peppercorns. Simmer 2 hours, skimming every half hour or so. Strain and cool. This stock will keep in the refrigerator for 5 days or in the freezer for 2 months.

6 pounds chicken parts
    (wings, necks and
    backs)*
2 onions, roughly chopped
3 stalks celery, roughly
    chopped
2 carrots, roughly chopped
2 bay leaves
3 sprigs thyme
Handful parsley stems
2 teaspoons whole black
    peppercorns

*Note: Wings have the most meat and lend the best flavor to the broth.

rich (double) chicken stock

Yet another option is to make a rich stock known as a *double stock*. A very lovely, intense sauce can be made by roasting a bit of cured ham like prosciutto or Serrano ham in a little olive oil in a hot oven with a carrot, an onion, and a few cloves of garlic. Add a pound of chicken wings (chopped with a cleaver in half or in thirds), and cook them until they are nicely browned. Transfer this to a stockpot and add a batch of the basic chicken stock (where originally you would add cold water) and a few more aromatics—a pinch of black peppercorns, a bay leaf, and a sprig of thyme. Cook for 40 minutes. Strain and cool. This stock is great for risottos and pan sauces.

fish stock or fish fumet

1 tablespoon olive oil

1 large leek, well rinsed and thinly sliced

1 onion, thinly sliced

2 stalks celery, thinly sliced

½ small bulb fennel, thinly sliced

1 small carrot, thinly sliced

½ teaspoon whole black peppercorns

½ teaspoon whole coriander seed

1 strip fresh orange peel

3 pounds whitefish bones, rinsed under cold water and cut into 3-inch pieces, all traces of blood removed

1 cup dry white wine

2 bay leaves

2 sprigs thyme

Sea salt, if desired

I make this stock, also known as *fumet,* when I want to have a really full-flavored fish dish. Sometimes chicken stock will work nicely in place of fumet, but when the flavors of the fish are delicate, the chicken stock is too strong, and plain water is uninteresting. Use only lean whitefish bones (snapper, halibut, sole, flounder), not salmon, tuna, mackerel, or any oil-fish bones, which will make an overly strong-tasting and cloudy fumet.

YIELDS 1½–2 QUARTS

Heat the olive oil in a heavy pot that is large enough to accommodate all ingredients and 3 quarts of water. Sweat the leek, onion, celery, fennel, and carrot until soft, about 5–8 minutes over medium heat, with the pot half covered. Add the peppercorns, coriander seed, and orange peel and sweat 1 minute longer. Add the fish bones, white wine, herbs and salt if using, and cover. Sweat for 20 minutes. Remove cover and add 2 quarts of cold water. Raise heat and bring fumet to a boil, skim any foam off the top, and reduce heat to a simmer. Simmer 20 minutes. Turn off the heat and let stock settle for 20 minutes so any particles that would make it cloudy will sink to

the bottom. Ladle the fumet from the top into a sieve lined with cheesecloth or a coffee filter. Chill. The fumet will keep up to 5 days in the fridge or 2 weeks in the freezer.

veal stock

Veal stock is my secret weapon for making rich, satiny, intensely flavored sauces in my home kitchen as well as at work. The gelatin in the bones is released into the stock and lends a wonderful body and sheen to any braised or sautéed dishes. I simply reduce the veal stock until it is concentrated, then use what I need for the next day or two and freeze the rest. It will keep up to four months in the freezer. It's a bit of a project, but a very satisfying one when you know that your "secret weapon" is just inside the freezer door. A variation on the basic veal stock is demi-glace, which is a roux-thickened secondary sauce. I find demi-glace old-fashioned and not really necessary, since the veal stock thickens nicely as it reduces. I also like the lighter and clearer qualities of a simply reduced stock.

MAKES ABOUT 2 QUARTS

Preheat oven to 400°F. Put the veal bones and the trim from flanks, if using, into a large roasting pan and roast until well browned, about 40 minutes. Dilute the tomato paste in a little water to create a consistency that can be brushed on the bones. Brush the bones with the paste, add the carrots, onions, and celery, and continue roasting until the vegetables have browned, about 30 minutes.

Transfer the bones and vegetables to a large stockpot. Deglaze the fond with the wine, scraping up all the browned bits. Transfer all these juices to the stockpot. Add the garlic, bay leaves, peppercorns, and parsley stems to the pot, as well as 4 quarts of cold water.

Bring to a boil over high heat, reduce heat to a simmer, and skim off any foam that rises to the top. Leave uncovered and skim every 30 minutes for 4 hours. Strain the stock through a very fine sieve or cheesecloth into a smaller, clean saucepan. Slowly reduce by simmering until the veal stock is half its volume—about 2 hours. Strain again and cool over an ice bath.

8–10 pounds veal bones, cracked and cut into 3-inch pieces

1–2 pounds veal scraps or trim from the flanks (optional—use if your butcher has them)

¼ cup tomato paste

3 carrots, peeled and roughly chopped

3 onions, roughly chopped

5 stalks celery, roughly chopped

2 cups dry red or white wine

6 cloves garlic, smashed with the side of a knife

3 bay leaves

1 teaspoon black peppercorns

Small handful parsley stems

NOTE: Veal stock is very high in protein and prone to spoiling if not handled carefully. This means you need to chill it quickly, storing it no more than 4 days in the fridge and up to 4 months in the freezer. Veal stock that is approaching its fourth day in the fridge can be boiled, recooled, and stored for another 4 days.

‹ weighing your options ›

You can add additional flavorings depending on how you want to use the resulting stock. For example, the addition of ginger, lemongrass, and cilantro stems lends the broth a bright, Asian-influenced flavor. Alternately, the addition of garlic, mushroom stems, and a few crushed tomatoes yields a fuller-flavored and richer broth for risotto or a hearty bean or lentil soup.

court bouillon

3 cups cold water
1 cup white wine
Juice of 1 lemon
1 onion, sliced
1 carrot, peeled and sliced
1 rib celery, peeled and sliced
¼ bulb fennel, sliced
1 clove garlic, smashed with the back of a knife
1 bay leaf
1 sprig thyme
Small handful parsley, leaves and stems
½ teaspoon whole black peppercorns
½ teaspoon whole coriander seeds
Sea salt to taste

A court bouillon is a simple stock made for poaching vegetables, fish, and shellfish. It's so easy to put together that I make it just when I need it and don't bother to store any in the freezer.

MAKES 1 QUART

Place all ingredients except the salt into a stockpot, bring to a boil, reduce to a simmer, and cook for 20 minutes. Strain, cool, and season to taste with salt.

how to open an oyster

Opening oysters reminds me a little of shucking pistachio nuts—some open effortlessly, and others reduce me to a tight-lipped frenzy of prying and muttering. I've learned over the years that simple brute strength is not the answer—you need good technique. Here, then, are my tips for successful oyster openings.

1. Scrub the oysters well under running cold water. Then let them relax again in the fridge before attempting to open them. Oysters are living creatures, and all that jostling from being scrubbed will cause them to tense up and hence be harder to open.

2. Place the oyster with its flat side up on a dish towel and press down with the flat of your palm (use your weaker hand; your primary hand will wield the oyster knife) over the oyster. This technique will lessen the chances of having an errant oyster knife cut into your hand.

3. Insert the tip of the oyster knife into the hinge of the oyster—this looks sort of like the stem end of a plant.

4. Twist your wrist back and forth while exerting slow, gentle pressure into the hinge until you feel the top shell "pop." Now slide the knife along the top of the shell to sever the top adductor muscle. Remove the top shell, then slide the knife gently under the oyster to release the bottom adductor.

5. Check the oyster for freshness. The oyster should be full of clear brine (the liquor), smell only of the sea, and be free of any bits of shell or grit. Serve immediately or as soon as possible on a bed of crushed ice, being careful to nestle the oyster firmly in the ice to avoid spilling the precious juices.

spatchcocking

Spatchcocking is the term used for splitting and flattening a whole, small bird so it can be quickly cooked. Typically baby chickens, squab, quail, and guinea fowl are candidates for spatchcocking.

Set the bird on a cutting board with the neck opening facing away from you. Place the tip of your knife along one side of the backbone at the neck and firmly cut down along the backbone with a sawing motion all the way down the length of the back. Repeat on the other side of the backbone until you can pull the backbone out in 1 piece.

Open up the bird by pressing down on the center of the breast bone to flatten the bird. The soft cartilage of the breast bone will pop out slightly. Run the tip of your knife around the contours of the breast bone and remove.

Leave the rib bones attached until the bird is cooked—the bones will protect the meat from drying out and are very easily pulled off the breast once the meat is cooked.

basil oil

MAKES APPROXIMATELY 2 CUPS

2 large bunches basil, nice green leaves only— discard the stems
1 cup canola oil
1 cup olive oil

Bring 2 quarts of water to a boil. Plunge the basil leaves into the boiling water and count to 15 seconds. Remove the leaves and immediately drop them into an ice bath to fix the green color. Drain the leaves on paper towels and gently squeeze the leaves to remove as much water as possible.

Drop the basil in a blender and pour both oils over them. Puree on medium speed and run the blender continuously for 4 minutes. This will extract the maximum color and flavor from the basil. Pour the basil oil into a sieve lined with a coffee filter and let the oil drip slowly through the filter overnight in the fridge. Don't press on the solids— this will yield a murky oil instead of the brilliant emerald green that you will get by letting gravity do its work.

quatre épices—four spices

This spice mixture is traditionally used to season pâtés, terrines, and foie gras. I've given you the traditional mixture as well as my own twist on an old theme. I love both combinations but prefer my mixture for a quick seasoning of things like salmon, chicken, and duck, and I rely on the traditional mixture for foie gras preparations where I think the pepper and cardamom would be too forceful.

Stir all 4 spices together (whichever recipe you choose), and use immediately.

traditional quatre épices

¼ teaspoon ground cinnamon

¼ teaspoon ground allspice

¼ teaspoon ground cloves

¼ teaspoon ground nutmeg

my quatre épices

½ teaspoon freshly ground coriander seed

⅛ teaspoon ground cardamom

¼ teaspoon ground black pepper

¼ teaspoon ground nutmeg

cleaning whole foie gras

Place the foie gras on a large, clean dish towel, as the liver is pretty slippery to work with. The liver consists of 2 lobes—1 large and 1 small. Separate the lobes by pulling them apart gently with your hands—use the tip of a paring knife to sever the membranes or blood vessels that the lobes have in common.

Using the paring knife, trim away the membrane that covers the lobes and scrape off any dark spots with the side of the knife; this could be bile and would taste bitter if left on the liver.

Start with the smaller lobe and use the tip of the knife to find the large blood vessel that runs through the length of the lobe. Pull gently on the blood vessel as you uncover it, pulling out any white sinews as you go. You may have to dig quite deep, but don't worry—the foie gras is very malleable, and you can reform it when you've finished removing veins.

Repeat this process with the larger lobe. After reforming the liver as best as you can, chill it to firm it up before cooking.

Foie gras that comes vacuum packed has a 10-day shelf life if unopened.

asian ingredients and japanese mandolines (benriner brand)

Katagiri
www.katagiri.com
224 East 59th Street
New York, NY 10022
212-755-3566

Kam Man Food
www.kammanfood.com
200 Canal Street
New York, NY 10013
212-571-0330

middle eastern ingredients

Sahadi Importing Company
www.sahadis.com
187 Atlantic Avenue
Brooklyn, NY 11210
718-624-4550

american and international specialties, smoked fish, and caviar

Balducci's
www.balduccis.com
10 stores throughout the
    Northeast and
    Mid-Atlantic
1-800-346-8763

Russ and Daughters
www.russanddaughters.com
179 E. Houston Street
New York, NY 10002
212-475-4880

Sterling Caviar
www.sterlingcaviar.com
1-800-525-0333

mexican ingredients

The Kitchen
218 Eighth Avenue
New York, NY 10011
212-243-4433

The Chile Shop
www.thechileshop.com
109 East Water Street
Santa Fe, NM 87501
505-983-6080

naturally raised meats and game

D'Artagnan
www.dartagnan.com
280 Wilson Avenue
Newark, NJ 07105
1-800-327-8246
Extensive range of naturally
    raised meats and
    prepared foods

Fancy Meats from Vermont
Lydia Ratcliff
2604 East Hill Road
Andover, VT 05143
802-875-3159
Baby lambs, baby goats, pigs,
    veal, chickens, ducks,
    venison, cheeses

Listings of Catskills Region
Small Farms
www.farmtotable.com

Niman Ranch
www.nimanranch.com
510-808-8246
Naturally raised pork and beef

Pipestone Family Farms
www.pipestonefamily
    farms.com
1-866-767-8875
Naturally raised pork from
    purebred lines

Stone Church Farm
www.stonechurchfarm.com
P.O. Box 215
Rifton, NY 12471
914-658-3243
Rare breeds of ducks
    and squab

spices

Kalustyan's
www.kalustyans.com
123 Lexington Avenue
New York, NY 10016
212-685-3888

Penzeys Spices
www.penzeys.com
P.O. Box 924
Brookfield, WI 53008
1-800-741-7787

seafood

Fish Tales
191A Court St.
Brooklyn, NY 11201
718-246-1346

new england oysters and clams

Rulon Wilcox
Great Island Oyster Co.
746 Great Island Road
P.O. Box 885
West Yarmouth, MA 02673
508-775-7867
(Where my parents get
their oysters)

Cotuit Oyster Co.
www.cotuitoystercompany
.com
26 Little River Rd.
Cotuit, MA 02635
508-428-6747

authentic virginia hams

R. M. Felts Packing Co.
Ivor, VA 23866
757-859-6131

Gwaltney, Inc.
P.O. Box 489
Smithfield, VA 23430
804-399-0417

vermont cobb-smoked hams and country bacon

Harrington Ham Co.
Main Street
Richmond, VT 05477
802-434-3411

sausages

Salumeria Biellese
www.salumeriabiellese.com
378 Eighth Avenue
New York, NY 10001
212-736-7376

Schaller and Weber
www.schallerweber.com
1-800-847-4115

wild mushrooms and truffles

Marche Aux Delices
www.auxdelices.com
1-888-547-5471

Urbani Truffles
www.urbaniusa.com
718-392-5050

chocolate

Jacques Torres
www.mrchocolate.com
718-875-9772

Scharffen Berger
www.scharffenberger.com
510-981-4050

Valrhona
www.valrhona.com

Michel Cluizel
www.cluziel.com
(Web site in French)

artisanal cheeses

Balducci's
www.balduccis.com
1-800-346-8763
10 stores throughout the
Northeast and
Mid-Atlantic

Dean & Deluca
www.dean-deluca.com
New York, NY (and several
locations nationwide)
212-226-6800
1-800-999-0306

Artisanal
www.artisanalcheese.com
New York, NY
212-239-1200
1-877-797-1200

Murray's Cheese
www.murrayscheese.com
254 Bleecker Street
New York, NY
212-243-0991

Whole Foods
www.wholefoods.com
Austin, TX (and multiple
locations nationwide)
512-477-4455
1-888-945-3637

Zingerman's
www.zingermans.com
Ann Arbor, MI
734-663-3354
1-888-636-8162

kitchenware

Bridge Kitchenware
www.bridgekitchenware.com
214 East 52nd St.
New York, NY

Broadway Panhandler
www.broadwaypanhandler
.com
477 Broome Street
New York, NY
212-966-3434

Sur La Table
www.surlatable.com
Many locations
1-800-243-0852

Williams-Sonoma
www.williams-sonoma.com
Many locations
800-541-2233

Andrews, Mrs. Lewis R., and Mrs. J. Reaney Kelly. *Maryland's Way: The Hammond-Harwood House Cookbook.* Annapolis, Md., 1963.

Bastianich, Lidia Matticchio. *Lidia's Italian-American Kitchen.* New York: Knopf, 2003.

Bertoli, Paul, with Alice Waters. *Chez Panisse Cooking.* New York: Random House, 1998.

Child, Julia, Simone Beck, and Louisette Bertholle. *Mastering the Art of French Cooking.* New York: Knopf, 1961.

Peterson, James. *Fish & Shellfish: The Cook's Indispensable Companion.* New York: William Morrow & Company, 1996.

Schneider, Elizabeth. *Uncommon Fruits and Vegetables: A Common Sense Guide.* New York: Harper & Row, 1986.

Waters, Alice. *Chez Panisse Fruit.* New York: HarperCollins, 2002.

Wells, Patricia. *Patricia Wells at Home in Provence.* New York: Scribner, 1996.

Wells, Patricia, and Joel Robuchon. *Simply French: Patricia Wells Presents the Cuisine of Joel Robuchon.* New York: Hearst Books, 1991.

White, Jasper. *Jasper White's Cooking from New England: More Than 300 Traditional and Contemporary Recipes.* Newton, Mass.: Biscuit Books, 1989.

KATY'S ACKNOWLEDGMENTS

I am tremendously grateful to Judith Jones for seeing something in Andrea and me that she wanted to pursue. Our first proposal for this book was on a German theme, and Judith steered us away from that book to the one I've always wanted to write. She graciously accepted the manuscript chapter by chapter since we were nervous neophytes with this, our first effort.

It's not every day that you get the chance to publicly thank all the people who have had an impact on your life, so here goes.

Thank you, Andrea, for your infectious optimism and incredible energy, which made this book a project I couldn't resist.

Big thanks to Stacey Glick, our agent, who made me feel that the world indeed wanted and needed another cookbook. Your enthusiasm for this project propelled me forward.

Thank you, Quentin Bacon, for taking such lovely photographs for this book.

I've been cooking professionally for close to twenty years, and have learned from some of the best chefs in the country. Just as I watched my mother as a child, I learned so much just watching these talented cooks move around their kitchens. It's been a fascinating journey, and I thank these chefs for guiding me along the way: Bobby Flay, Barry Wine, Ben Wood, Susan Vanderbeek, Joann Killeen, and George Germon.

And I'd like to thank the chefs that I didn't get the chance to work with but nevertheless spent time with and learned from either in person or only through their wonderful books and restaurants: Jimmy Bradley, Bruce Bromberg, Eric Bromberg, Alice Waters, Mario Batali, Lidia Bastianich, Jasper White, Daniel Boulud, and Jean-Georges Vongerichten.

I'm so grateful to all the fabulous cooks I've worked with in so many kitchens. These people inspired me, teased me, challenged me, and in general made a tough job a hell of a lot of fun: Larry Manheim, Neil Manacle, Teresa Scala, Barbara Esmonde, Ellen D'Aleo, Amir Ilan, Margaret Morse, Marc Aumont, Anna Utevsky, Glory Mongin, Yasmin Lozada, Dominique Andrews, and Al Soto.

My deepest gratitude and admiration go to my sous chefs, who supported me and allowed my culinary dreams to become a reality. They're all terrific chefs in their own right now: Ivan Orkin, who lives and breathes food and who loves to talk about it more than anyone I've ever met; Kevin Roth, whose terrific palate and loyalty over the years has been so precious to me; Marc Van Steyn, whose amazing discipline and athletic and precise movements in the kitchen inspired us all; Matt Weingarten, who finds the right balance between an intellectual and emotional approach to creating great food; and Sani Hebaj, who brought a thirst for knowledge and a big heart into my kitchen.

Very special thanks to Dana Cowin and her staff at *Food & Wine* magazine for always being in my corner, and for keeping me in touch with some of the best chefs around—even if we do stink at softball.

I'm very grateful to the grande dames of food writing, who have understood and praised my work over the years, allowing me to reach an appreciative audience: Gael Greene, Florence Fabricant, Ruth Reichl, Marian Burros, and Gillian Duffy.

And thanks to so many other food writers and editors who have engaged with me and other chefs in a wonderful and exciting dialogue: Steve Cuozzo, Pascal LeDraoulec, Susan Westmoreland, Coleman Andrews, Sam Gugino, Thomas Matthews, Sam Sifton, Francis Boswell, Robin Raisfeld, Kathryn Matthews, Maura Hodgson, Amy Albert, and Bob Lape.

Warm thanks to Mildred Amico of the James Beard Foundation, who has always been a terrific support—she's my fairy godmother.

Thank you, Danny Meyer, for keeping me on your radar screen and for generously sharing some of your valuable insights.

Thank you, Arlene Feltman-Sailhac, for sharing your wonderful students with me and helping me get over my stage fright.

Warmest thanks to Bert Sonnenfeld and Noel Reilly-Fitch, high-powered über-foodies whose company I thoroughly enjoy and who always make a beeline for wherever I'm cooking when they fly in from L.A. or Paris. I'll always have beet chips at the bar for you, Bertie.

My most heartfelt thanks to Steven Hall and Sam Firer for always being there when I needed you—you provided a lifeline when I felt cut off. And for making me feel like I'm your favorite chef. You guys are the best.

Thank you, Diana Barnett, for never allowing me to stop believing in myself as a cook.

Warmest thanks to Peter Lucania, who contributed his amazing knowledge and skills to the cocktail section of this book. And for gently telling me what he and the wait staff really thought of my dishes. I thoroughly enjoyed deconstructing every new menu with him under the mild anesthetic of one of his killer martinis.

I'm very grateful to Sam Roberts, Jim English, and Jason Ungar, who owned and operated Quilty's. Thanks for letting me have free rein in the kitchen to explore and pursue my culinary vision, and for creating the kind of place where I would want to be a regular—convivial, warm, and generous. And thanks too for surrounding us with a great front-of-the-house staff, who were very loyal and devilishly funny.

Thank you, Mark Ordan, for helping me write the next chapter in my career. It's already been an exciting transition.

A tremendous thank-you to the farmers, artisans, and committed merchants who bring great food to our tables. Thank you to everyone at D'Artagnan, Dairyland, Wild Edibles, Riviera Produce, Upstate Farms, Jobaggy Meats, Stone Church Farm, Vermont Quality Meats, and Barry Lutsky.

But most of all, my deepest love and gratitude to my husband, Michael Amendolara, and my son, Luke Amendolara, who make everything I do make sense.

Writing this book with Katy has really spoiled me. I will probably never work with another chef with as much natural given talent. Aside from being a wildly gifted chef, she is an incredible storyteller, a beautiful writer, a ton of fun to work with, and a wonderful friend. I am so grateful to have spent the past two years working with her, though it is hard to call it work, because we really did have a great time. (You are supposed to drink lots of wine while writing a cookbook, right?) In all seriousness, I am truly honored to have been able to help her write this book and to bring her recipes and her memories to life.

This project could not have happened without the support and vision of Judith Jones, our phenomenal editor. She has helped us create a book that we hope will inspire you to cook, to laugh, to share, and to learn.

But before we could even get in the same room with Judith, we had to find the right agent to represent us. We hit the jackpot with Stacey Glick, who taught us the ropes, always gave it to us straight, steered our proposal in the right direction, and believed in us, and in our book, even when we were not so sure anyone else would. Thank you.

There are many people who helped me take the "right" turns in life—even those turns that seemed fairly harrowing at the time—so it is nice to have the opportunity to thank them in front of the world (or at least anyone willing to pick up this book). I started my career as a corporate lawyer, and ended up a writer thanks to the steady love and eternal encouragement of my amazing friends—Susie Ter-Jung, Jamie Krulewitz, Diana Barnett, Steven Hall, Stacey Levine, Debbie Davidson, and Court Golumbic.

I'd also like to thank two incredible writers in my life who have been a constant source of support and who have never let me give up on the dream—Kathy Squires and Julie Besonen. A huge thank-you also goes to Sam Sifton for giving me a chance nobody else would.

To my brother David, whom I adore for his unwavering support and friendship, but who rarely eats anything that contains evil fat molecules (he is a serious athlete): I hope these recipes will inspire you to cook and to eat—a lot!

To my dad, who seems to have gotten over my fall from grace as a fancy lawyer, I send a wave of gratitude for teaching me how to soar.

Yes, you have to save the best for last: my mom, who is my rock. I am so grateful for your wisdom, your support, and your amazing love. I know how lucky I am to have been born to you. You are like no other.

italicized page numbers indicate photographs

Al Forno restaurant, 6–7, 296

almonds

almond-crusted fried squid with thyme, 134–5

almond-garlic-thyme butter, 45

apple tarts with almond-ginger streusel, 297–8

chile-roasted almonds, 135

dried fig and almond chutney, 273

quark cheesecake on a spiced nut crust, 302–3

sweet and hot peppers with almonds, 238

Amendolara, Zeke, 46

Amico, Mildred, 15

anchovies

anchovy vinaigrette, 39

garlic-anchovy mayonnaise, 270

apples

apple cider mignonette, 42–3

apple cider sauce, 136–7

apple tarts with almond-ginger streusel, 297–8

celery root and apple remoulade, 275

cold fillet of beef with grated apple and blackberry-horseradish sauce, 44

grated apple and horseradish cream, 275

medallions of pork breaded in crushed gingersnaps with apples and sage, 202–3

oven-roasted grouper with cabbage, apples, and warm carrot-caraway dressing, 158–9

artichokes

grilled or roasted baby artichokes with lemon-cracked pepper aioli, 52–3

arugula

arugula with grilled peaches, goat cheese, and country ham, 98–9

beef tartare with anchovy vinaigrette and arugula, 38–9

asparagus

asparagus vinaigrette with lemon-pistachio dressing and Manchego cheese, 106–7

cooking technique, 107

morel and asparagus fricassee, 225

avocados

avocado-sesame relish, 76–7

salmon carpaccio with red onion, orange, and avocado, 104–5

bacon

applewood-smoked bacon, 225

baby brussels sprouts with bacon, chestnuts, and pomegranate seeds, 242

frisée salad with bacon-wrapped sea scallops, 100–1

pancetta-wrapped duck breast with verjuice and green peppercorn sauce, 186–7

parsley-stuffed shrimp with speck and horseradish-lemon sauce, 32–3

basil

basil oil, 322

quinoa salad with pine nuts, dried cherries, and basil, 248

basil (*continued*)

steamed mussels with toasted garlic, saffron, and basil, 129

summer squash soup with white beans, mango, and basil, 80–1

tomato, basil, and caper salsa, 267

warm lobster salad with golden potatoes, papaya, and basil, 110–12

barbecue sauce, chipotle, 204–5

beans

monkfish with cassoulet beans, 152–3

sesame-roasted green beans, 237

summer squash soup with white beans, mango, and basil, 80–1

sweet corn and fava bean succotash, 230

Beard House, 108, *111*

beef

beef short ribs braised in Amarone with dried cherries and black olives, 216–17

beef tartare with anchovy vinaigrette and arugula, 38–9

beef tenderloin with marrow toasts and spiced tomato chutney, 214–15

cold fillet of beef with grated apple and blackberry-horseradish sauce, 44

goulash soup, 88

grilled flank steak in smoked chile and lime marinade, 218–19

pan-roasted New York strip steak with balsamic vinegar, 220–1

beets
    beet-pickled eggs with spice-
        seasoned salt, 31
    roasted baby beets in cayenne-
        buttermilk dressing, 118–19
Belgian endive
    braised Belgian endive with citrus
        cream and walnuts, 241
beurre noisette and variations, 281
Bittici, John, 216
blackberries
    blackberry and horseradish relish,
        130–1
    blackberry-horseradish sauce, 44
    warm berry and mango gratin in
        mascarpone chantilly, 306–7
breadings
    gingersnap breading, 202
    standard breading procedure, 197
bread pudding, chocolate, 311
brine, 206–7
Bromberg, Bruce and Erik, 15
browning technique, 55
brussels sprouts
    baby brussels sprouts with bacon,
        chestnuts, and pomegranate
        seeds, 242
butter, 255
    almond-garlic-thyme butter, 45
    beurre noisette and variations,
        281
    brown butter-cardamom dressing,
        108–9
    cardamom browned butter,
        130–1
    compound butters, 177
    "fortifying" butter for cooking,
        51
    lemon and herb compound
        butter, 175
    lemon-herb butter, 225
    marrow butter, 214
    red chile butter, 136
    truffle butter, 154–5
buttermilk
    cayenne-buttermilk dressing,
        118–19
butterscotch pots de crème, 291–2

cabbage
    oven-roasted grouper with
        cabbage, apples, and warm
        carrot-caraway dressing,
        158–9
cake, simple chocolate, 305
Calvados cream sauce, 182–3
capers
    chicken liver toasts with cognac-
        plumped golden raisins, fried
        capers, and shallots, 34–5
    my green sauce, 277
    smoked chile and caper
        remoulade, 271
    tomato, basil, and caper salsa,
        267
caraway seeds
    carrot-caraway dressing,
        158–9
    goat cheese spread with caraway
        and paprika, 37
cardamom
    brown butter-cardamom dressing,
        108–9
    cardamom browned butter,
        130–1
    gewürztraminer syrup, 304
    raspberry tarts with cardamom
        sugar, 299
carrots
    carrot-caraway dressing, 158–9
Catton, David, 8
cauliflower
    curried cauliflower soup with
        garnishes, 72
    roasted cauliflower gratin,
        240
caviar, 142
    lychee, cucumber, and caviar
        vinaigrette, 140–1
    salt-roasted fingerling potatoes
        with crème fraîche and caviar,
        28
cayenne
    cayenne-buttermilk dressing,
        118–19
    cinnamon-cayenne sugar cookies,
        315

celery root
    celery root and apple remoulade,
        275
    celery root puree, 232
    celery root soup with spiced pear
        and black truffle, 82–3
cheese
    arugula with grilled peaches, goat
        cheese, and country ham, 98–9
    asparagus vinaigrette with lemon-
        pistachio dressing and
        Manchego cheese, 106–7
    cheddar, 30
    goat cheese quesadillas with
        smoked salmon and kumquat
        relish, 50–1
    goat cheese spread with caraway
        and paprika, 37
    porcini potato gratin, 250
    quark cheesecake on a spiced nut
        crust, 302–3
    roasted cauliflower gratin, 240
    sharp cheddar and sherry crack-
        ers, 30
    smoked trout tartare with cucum-
        ber, feta, and dill, 27
    spaetzle gratin with browned
        onions, Gruyère, and ham, 254
    warm berry and mango gratin in
        mascarpone chantilly, 306–7
    Zeke's tyropitas, 46
cherries
    cherry and olive gremolata,
        216–17
    quinoa salad with pine nuts,
        dried cherries, and basil, 248
chestnuts
    baby brussels sprouts with bacon,
        chestnuts, and pomegranate
        seeds, 242
    glazed chestnuts, 234
chicken
    chicken liver toasts with cognac-
        plumped golden raisins, fried
        capers, and shallots, 34–5
    chicken stocks, 317–18
    grilled chicken in marjoram
        marinade, 178–9

chicken (continued)
  pan-roasted chicken thighs with Calvados cream and onion-sage confit, 182–3
  simple roast chicken, 174–7
  summer jambalaya with poussin, shrimp, spicy sausage, and sweet corn, 180–1
chiles
  chile-roasted almonds, 135
  cranberry relish with green chiles and kumquat, 272
  garlic-studded leg of lamb in red chile and cumin crust, 208–9
  red chile-basted shrimp in apple cider sauce, 136–7
  red chile butter, 136
  red chile croutons, 84–5
  red chile oil, 264
  salsa verde piccante, 278
  smoked chile and caper remoulade, 271
  smoked chile and lime marinade, 218–19
  yellow tomato, blistered chile, and mango salsa, 268
chipotle barbecue sauce, 204–5
chives
  citrus-chive dressing, 160–1
chocolate, 294–5
  bittersweet chocolate pots de crème, 290–1
  chocolate bread pudding, 311
  Mohr im Hemd, 301
  oatmeal, chocolate chip, and pecan cookies, 316
  simple chocolate cake, 305
chutneys, see condiments
cinnamon
  cinnamon-cayenne sugar cookies, 315
clams, 127
cocktail hour, love of, 62
cocktails, 62
  Grandma Sparks's eggnog, 66–7
  highballs, 65
  margaritas, 65–6
  martinis, 63–5

coconut milk
  coconut-curry dressing, 263
  coconut curry sauce, 188–9
  coconut-simmered fingerling potatoes, 251
condiments, 259
  avocado-sesame relish, 76–7
  blackberry and horseradish relish, 130–1
  celery root and apple remoulade, 275
  cranberry relish with green chiles and kumquat, 272
  cumin-cured cherry tomatoes, 276
  dried fig and almond chutney, 273
  fruited mustards, 274
  grated apple and horseradish cream, 275
  kumquat relish, 50–1
  lemon-cracked pepper aioli, 52–3
  mayonnaise and variations, 269–70
  muscat grape, black olive, and pine nut relish, 184–5
  nectarine salsa, 146
  onion-sage confit, 285
  papaya-ginger salsa, 279
  peach-radish salsa, 204–5
  pickled radishes, 265
  pickled wild mushrooms, 266
  port-plumped prunes, 280
  red pepper rouille, 91
  salsa verde picante, 278
  smoked chile and caper remoulade, 271
  spiced tomato chutney, 284
  tomato chutney, 214–15
  tomato salsas, 267–8
cookies
  cinnamon-cayenne sugar cookies, 315
  maple lace cookies, 314
  oatmeal, chocolate chip, and pecan cookies, 316
cooking tools, 93–5

coriander
  coriander hollandaise, 150–1
  fresh mint and coriander sauce, 271
corn
  summer jambalaya with poussin, shrimp, spicy sausage, and sweet corn, 180–1
  sweet corn and fava bean succotash, 230
  sweet corn soup with crispy shiitake mushrooms, 73–4
court bouillon, 320
couscous, macadamia nut, 243
crab, 126–7
  Grandma Sparks's Maryland crab cakes, 47
  soft-shell crab tempura with crushed blackberry and horseradish relish, 130–1
crackers, sharp cheddar and sherry, 30
cracklings, 189
Craft, Bob, 16
cranberries
  cranberry relish with green chiles and kumquat, 272
crème fraîche, 29
  lentil soup with red chile croutons and crème fraîche, 84–5
  salt-roasted fingerling potatoes with crème fraîche and caviar, 28
crepes, 40
croutons, 77
  red chile croutons, 84–5
cucumbers
  cucumber, sesame, and dill sauce, 149
  lychee, cucumber, and caviar vinaigrette, 140–1
  smoked trout tartare with cucumber, feta, and dill, 27
cumin
  cumin-cured cherry tomatoes, 276
  garlic-studded leg of lamb in red chile and cumin crust, 208–9

currants
  creamed spinach with sherried
    currants, 239
curry
  coconut-curry dressing, 263
  coconut curry sauce, 188–9
  curried cauliflower soup with
    garnishes, 72

Daguin, Ariane, 15
D'Aleo, Ellen, 13
deep-frying technique, 132
deglazing technique, 55
Dehillerin cookware shop, 93, 93
Del Favero, Paul, 15
Del Grande, Robert, 15
desserts, 287–9
  caramelized pineapple with vanilla
    bean and star anise sauce, 310
  chocolate bread pudding, 311
  cinnamon-cayenne sugar cookies,
    315
  frosted green grapes, 304
  gewürztraminer syrup, 304
  maple lace cookies, 314
  Mohr im Hemd, 301
  oatmeal, chocolate chip, and
    pecan cookies, 316
  pastry cream, 306
  pots de crème, 290–3
  quark cheesecake with a spiced
    nut crust, 302–3
  riesling poached pears with
    pistachio custard sauce, 312–13
  simple chocolate cake, 305
  strawberry-rhubarb shortcake,
    308–9
  tarts, 296–9
  warm berry and mango gratin in
    mascarpone chantilly, 306–7
dill
  cucumber, sesame, and dill sauce,
    149
  German butterball potato salad
    with dill, 249
  lemon-dill mayonnaise, 270
  smoked trout tartare with cucum-
    ber, feta, and dill, 27

dressings, 259
  aged sherry-walnut vinaigrette,
    261
  anchovy vinaigrette, 39
  apple cider mignonette, 42–3
  brown butter-cardamom dressing,
    108–9
  carrot-caraway dressing, 158–9
  cayenne-buttermilk dressing,
    118–19
  citrus-chive dressing, 160–1
  coconut-curry dressing, 263
  creamy herb vinaigrette, 114–15
  insider's guide to the vinaigrette,
    96–7
  juniper vinaigrette, 262
  lemon-pistachio dressing, 106–7
  lychee, cucumber, and caviar
    vinaigrette, 140–1
  sesame vinaigrette, 262
  spicy mushroom dressing, 260
duck
  duck simmered in coconut curry,
    188–9
  pancetta-wrapped duck breast
    with verjuice and green pepper-
    corn sauce, 186–7

eggplant
  spiced lamb meatballs in eggplant
    "leaves," 210–13
eggs
  beet-pickled eggs with spice-
    seasoned salt, 31
  Grandma Sparks's eggnog, 66–7
  red-flannel salmon hash with
    poached eggs and coriander
    hollandaise, 150–1
English, Jim, 16, 18
Esterhazy family, 287–8

Fabricant, Florence, 15
Fearing, Dean, 15
fennel
  cream of fennel soup with
    mussels, salmon, and shrimp,
    90–1
  fennel kraut, 231

fennel (continued)
  foie gras "bon bons" with fennel
    kraut and lingonberry sauce,
    60–1
  homemade gravlax with fennel,
    radish, and marinated
    chanterelles, 58–9
figs
  dried fig and almond chutney, 273
Firer, Sam, 16
fish and shellfish, 121–4
  almond-crusted fried squid with
    thyme, 134–5
  fish stock or fish fumet, 318–19
  Grandma Sparks's Maryland crab
    cakes, 47
  grilled whole fish, 164–5
  halibut baked in parchment with
    new potatoes, braised leeks,
    and truffle butter, 154–5
  Maine lobster in sherry-ginger
    sauce, 133
  monkfish with cassoulet beans,
    152–3
  oven-braised halibut in wild
    mushroom broth with baby
    herb and hazelnut salad, 166–7
  oven-roasted grouper with
    cabbage, apples, and warm
    carrot-caraway dressing, 158–9
  pancetta-wrapped tuna with red
    wine-braised onions, 162–3
  purchasing seafood, 126–7
  red snapper roasted on fleur de
    sel with a warm citrus-chive
    dressing, 160–1
  smoked trout tartare with cucum-
    ber, feta, and dill, 27
  soft-shell crab tempura with
    crushed blackberry and horse-
    radish relish, 130–1
  storing seafood, 128
  tuna tartare, 157
  warm lobster salad with golden
    potatoes, papaya, and basil,
    110–12
  see also mussels; oysters; salmon;
    scallops; shrimp

Flay, Bobby, 14–15, 16–17
foie gras
    cleaning technique, 323
    foie gras "bonbons" with fennel
        kraut and lingonberry sauce, 60–1
fond, 55, 221
Ford, Willy, 121
fraisage, 296
frisée
    frisée salad with bacon-wrapped
        sea scallops, 100–1
fruit-picking, 288–9
Fulton Fish Market, 124

garlic
    almond-garlic-thyme butter, 45
    garlic-anchovy mayonnaise, 270
    garlic-studded leg of lamb in red
        chile and cumin crust, 208–9
    germ removal, 37
    steamed mussels with toasted
        garlic, saffron, and basil, 129
gazpacho with avocado-sesame
    relish, 76–7
Germon, George, 296
ginger
    apple tarts with almond-ginger
        streusel, 297–8
    ginger-soy marinade, 192–3
    kabocha squash soup with
        lemongrass and ginger, 86–7
    papaya-ginger salsa, 279
    sherry-ginger sauce, 133
gingersnap breading, 202
goose, 172
goulash soup, 88
grapes
    fox grape poivrade, 222–4
    frosted green grapes, 304
    muscat grape, black olive, and
        pine nut relish, 184–5
gravlax (homemade) with fennel,
    radish, and marinated
    chanterelles, 58–9
Greek salad with roasted olives and
    rosemary-skewered shrimp,
    102–3
Greene, Gael, 15, 16

gremolata, cherry and olive, 216–17
grilling whole fish, 164–5
grill pans, 99
grouper
    oven-roasted grouper with
        cabbage, apples, and warm
        carrot-caraway dressing, 158–9

halibut
    halibut baked in parchment with
        new potatoes, braised leeks,
        and truffle butter, 154–5
    oven-braised halibut in wild
        mushroom broth with baby
        herb and hazelnut salad, 166–7
Hall, Steven, 16, 194
ham
    arugula with grilled peaches, goat
        cheese, and country ham, 98–9
    baked Smithfield ham and ham
        spread, 48–9
    composed salad of salsify, seckle
        pear, and Serrano ham in
        brown butter-cardamom
        dressing, 108–9
    spaetzle gratin with browned
        onions, Gruyére, and ham, 254
Hammer, Juergen and Gisela, 287
hazelnuts
    herb and hazelnut salad, 166–7
herbs
    creamy herb vinaigrette, 114–15
    fresh versus dried, 173
    herb and hazelnut salad, 166–7
    lemon and herb compound
        butter, 175
    lemon-herb butter, 225
    my green sauce, 277
highballs, 65
hollandaise, coriander, 150–1
honey
    wasabi-honey glaze, 145
horseradish
    blackberry and horseradish relish,
        130–1
    blackberry-horseradish sauce, 44
    grated apple and horseradish
        cream, 275

horseradish (continued)
    horseradish-lemon sauce, 33
    smoked salmon flutes with
        horseradish-papaya cream, 36
hunting, 170–1

Ilan, Amir, 13
immediacy of cooking, 7
ingredients, integrity of, 7

jambalaya with poussin, shrimp,
    spicy sausage, and sweet corn,
    180–1
juniper berries
    juniper, black pepper, and citrus
        dipping salt, 56
    juniper vinaigrette, 262

Kennedy, Philip, 7, 8
Kenney, Matthew, 15
knives, 94, 95
Kretchmer, Lawrence, 15
kumquats
    cranberry relish with green chiles
        and kumquat, 272
    kumquat relish, 50–1

lamb
    garlic-studded leg of lamb in red
        chile and cumin crust, 208–9
    spiced lamb meatballs in eggplant
        "leaves," 210–13
Langrock, Peter and Joann, 222–3
Le Cirque restaurant, 12–13
leeks
    chilled wild leek soup (vichys-
        soise), 92
    halibut baked in parchment with
        new potatoes, braised leeks,
        and truffle butter, 154–5
    wild leek risotto, 246–7
lemongrass
    kabocha squash soup with
        lemongrass and ginger, 86–7
lemons
    braised Belgian endive with citrus
        cream and walnuts, 241
    citrus-chive dressing, 160–1

lemons (*continued*)
  horseradish-lemon sauce, 33
  juniper, black pepper, and citrus
    dipping salt, 56
  lemon and herb compound
    butter, 175
  lemon-cracked pepper aioli, 52–3
  lemon-dill mayonnaise, 270
  lemon-herb butter, 225
  lemon-pistachio dressing, 106–7
  margaritas, 65–6
  seedless sections, technique for,
    268
  tomato and citrus salsa, 268
lentils
  lentil soup with red chile crou-
    tons and crème fraîche, 84–5
  pork chops smothered in lentils,
    200–1
  sautéed fillet of salmon on French
    lentils with mango and oil-
    cured olives, 144
Lewis, Peter, 8–9
limes
  citrus-chive dressing, 160–1
  juniper, black pepper, and citrus
    dipping salt, 56
  margaritas, 65–6
  seedless sections, technique for,
    268
  smoked chile and lime marinade,
    218–19
  tomato and citrus salsa, 268
lingonberries
  lingonberry sauce, 60–1
lobster, 111, 126–7
  cooking times, 110
  Maine lobster in sherry-ginger
    sauce, 133
  warm lobster salad with golden
    potatoes, papaya, and basil,
    110–12
lobster-catching, 122–3
Lucania, Peter, 18, 62
Luke, 3, 14, 19, *19, 87, 111, 313*
lychee nuts
  lychee, cucumber, and caviar
    vinaigrette, 140–1

macadamia nuts
  macadamia nut couscous, 243
Mainz, Germany, 4–5
mandolines, 95
mangoes
  sautéed fillet of salmon on French
    lentils with mango and oil-
    cured olives, 144
  spiced mango yogurt, 200–1
  summer squash soup with white
    beans, mango, and basil,
    80–1
  warm berry and mango gratin in
    mascarpone chantilly, 306–7
  yellow tomato, blistered chile,
    and mango salsa, 268
Manheim, Larry, 14
maple lace cookies, 314
margaritas, 65–6
marinades and rubs, 191
  ginger-soy marinade, 192–3
  marjoram marinade, 178–9
  smoked chile and lime marinade,
    218–19
marjoram
  marjoram marinade, 178–9
marrow butter, 214
martinis, 63–5
mayonnaise
  basic mayonnaise, 269
  garlic-anchovy mayonnaise, 270
  lemon-dill mayonnaise, 270
McPhee, Danny, 5
meat, 169–72
  fried rabbit with whole-grain
    mustard sauce, 194–6
  garlic-studded leg of lamb in red
    chile and cumin crust, 208–9
  rabbit sausage, 198–9
  spiced lamb meatballs in eggplant
    "leaves," 210–13
  venison dishes, 222–5
  see also beef; pork
Mesa Grill, 14–15
Michael, 3, *12,* 13, 20, 171, *221,*
  307
Milchbrot (rolls made with milk), 5
Miller, Bryan, 11

mint
  fresh mint and coriander sauce,
    271
  orange and radish salad with
    mint, 229
  sugar snap peas with browned
    shallots, pancetta, and mint,
    236
mise en place, 113
Mohr im Hemd, 301
monkfish
  monkfish with cassoulet beans,
    152–3
mushrooms
  homemade gravlax with fennel,
    radish, and marinated
    chanterelles, 58–9
  morel and asparagus fricassee, 225
  palatschinken with fresh porcini
    and pine nuts, 40–1
  pan-roasted morels, 54–5
  pickled wild mushrooms, 266
  porcini potato gratin, 250
  sautéed wild mushrooms, 233
  spicy mushroom dressing, 260
  sweet corn soup with crispy
    shiitake mushrooms, 73–4
  wild mushroom broth, 166–7
  see also truffles
mussels, 127
  cream of fennel soup with mus-
    sels, salmon, and shrimp, 90–1
  roasted black mussels with
    almond-garlic-thyme butter, 45
  steamed mussels with toasted
    garlic, saffron, and basil, 129
mustard
  fruited mustards, 274
  whole-grain mustard sauce, 194–6

Nathan, Andrew, 15
nectarines
  nectarine salsa, 146
nuts
  baby brussels sprouts with bacon,
    chestnuts, and pomegranate
    seeds, 242
  glazed chestnuts, 234

nuts (*continued*)
    herb and hazelnut salad, 166–7
    lemon-pistachio dressing, 106–7
    lychee, cucumber, and caviar
      vinaigrette, 140–1
    macadamia nut couscous, 243
    oatmeal, chocolate chip, and
      pecan cookies, 316
    pistachio custard sauce, 312–13
    toasting technique, 107
    see also almonds; pine nuts;
      walnuts

oatmeal
    oatmeal, chocolate chip, and
      pecan cookies, 316
olive oil, 78–9
olives
    cherry and olive gremolata,
      216–17
    Greek salad with roasted olives
      and rosemary-skewered
      shrimp, 102–3
    muscat grape, black olive, and
      pine nut relish, 184–5
    my green sauce, 277
    sautéed fillet of salmon on French
      lentils with mango and oil-
      cured olives, 144
onions
    onion-sage confit, 182, 285
    pancetta-wrapped tuna with red
      wine-braised onions, 162–3
    salmon carpaccio with red onion,
      orange, and avocado, 104–5
    spaetzle gratin with browned
      onions, Gruyére, and ham,
      254
    summer tomato and sweet onion
      salad with creamy herb vinai-
      grette, 114–15
oranges
    braised Belgian endive with citrus
      cream and walnuts, 241
    citrus-chive dressing, 160–1
    gewürztraminer syrup, 304
    juniper, black pepper, and citrus
      dipping salt, 56

oranges (*continued*)
    marsala pots de crème with
      orange zest, 292–3
    orange and radish salad with
      mint, 229
    salmon carpaccio with red onion,
      orange, and avocado, 104–5
    seedless sections, technique for,
      268
    tomato and citrus salsa, 268
Otter Creek Café, 10–11
oysters, 127
    chilled oysters on the half shell
      with apple cider mignonette
      and grilled spicy sausage, 42–3
    opening technique, 321
    oysters in gewürztraminer cream,
      138–9

palatschinken with fresh porcini
    and pine nuts, 40–1
Palio restaurant, 12
pans, 95
papayas
    papaya-ginger salsa, 279
    smoked salmon flutes with
      horseradish-papaya cream, 36
    warm lobster salad with golden
      potatoes, papaya, and basil,
      110–12
paprika
    goat cheese spread with caraway
      and paprika, 37
pastry cream, 306
peaches
    arugula with grilled peaches, goat
      cheese, and country ham, 98–9
    peach-radish salsa, 204–5
pears
    celery root soup with spiced pear
      and black truffle, 82–3
    composed salad of salsify, Seckel
      pear, and Serrano ham in
      brown butter-cardamom
      dressing, 108–9
    riesling poached pears with
      pistachio custard sauce,
      312–13

peas
    green pea and sorrel soup, 89
    sugar snap peas with browned
      shallots, pancetta, and mint,
      236
pecans
    oatmeal, chocolate chip, and
      pecan cookies, 316
peppers
    red pepper rouille, 91
    sweet and hot peppers with
      almonds, 238
    see also chiles
Peterson, James, 127
phyllo dough, 46
pickles, *see* condiments
pineapples
    caramelized pineapple with
      vanilla bean and star anise
      sauce, 310
pine nuts
    muscat grape, black olive, and
      pine nut relish, 184–5
    palatschinken with fresh porcini
      and pine nuts, 40–1
    quinoa salad with pine nuts,
      dried cherries, and basil, 248
pistachios
    lemon-pistachio dressing,
      106–7
    pistachio custard sauce,
      312–13
poivrade, fox grape, 222–4
pomegranate seeds
    baby brussels sprouts with bacon,
      chestnuts, and pomegranate
      seeds, 242
Ponzek, Debra, 15
pork
    brined pork roast "wild boar"
      style, 206–7
    chipotle barbecued pork with
      peach- radish salsa, 204–5
    medallions of pork breaded in
      crushed gingersnaps with
      apples and sage, 202–3
    pancetta-wrapped tuna with red
      wine-braised onions, 162–3

pork (*continued*)
  pork chops smothered in lentils,
    200–1
  sugar snap peas with browned
    shallots, pancetta, and mint,
    236
  see also bacon; ham
Portale, Alfred, 15
potatoes
  coconut-simmered fingerling
    potatoes, 251
  German Butterball potato salad
    with dill, 249
  halibut baked in parchment with
    new potatoes, braised leeks,
    and truffle butter, 154–5
  my homemade potato chips, 57
  porcini potato gratin, 250
  salt-roasted fingerling potatoes
    with crème fraîche and caviar,
    28
  warm lobster salad with golden
    potatoes, papaya, and basil,
    110–12
pots, 95
pots de crème, 290–3
poultry, 169–72
  duck simmered in coconut curry,
    188–9
  grilled quail with warm muscat
    grape, black olive, and pine nut
    relish, 184–5
  pancetta-wrapped duck breast
    with verjuice and green pepper-
    corn sauce, 186–7
  spatchcocked squab with star
    anise, ginger, and soy, 192–3
  see also chicken
Pratt, Melanie, 222
prunes
  port-plumped prunes, 280
Pyles, Stephen, 15

quail
  grilled quail with warm muscat
    grape, black olive, and pine nut
    relish, 184–5
quatre épices, 323

quesadillas (goat cheese) with
    smoked salmon and kumquat
    relish, 50–1
Quileute Indians, 123
Quilted Giraffe restaurant, 13, 14
Quilty's restaurant, 7, 16–18, *19*
quinoa
  quinoa salad with pine nuts,
    dried cherries, and basil, 248

rabbit
  fried rabbit with whole-grain
    mustard sauce, 194–6
  rabbit sausage, 198–9
radishes
  homemade gravlax with fennel,
    radish, and marinated
    chanterelles, 58–9
  orange and radish salad with
    mint, 229
  peach-radish salsa, 204–5
  pickled radishes, 265
raisins
  chicken liver toasts with
    cognac-plumped golden
    raisins, fried capers, and
    shallots, 34–5
raspberries
  raspberry tarts with cardamom
    sugar, 299
  warm berry and mango gratin
    in mascarpone chantilly,
    306–7
red snapper, 161
  red snapper roasted on fleur de
    sel with a warm citrus-chive
    dressing, 160–1
Reichl, Ruth, 18
relishes, *see* condiments
resting, 190
rhubarb
  strawberry-rhubarb shortcake,
    308–9
rice
  summer jambalaya with poussin,
    shrimp, spicy sausage, and
    sweet corn, 180–1
  see also risotto

risotto
  risotto with oven-cured tomatoes,
    244–5
  wild leek risotto, 246–7
roasting fish, 160
Roberts, Sam, 16, 18
rosemary
  Greek salad with roasted olives
    and rosemary-skewered
    shrimp, 102–3
Roth, Kevin, 17
rubs, *see* marinades and rubs

sachets, 75
saffron
  steamed mussels with toasted
    garlic, saffron, and basil, 129
sage
  medallions of pork breaded in
    crushed gingersnaps with
    apples and sage, 202–3
  onion-sage confit, 182, 285
salads, 69, 96–7
  arugula with grilled peaches, goat
    cheese, and country ham, 98–9
  asparagus vinaigrette with lemon-
    pistachio dressing and
    Manchego cheese, 106–7
  composed salad of salsify, Seckel
    pear, and Serrano ham in
    brown butter-cardamom
    dressing, 108–9
  frisée salad with bacon- wrapped
    sea scallops, 100–1
  German Butterball potato salad
    with dill, 249
  Greek salad with roasted olives
    and rosemary-skewered
    shrimp, 102–3
  herb and hazelnut salad, 166–7
  orange and radish salad with
    mint, 229
  quinoa salad with pine nuts,
    dried cherries, and basil, 248
  roasted baby beets in cayenne-
    buttermilk dressing, 118–19
  salmon carpaccio with red onion,
    orange, and avocado, 104–5

salads (*continued*)

    seasonal country salad with
        spiced walnuts, 116–17
    summer tomato and sweet onion
        salad with creamy herb vinai-
        grette, 114–15
    warm lobster salad with golden
        potatoes, papaya, and basil,
        110–12
    see also dressings
salmon, 143
    cream of fennel soup with mus-
        sels, salmon, and shrimp, 90–1
    goat cheese quesadillas with
        smoked salmon and kumquat
        relish, 50–1
    grilled salmon with wasabi-
        honey glaze, 145
    homemade gravlax with fennel,
        radish, and marinated
        chanterelles, 58–9
    oven-steamed fillet of salmon with
        zucchini "pappardelle," 147–8
    paillard of salmon "unilateral"
        with sel gris and nectarine
        salsa, 146
    red-flannel salmon hash with
        poached eggs and coriander
        hollandaise, 150–1
    salmon carpaccio with red onion,
        orange, and avocado, 104–5
    sautéed fillet of salmon on French
        lentils with mango and oil-
        cured olives, 144
    smoked salmon flutes with
        horseradish-papaya cream, 36
salsas, *see* condiments
salsify, 109
    composed salad of salsify, seckle
        pear, and Serrano ham in
        brown butter-cardamom
        dressing, 108–9
salt, 29
    juniper, black pepper, and citrus
        dipping salt, 56
    paillard of salmon "unilateral"
        with sel gris and nectarine
        salsa, 146

salt (*continued*)

    red snapper roasted on fleur de
        sel with a warm citrus-chive
        dressing, 160–1
    spice-seasoned salt, 31
sauce pans with lids, 95
sauces
    apple cider sauce, 136–7
    beurre noisette and variations, 281
    blackberry-horseradish sauce, 44
    Calvados cream sauce, 182–3
    chipotle BBQ sauce, 204–5
    coconut curry sauce, 188–9
    coriander hollandaise, 150–1
    cucumber, sesame, and dill sauce,
        149
    fond for, 221
    fox grape poivrade, 222–4
    fresh mint and coriander sauce,
        271
    gewürztraminer sauce, 138–9
    horseradish-lemon sauce, 33
    lingonberry sauce, 60–1
    my green sauce, 277
    pistachio custard sauce, 312–13
    sherry-ginger sauce, 133
    "skin" formation, prevention of,
        224
    vanilla bean and star anise sauce,
        310
    verjuice and green peppercorn
        sauce, 186–7
    whole-grain mustard sauce, 194–6
    yogurt sauce, 212
sausages
    chilled oysters on the half shell
        with apple cider mignonette
        and grilled spicy sausage, 42–3
    rabbit sausage, 198–9
    summer jambalaya with poussin,
        shrimp, spicy sausage, and
        sweet corn, 180–1
scallops, 127
    frisée salad with bacon- wrapped
        sea scallops, 100–1
    seared sea scallops with a cool
        cucumber, sesame, and dill
        sauce, 149

scallops (*continued*)

    sea scallop carpaccio with lychee,
        cucumber, and caviar vinai-
        grette, 140–1
"Seasonal American" style of
    cooking, 17, 20–2
Sendel, Jan, 220
sesame oil
    avocado-sesame relish, 76–7
    cucumber, sesame, and dill sauce,
        149
    sesame-roasted green beans, 237
    sesame vinaigrette, 262
shallots
    chicken liver toasts with cognac-
        plumped golden raisins, fried
        capers, and shallots, 34–5
    sugar snap peas with browned
        shallots, pancetta, and mint,
        236
shortcake, strawberry-rhubarb,
    308–9
shrimp, 127
    broiled shell-on shrimp with
        juniper, black pepper, and
        citrus dipping salt, 56
    cream of fennel soup with mus-
        sels, salmon, and shrimp, 90–1
    Greek salad with roasted olives
        and rosemary-skewered
        shrimp, 102–3
    parsley-stuffed shrimp with speck
        and horseradish-lemon sauce,
        32–3
    red chile-basted shrimp in apple
        cider sauce, 136–7
    summer jambalaya with poussin,
        shrimp, spicy sausage, and
        sweet corn, 180–1
side dishes, 227–8
    baby brussels sprouts with bacon,
        chestnuts, and pomegranate
        seeds, 242
    black pepper and parsley spaetzle,
        252–3
    braised Belgian endive with citrus
        cream and walnuts, 241
    celery root puree, 232

side dishes (*continued*)
coconut-simmered fingerling potatoes, 251
creamed spinach with sherried currants, 239
fennel kraut, 231
German butterball potato salad with dill, 249
glazed chestnuts, 234
macadamia nut couscous, 243
orange and radish salad with mint, 229
porcini potato gratin, 250
quinoa salad with pine nuts, dried cherries, and basil, 248
risotto with oven-cured tomatoes, 244–5
roasted cauliflower gratin, 240
sautéed wild mushrooms, 233
sesame-roasted green beans, 237
spaetzle gratin with browned onions, Gruyére, and ham, 254
squash roasted in foil packages, 235
sugar snap peas with browned shallots, pancetta, and mint, 236
sweet and hot peppers with almonds, 238
sweet corn and fava bean succotash, 230
wild leek risotto, 246–7
small plates and snacks, 25–6
baked Smithfield ham and ham spread, 48–9
beef tartare with anchovy vinaigrette and arugula, 38–9
beet-pickled eggs with spice-seasoned salt, 31
broiled shell-on shrimp with juniper, black pepper, and citrus dipping salt, 56
chicken liver toasts with cognac-plumped golden raisins, fried capers, and shallots, 34–5
chilled oysters on the half shell with apple cider mignonette and grilled spicy sausage, 42–3

small plates and snacks (*continued*)
cold fillet of beef with grated apple and blackberry-horseradish sauce, 44
foie gras "bon bons" with fennel kraut and lingonberry sauce, 60–1
goat cheese quesadillas with smoked salmon and kumquat relish, 50–1
goat cheese spread with caraway and paprika, 37
Grandma Sparks's Maryland crab cakes, 47
grilled or roasted baby artichokes with lemon-cracked pepper aioli, 52–3
homemade gravlax with fennel, radish, and marinated chanterelles, 58–9
my homemade potato chips, 57
palatschinken with fresh porcini and pine nuts, 40–1
pan-roasted morels, 54–5
parsley-stuffed shrimp with speck and horseradish-lemon sauce, 32–3
roasted black mussels with almond-garlic-thyme butter, 45
salt-roasted fingerling potatoes with crème fraîche and caviar, 28
sharp cheddar and sherry crackers, 30
smoked salmon flutes with horseradish-papaya cream, 36
smoked trout tartare with cucumber, feta, and dill, 27
Zeke's tyropitas, 46
snacks, *see* small plates and snacks
Solstice restaurant, 16–17
sorrel
green pea and sorrel soup, 89
soups, 69
as braising liquids, 167
celery root soup with spiced pear and black truffle, 82–3

soups (*continued*)
chilled wild leek soup (vichyssoise), 92
cream of fennel soup with mussels, salmon, and shrimp, 90–1
curried cauliflower soup with garnishes, 72
foolproof guide to making soup, 70–1
gazpacho with avocado-sesame relish, 76–7
goulash soup, 88
green pea and sorrel soup, 89
kabocha squash soup with lemongrass and ginger, 86–7
lentil soup with red chile croutons and crème fraîche, 84–5
summer squash soup with white beans, mango, and basil, 80–1
sweet corn soup with crispy shiitake mushrooms, 73–4
thinned out for braising, 167
soy sauce
ginger-soy marinade, 192–3
spaetzle
black pepper and parsley spaetzle, 252–3
spaetzle gratin with browned onions, Gruyère, and ham, 254
Sparks, Katy, 4, 6, 9, 12, 32, 111, 221, 228, 254
"belly tour" of France, 7–8
childhood of, 3–6
college studies, 6
cookbook philosophy, 20–3
culinary career, 6–7, 8–19
"Seasonal American" style of cooking, 17, 20–2
in Vienna, 287–8
Sparks, Kim, 3–4, 4, 7, 121, 122–3, 122, 172
Sparks, Liza, 3, 5, 171
Sparks, Michael, 121
Sparks, Sue, 3, 4–5, 5, 7, 25, 26, 121, 233
Sparks farm in Vermont, 3–4, 26, 170

spatchcocking, 192, 322
spinach
    creamed spinach with sherried
        currants, 239
squab
    spatchcocked squab with star
        anise, ginger, and soy, 192–3
squash
    kabocha squash soup with
        lemongrass and ginger, 86–7
    squash roasted in foil packages,
        235
    summer squash soup with white
        beans, mango, and basil, 80–1
squid
    almond-crusted fried squid with
        thyme, 134–5
star anise
    ginger-soy marinade, 192–3
    vanilla bean and star anise sauce,
        310
stocks, 70
    chicken stocks, 317–18
    court bouillon, 320
    fish stock or fish fumet, 318–19
    fortifying stock with rabbit
        forelegs, 195
    veal stock, 319–20
strawberries
    strawberry-rhubarb shortcake,
        308–9
Strong, Andrea, 20, 23, 32
succotash, sweet corn and fava
    bean, 230
sweating process, 70–1

tarts, 296–9
temperature-testing technique, 209
tempura batter, 131
thyme
    almond-crusted fried squid with
        thyme, 134–5
    almond-garlic-thyme butter, 45
tomatillos
    salsa verde piccante, 278
tomatoes
    cumin-cured cherry tomatoes,
        276

tomatoes (continued)
    risotto with oven-cured tomatoes,
        244–5
    spiced tomato chutney, 284
    summer tomato and sweet onion
        salad with creamy herb vinai-
        grette, 114–15
    tomato, basil, and caper salsa,
        267
    tomato and citrus salsa, 268
    tomato chutney, 214–15
    yellow tomato, blistered chile,
        and mango salsa, 268
trout
    smoked trout tartare with cucum-
        ber, feta, and dill, 27
truffles
    celery root soup with spiced pear
        and black truffle, 82–3
    truffle butter, 154–5
    truffle oil, 156
tuna
    pancetta-wrapped tuna with
        red wine-braised onions,
        162–3
    tuna tartare, 157
turkeys, wild, 171–2

Unger, Jason, 16

Vanderbeek, Susan, 8, 10
vanilla beans
    vanilla bean and star anise sauce,
        310
veal stock, 319–20
vegetable buying tips, 256–7
vegetable dishes, see side dishes
venison dishes, 222–5
verjuice
    verjuice and green peppercorn
        sauce, 186–7
vinaigrettes, insiders guide to, 96–7;
    see also dressings
vinegar
    creamed spinach with sherried
        currants, 239
    homemade flavored vinegars,
        282–3

vinegar (continued)
    pan-roasted New York strip
        steak with balsamic vinegar,
        220–1
    sherry-ginger sauce, 133
walnuts
    aged sherry-walnut vinaigrette,
        261
    braised Belgian endive with citrus
        cream and walnuts, 241
    Mohr im Hemd, 301
    quark cheesecake on a spiced nut
        crust, 302–3
    seasonal country salad with
        spiced walnuts, 116–17
wasabi
    wasabi-honey glaze, 145
Waxman, Jonathan, 15
Whidbey Island party, 8–10
Wilcox, Rulon, 138
wine
    beef shortribs braised in Amarone
        with dried cherries and black
        olives, 216–17
    gewürztraminer sauce, 138–9
    gewürztraminer syrup, 304
    marsala pots de crème with
        orange zest, 292–3
    pancetta-wrapped tuna with
        red wine-braised onions,
        162–3
    port-plumped prunes, 280
    Riesling poached pears with
        pistachio custard sauce,
        312–13
    sharp cheddar and sherry crack-
        ers, 30
Wine, Barry, 13, 14
Wood, Ben, 10–11

yogurt
    spiced mango yogurt, 200–1
    yogurt sauce, 212

zucchini
    oven-steamed fillet of salmon
        with zucchini "paparadelle,"
        147–8

A NOTE ABOUT THE AUTHORS

Katy Sparks grew up in the Champlain Valley of Vermont. She attended the cooking school at Johnson & Wales University in Providence, Rhode Island, and had her early training in that city at Al Forno before moving to Seattle. She later worked at the celebrated Quilted Giraffe in New York before opening Quilty's in SoHo. She lives with her family in Brooklyn, New York.

Andrea Strong is a freelance writer whose work has appeared in *The New York Times, New York* magazine, *New York Post, Time Out New York, Gourmet, Real Simple,* and *Food & Wine.* She is the creator and author of The Strong Buzz, a weekly blog (www.thestrongbuzz.com) devoted to New York City's restaurant and food scene. She lives in Manhattan.